The Wonder of the Eucharist

More Voices from the Twentieth Century

Dennis J. Billy, C.Ss.R.

En Route Books and Media, LLC
Saint Louis, MO

En Route Books and Media, LLC
5705 Rhodes Avenue
St. Louis, MO 63109
contact@enroutebooksandmedia.com

Cover Credit: Sebastian Mahfood

Copyright 2022 Dennis J. Billy, C.Ss.R.

ISBN-13: 978-1-956715-76-7
LCCN: 2022943365

All rights reserved. No part of this book may be reproduced, stored in a retrieval system, or transmitted in any form, or by any means, electronic, mechanical, photocopying, or otherwise, without the prior written permission of the author.

In memory of
Michael Woltmann
("Wally")
1953-2016,
Who always loved
A good story.

"I write to discover
what I know."

Flannery O'Connor

Acknowledgments

Parts of this book were previously published as: "Robert Hugh Benson on the Eucharist," *Emmanuel* 125/3(May/June, 2019): 155-63 [Voice Two]; "Charles Williams on the Eucharist," *Emmanuel* 127(March/April, 2021): 89-97 [Voice Five]; "J. R. R. Tolkien on the Eucharist," *Emmanuel* 125/6(November/December, 2019): 370-77 [Voice Six]; "Catherine de Hueck Doherty on the Eucharist," *Emmanuel* 125/4(July/August, 2019): 222-30 [Voice Seven]; "C. S. Lewis on the Eucharist," *Emmanuel* 127 (January/ February, 2012): 13-21 [Voice Nine]; "Caryll Houselander on the Eucharist," *Emmanuel* 126(March/April, 2020): 83-91 [Voice Ten]; "Graham Greene and the Eucharist," *Emmanuel* 127(May/June, 2021): 159-68 [Voice Twelve]; "Rumer Godden on the Eucharist," *Emmanuel* 127/5 (September/October, 2021): 291-300 [Voice Thirteen]; "Walker Percy on the Eucharist," *Emmanuel* 127/4 (July/ August, 2021): 229-37 [Voice Fourteen]; "J. F. Powers on the Eucharist, " *Emmanuel* 127/6 (November/ December, 2021): 364-73 [Voice Fifteen]; "Flannery O'Connor on the Eucharist," *Emmanuel* 126/1 (January/ February, 2020): 11-20 [Voice Sixteen]; "Basil Pennington on the Eucharist," *Emmanuel* 125/1(January/February, 2019): 21-30 [Voice Seventeen]; "Henri Nouwen on the Eucharist," *Emmanuel* 125/2(March/April, 2019): 87-95 [Voice Eighteen]; "Ron Hansen on the Eucharist," *Emmanuel* (Final

Issue, 2021), https://emmanuelpublishing.org/article-categories/final-issue/ron-hansen-on-the-eucharist/ [Voice Twenty]." Except for those within direct quotations from the authors studied, all Scriptural citations come from *Holy Bible: New Revised Standard Version with Apocrypha* (New York/Oxford: Oxford University Press, 1989). All Vatican documents are available online on the website of the Holy [See http://w2.vatican.va/content/vatican/en.html.] In keeping with the book's popular tone, footnotes have been kept to a minimum. The strictly historical material in the book is not original to the author.

Table of Contents

Acknowledgments i
Introduction 1
Voice One Hilaire Belloc: *The Path to Rome* 5
Voice Two Robert Hugh Benson: *The Lord of the World* .. 21
Voice Three G. K. Chesterton: *The Ball and Cross* 37
Voice Four Georges Bernanos: *A Diary of a Country Priest* 55
Voice Five Charles Williams: *The Principle of Coinherence* 71
Voice Six J. R. R. Tolkien: *A Letter to His Son* 87
Voice Seven Catherine de Hueck Doherty: *Poustinia and Sobernost* 101
Voice Eight Myles Connolly: *Mr. Blue* 115
Voice Nine C. S. Lewis: *Letters to Malcolm* 133
Voice Ten Caryll Houselander: *A Rocking Horse Catholic* 151
Voice Eleven Evelyn Waugh: *Brideshead Revisited* 167
Voice Twelve Graham Greene: *The Power and the Glory* 185
Voice Thirteen Rumer Godden: *In This House of Brede* .. 203
Voice: Fourteen Walker Percy: *Love in the Ruins* 221
Voice Fifteen J. F. Powers: *Morte-D'Urban* 239
Voice Sixteen Flannery O'Connor: *A Temple of the Holy Ghost* 257

Voice Seventeen Basil Pennington: *Wine of Faith, Bread of Life* 275
Voice Eighteen Henri Nouwen: *With Burning Hearts* 291
Voice Nineteen Jon Hassler: *North of Hope* 307
Voice Twenty Ron Hansen: *Mariette in Ecstasy* 327
Conclusion 345

Introduction

This book is the fourth volume of my voices on the Eucharist series. In the previous three volumes, I covered the early Church Fathers, the saints and mystics through the ages, and the major twentieth-century theological voices on the Eucharist.[1] The present volume continues my reflection on the Eucharist in the twentieth century and is aptly called, *The Wonder of the Eucharist: More Voices from the Twentieth Century*.

My intention here is to examine some of the major literary voices from the past century who deepened our understanding of the Eucharist by embedding it in their short stories, novels, memoirs, and spiritual writings. Since the Gospels themselves come down to us in narrative form, I thought it would be helpful to see how some well-known (mostly Catholic) novelists and creative writers presented the Eucharist in their works. Each of the authors has a distinct literary voice and style that resonate with the Church's deep spiritual tradition. The result is a beautifully nuanced

---

[1] See Dennis Billy, *The Beauty of the Eucharist: Voices from the Church Fathers* (Hyde Park, NY: New City Press, 2010; Idem, *The Mystery of the Eucharist: Voices from the Saints and Mystics* (Hyde Park, NY: New City Press, 2014); Idem, *The Meaning of the. EucharistVoices from the Twentieth Century* (St. Louis, MO: En Route Books and Media, 2019).

harmony that challenges the mind and moves the heart to wonder.

With few exceptions (Benson, Nouwen, Pennington), most of the authors presented in these pages are not trained theologians or clergy, but members of the laity involved in teaching, journalism, creative writing, film, and similar literary pursuits. With few exceptions (Lewis, Williams) most are either cradle Catholics or converts to the Catholic faith. One in particular (Houselander) converted during childhood and describes herself as a "Rocking Horse Catholic." Some of the authors (Tolkien, Connolly), were devout, practicing Catholics; others led rather questionable moral lives and did not like being referred to as a "Catholic novelist" (Greene). Some of these authors were long-lived (Belloc, Doherty), while others died rather young, before reaching their full potential (Benson, Houselander, O'Connor). With one exception (Bernanos), all the authors selected for this volume are American or British, a deliberate choice that reflects my own interests in English literature. Some were close friends (Belloc and Chesterton; Tolkien and Lewis); others were loners and liked to stay out of the limelight (Powers). With one exception (Hansen), all were born in the seventy-five-year span between 1870 and 1945, are now deceased, and, for the most part, wrote their major works either before the Second Vatican Council or during its tumultuous spiritual aftermath. Their lives span an arc of almost 150 years, and their writings impacted the literary world of the twentieth century and beyond. For the most part, the chapters have been arranged in chronological order according to the years of the authors' births.

As in the previous volumes, each of the twenty chapters (or "voices,") begins with a brief biographical sketch of the Catholic author under consideration and a summary of his or her spiritual and/or theological outlook. A presentation of his or her teaching on the Eucharist follows with accompanying observations, a conclusion, and a series of reflection questions. This loose underlying structure unifies the whole, while at the same time allowing each chapter to stand by itself and, if need be, read alone. The reflection questions in particular are meant to encourage readers to explore the issues raised by these thinkers and to find their relevance for their own lives. My hope is that such reflection will deepen the reader's understanding of the Eucharist and help them to find its significance for their lives.

The voices within these pages give witness to the abiding yet ever elusive presence of the God who calls himself, "Emmanuel, which means, God with us" (Mt 1:23). The words they speak suggest that no narrative presentation, however creative or sustained, can exhaust the mystery that the sacrament brings into our midst and invites us to share. To ponder the meaning of the Eucharist, in other words, requires an open mind, a humble heart, and a willingness to explore the darkened pathways of the soul that only faith in Christ can illumine. Their voices encourage us to ponder the mystery of the sacrament and discover its significance in the narrative of our own earthly sojourn.

Voice One

Hilaire Belloc
The Path to Rome

Hilaire Belloc (1870-1953), an Anglo-French Roman Catholic author, was one of the most accomplished men of letters of the twentieth century. He was born in La Celle-Saint-Cloud, France and fled to England with his family during the Franco-Prussian war. He studied at the Oratory School in Birmingham, served in the French military, and eventually matriculated at Balliol College, Oxford and graduated from there with first-class honors in history in 1894. He became a naturalized citizen of Great Britain in 1902, while retaining his French citizenship, was president of the Oxford Union, and sat as a member of Parliament from 1906-10. He is remembered as a master of light verse, especially for his *Cautionary Tales for Children* (1908), a book that has never gone out of print, and *The Path to Rome* (1902), considered by many his best and most memorable work. His other accomplishments include such titles as: *A Bad Child's Book of Beasts* (1896), *Sonnets* (1896), *Mr. Clutterbuck's Election* (1908), *A Change in the Cabinet* (1909), *Pongo and the Bull* (1910), *The French Revolution* (1911), *The Party System* (1911), *History of England* (1915), *The Two Maps of, Europe* (1915), *Europe and Faith* (1920), *Oliver*

Cromwell (1927), *James II* (1928), *Wolsey* (1930), *Crammer* (1931), *Napoleon* (1932), *The Great Heresies* (1938), *Charles II* (1940), and a host of others.[1] A close friend and colleague of G. K. Chesterton, he suffered a stroke in 1942 and was incapacitated until his death some eleven years later. A devout Catholic for his entire life, his views on the Eucharist flow from his intransigent faith, dogged, perseverance, and overall zest for life.

Belloc's Spiritual Outlook

An ardent Catholic and defender of the faith, Belloc had a sacramental view of life that saw God's presence in all aspects of life.[2] Catholicism, he believed, was the true religion, and all other explanations of the meaning of existence paled in comparison. In *The Path to Rome*, a memoir based on a walking pilgrimage through France, Switzerland and Italy, he writes: "The Catholic Church makes men. By which I do not mean boasters and swaggerers, nor bullies nor ignorant fools, who, finding themselves comfortable, think that their comfort will be a boon to others, and attempt (with singular

---

[1] For a biography of Belloc, see Joseph Pearce, *Old Thunder: A Life of Hilaire Belloc* (London: HarperCollins, 2002). For a complete list of Belloc's writings, see "Hilaire Belloc Bibliography," https://wikivisually.com/wiki/Hilaire_Belloc_bibliography .

[2] See, for example, Hilaire Belloc, "On Sacramental Things," in *On Something*(London: Methuen & Co. LTD, 1910), 257-265.

unsuccess) to force it on the world; but men, human beings, different from the beasts, capable of firmness and discipline and recognition; accepting death; tenacious."[3]

Catholicism, for him, not only shaped the hearts of men, but also the world in which they lived. In his mind, it has inspired the greatest works of music, art, and literature, yet has done so with a certain sense of carelessness, since she lays her foundations in something other— a deep sense of the transcendent. He continues: "Have you ever noticed that all the Catholic Church does is thought beautiful and loveable until she comes out into the open, and then suddenly she is found by her enemies (which are the seven capital sins, and the four sins calling to heaven for vengeance) to be hateful and grinding?"[4] Catholicism, he held, was inextricably tied to European civilization: "She is Europe and all our past. She is returning."[5]

Catholicism, according to Belloc, embraced all of humanity and was universal in the truest sense of the word. Near the end of *The Path to Rome*, he tells the fictitious story of a certain American (a Mr. Benjamin Franklin Hard) who, having traveled to Europe, became fascinated with the faith: "He studied the Catholic Church with extreme interest. He watched High Mass at several places (hoping it might be

---

[3] Hilaire Belloc, *The Path to Rome* (New York: Image Books, 1956), 213.
[4] Ibid.
[5] Ibid., 214.

different). He thought it was what it was not, and then, contrariwise, he thought it was not what it was. He talked to poor Catholics, rich Catholics, middle-class Catholics, and elusive, well-born, penniless, neatly dressed, successful Catholics; also to pompous, vain Catholics; humble, uncertain Catholics; sneaking, pad-footed Catholics; healthy, howling, combative Catholics; doubtful, shoulder-shrugging, but devout Catholics; fixed, crabbed, and dangerous Catholics; easy, jovial, and shone-upon-by-the-heavenly-light Catholics; subtle Catholics; strange Catholics, and (*quod tibi manifeste absurdum videtur*) intellectual, *pince-nez*, jejune, twisted, analytical, yellow, cranky, and introspective Catholics: in fine, he talked to all Catholics. And when I say 'all Catholics,' I do not mean that he talked to every individual Catholic, but that he got a good, integrative grip of the Church militant, which is all that the words connote."[6] Hilaire Belloc, we might say, was a thoroughly Catholic Catholic. His spiritual outlook was entirely shaped by his Catholic faith and all that that entailed.

Belloc on the Eucharist

The Eucharist, for Belloc, was the sacrament around which all else revolved. In his Preface to *The Path to Rome*, he describes what he intended to do on each day of his pil-

---

[6] Ibid., 251-52.

grimage: "I will start from the place where I served in arms for my sins; I will walk all the way and take advantage of no wheeled thing; I will sleep rough and cover thirty miles a day, and I will hear Mass every morning; and I will be present at high mass in St. Peter's on the Feast of St. Peter and St. Paul."[7] Although he readily admits that circumstances would not allow him to fulfill every aspect of this pilgrim's itinerary, it is clear that he considers the Mass an integral part of his earthly sojourn. The importance, for Belloc, of hearing Mass during his pilgrimage to Rome (and by extension throughout his life) comes through on the third day of his journey when the opportunity on the feast of Corpus Christi considered the Mass an integral part of his earthly sojourn. It was as essential the soul, as food and drink were to the body.[8]

Early on in his journey to Rome, Belloc writes: "In the first village I came to I found that Mass was over, and this justly annoyed me; for what is a pilgrimage in which a man cannot hear Mass every morning?"[9] He also opines on the purely temporal comfort of beginning the day by going to Mass (what the monks of old would have called a "carnal feeling") and attributes this experience to a number of things. To begin with, starting each day with a half-an-hour of silence and recollection allows one to put the cares of the

---

[7] Ibid., 8.
[8] Ibid, 60.
[9] Ibid., 38.

day in perspective. What is more, the careful and rapid ritual of the Mass calms one's mind and gives one a sense of singular repose. The surroundings at the Mass, moreover, inspire good and reasonable thoughts and insulate a person from the misery and threats of the outer world. Finally (and most importantly), by attending Mass each morning, a person does what so much of the human race has done for thousands and thousands of years.[10] The Mass, for him, offered natural and well as supernatural benefits to those who heard it on a regular basis.

Belloc's pilgrimage to Rome is dotted by various visits to churches in the small towns and villages. Sometimes he is able to hear Mass. More often than not it is a low Mass. On rare occasions it is a High Mass. One day, he happens across the Corpus Christi procession celebrated in a small French village.[11] On another occasion, he gives his readers an indication of the morning bustle of priests trying to celebrate their early Latin Mass: "Here, as I heard a bell, I thought I would go up and hear Mass; and I did so, but my attention at the holy office was distracted by the enormous number of priests that I found in the church, and I have wondered painfully ever since how so many came to be in a little place like Giromagny. There were three priests at the high altar, and nearly one for each chapel, and there was such a buzz of

---

[10] Ibid., 59.
[11] Ibid., 45-46.

Masses going on, beginning and ending....With all this there were few people at Mass so early; nothing but these priests going in and out, and continual little bells."¹² Like the rising of the sun and its setting, Holy Mass and devotion to the Blessed Sacrament are a provide constant (and at times confusing) backdrop against which his journey to Rome unfolds.

Belloc also marvels at the lonely chapels in the French countryside that might have Mass celebrated there only once a year, if that: "The rest of the time they stand empty, and some of the older or simpler, one might take for ruins. They mark everywhere some strong emotion of supplication, thanks, or reverence, and they anchor these wild places to their own past, making them up in memories what they lack in multitudinous life."¹³ What comes across throughout the memoir is that the Mass, and what happens during it, is an important part of Belloc's spiritual and earthly pilgrimage. For him, the two— like body are soul— are intimately related and are separated only at death.

Some Further Insights

While by no means exhaustive, this brief summary of Belloc's views toward the Eucharist as depicted in his classic (and most popular) work, *The Path to Rome*, offers an

---

¹² Ibid., 71.
¹³ Ibid., 57-58.

opportunity to delve a bit mor deeply into his deep convictions about Catholicism and the role it plays on the world stage. The following remarks seek to his understanding of the Eucharist in a little more depth.

First, it is interesting to note that Belloc refers, again and again, to "hearing" Mass, rather than" attending" or simply "going to" Mass. What is unusual about this expression is that in the pre-Vatican II era, when Mass was in Latin and the priest had his back to the people, most of the ritual could not be heard. What was heard was silence. People often prayed their own private devotions or followed along in a Missal, but very little of the words of the Mass as uttered by the priest could be heard. This would be especially true if a person were sitting (or kneeling, as the case may be) near the rear of the church, where Catholics would normally tend to gravitate. "Faith comes through hearing," the Apostle Paul tells us (Rom 10:17). But to hear Mass does not necessarily mean that one understands it. In Belloc's case, he most certainly would have since he was as fluent in Latin as he was in English and French. Still, his choice of words is fascinating. One wonders if, by "hearing" Mass, that is, by listening to the silence of the ritual, those present are touched by God in a way that goes deeper than words. Since words spring from silence and can only be distinguished against the backdrop oof silence from which they come, it may very well be the case.

The importance, for Belloc, of hearing Mass during his pilgrimage to Rome (and by extension throughout his life) comes through on the third day of his journey when the opportunity on the feast of Corpus Christi: "I cried out profanely," he writes, "'Devil take me! It is Corpus Christi, and my third day out. It would be a wicked pilgrimage if I did not get to Mass at last.' For my first day (if you remember) I had slept in a wood beyond Mass-time, and my second (if you remember) I had slept in a bed. But this third day, a great Feast into the bargain, I was bound to hear Mass."[14] Although Belloc does not keep his vow of attending Mass at the outset of every day of his pilgrimage (an impractical possibility given the isolated territories he would traverse along the way), his intention to do so is as firm as ever. There is an obvious lesson to be learned here. In the course of life, there will be times when attending Mass is not possible and, in some cases, even to be discouraged (e.g., old age, illness, a pandemic, threats to the common good). Still, the desire to attend is itself a good thing and possibly even meritorious. Today, those unable to receive attend Mass or receive Holy Communion can take advantage of things such a livestreaming and acts of spiritual communion. Although they are not the same as actually being there, they can help a person to stay in touch with and benefit from the wellspring of the Catholic faith.

Belloc's sacramental view of life enables him to draw a close connection between his pilgrimage to Rome and his journey to heaven. He states very clearly near the beginning of his

---

[14] Ibid., 60.

memoir "…what is a pilgrimage in which a man cannot hear Mass every morning?"[15] Mass and the Eucharist are, for him, the link between the human and the divine, heaven and earth, the City of God and the City of Man. Although circumstances do not allow him to keep his vow of hearing Mass every morning while on his walking pilgrimage to Rome, his desire to do so never wavers, and he takes advantage of doing so whenever the opportunity arises. Mass, for him, represents God's journey to our world so that he might join himself to us and take on his journey back to the Father. The Mass cannot be properly understood outside the context of the Incarnation and Christ's paschal mystery. Jesus, the Bread of Life, is the manna from heaven that gives us strength as we wander along in our earthly pilgrimage. When seen in this light, the path to Rome is a symbol of our journey to the heavenly Jerusalem. The great emphasis that Belloc places on bread, wine, and table fellowship is itself a symbol of the Eucharist, which itself is a reflection of the Messianic banquet.

At one point in his journey, Belloc finds himself in Milan attending an Ambrosian Mass: "…I stood in the crypt of the cathedral to hear the Ambrosian Mass, and it was (as I had expected) like any other, save for a kind of second lavabo before the Elevation. To read the distorted stupidity of the north one might have imagined that in the Ambrosian ritual

---

[15] Ibid., 38.

the priest put a *non* before the *credo*, and *nec's* at each clause of it, and renounced his baptismal vows at the *kyrie*; but the Milanese are Catholics like any others, and the northern historians are either liars or ignorant men. And I know three that are both together."[16] Here, we are reminded that the Catholic Church has various rites associated with it (both Eastern and Western), each of which is deeply rooted in history, tradition, and the practice of the faith. The Ambrosian (or Milanese) rite is a Catholic liturgical Western rite that differs from the Roman rite in some respects but, as Belloc duly points out, is fully Catholic in every respect. Since they belong by far to the largest rite in the Church, Roman-rite Catholics need to take care not to look down upon or denigrate in any way the many other rites (including the Ambrosian) that form a part of the Church spiritual heritage. To do so, would be to misunderstand the universal dimensions of Catholicism and the commission the Church has to spread the Gospel and make disciples of all nations (Mt 28:19).

Finally, Belloc has a profound understanding of the efficacy of Christian worship. Toward the end of the memoir, he imagines a possible conversation between the Eternal Father and St. Michael the Archangel. At one point, God, the Father views humanity from afar and has this to say: "'But I notice one odd thing. Here and there are some not doing as the rest, or attending to their business, but throwing themselves into

---

[16] Ibid., 182-83.

all manner of attitudes, making the most extraordinary sounds, and clothing themselves in the quaintest of garments. What is the meaning of that?' 'Sire!' cried St. Michael, in a voice that shook the architraves of heaven, 'they are worshiping You!' 'Oh! They are worshiping *me*! Well, that is the most sensible thing I have heard of them yet, and I altogether commend them. *Continuez,*' said the Padre Eterno, *'continuez!'* And since then all has been well with the world; at least where *ils continuent*"[17] The celebration of Mass, Belloc maintains, is essential for the world's well-being. Although the ritual may seem odd (even mysterious), it represents the authentic worship of Christ and his mystical body, the Church. Its celebration, wherever and whenever it takes place, is a sign that all is (and shall be well) with the world.

Conclusion

Hilaire Belloc, one of the great English authors of the twentieth century, wrote in many literary genres: poetry, novels, essays, histories, apologies, memoirs—to name but a few. His literary output was enormous and the impact it had on world of his day (and particularly the Catholic one) was substantial. Although his influence has diminished over the time, he is still remembered for what now considered a classic work of English literature, *The Path to Rome*; his

---

[17] Ibid., 267.

friendship with G. K. Chesterton, whom pundits today refer to in the singular as "The Chesterbelloc," a name given them by George Bernard Shaw; and works for children such as *Cautionary Tales for Children*, which has never gone out of print.

Belloc's spiritual outlook was thoroughly Catholic in the best sense of the word. He had a sacramental view of reality that sensed the sacred in the midst of the ordinary; he viewed life as a journey upon which all men and women were called to embark; he revered Catholicism's universal dimensions and relished the different types of persons who gathered under it doctrinal, moral, and spiritual umbrella; he was conscious of the great heights that we could reach through the assistance of God's grace, yet also understood the weakness of the human condition and the sinful tendencies that haunt the human heart. A devout Catholic with both feet firmly planted on the ground, he believed in the fundamental goodness of creation and was an adversary of any kind of dualism that would separate the body from the soul or look upon the simple pleasures of life (like a good wine at a good meal) as gifts from God too help us through the difficulties of life's journey.

The Mass, for Belloc, was one such gift, one that conveyed both natural and supernatural benefits. It provided a quiet moment at the beginning of the day that would help us put things in perspective and remember where we came from and where we were bound. It provided food for the journey to our heavenly homeland and helped us get in touch with the mystery of the divine presence that underlies all things. It put us in touch with our earthly forebearers and the ritual they performed for thousands and thousands of years. Most of all, it immersed us in the sacrifice of Christ's death on the cross and gave us he body and blood as food for the journey. "What is a pilgrimage in which a man cannot hear Mass every morning?" What he states about his pilgrimage to Rome can just as easily apply to his pilgrimage through life. The Mass and the Blessed Sacrament it gives us represent all that is deepest, most precious, and life-giving about the Catholic faith. Without them, the journey (be it to Rome or elsewhere) would be impossible for us to dream of, undertake, or ever hope to complete.

Reflection Questions

- Have you ever made a long pilgrimage by foot? If not, would you like to? If so, where would you go? Where would be your starting point? What would be your destination? What is it about a pilgrimage by foot that engages the imagination? What is it about pilgrimages in general that speak to us about the meaning of life?
- To what extent can Life itself be likened to a walking pilgrimage? What similarities does it share with pilgrimages in general? How are the two dissimilar? Do

you view your life as a journey? Do you view it as a spiritual journey? What is the purpose of your earthly pilgrimage? What do you consider your final destination to be? Do you hope one day to get there?

- What role does the Eucharist play in your spiritual journey? Is it an important part of your spiritual practice? Do you look upon it as something essential for the journey or a mere accessory? Do you look upon it as your daily bread? Do you look upon it as the source and summit of your life? Do you miss it when you are unable to attend? Can you do without it?

Voice Two

Robert Hugh Benson
Lord of the World

Robert Hugh Benson (1871-1914) was one of the bright lights of the Catholic literary revival in Great Britain in the early part of the twentieth century. The son of E. W. Benson (d. 1896), the Anglican Archbishop of Canterbury, he was educated at Eton College, studied classics and theology at Trinity College, Cambridge, and was ordained an Anglican priest at the age of twenty-five. His conversion to Catholicism in 1903 caused an uproar in the Anglican circles of the day and became the subject of much controversy. He went to Rome to study for the Catholic priesthood, was ordained in 1904, ministered as University Chaplain at Cambridge in 1908, and named a Monsignor in 1911. The author of many novels, plays, poetry, and spiritual works, his better-known works include *Lord of the World* (1907), *The Paradoxes of Catholicism* (1913), and *Confessions of a Convert* (1913). The first of the works is widely considered the world's first dystopian novel; the second demonstrates the breadth of his theological knowledge and his popularity as a preacher; the third numbers among the great classic in the literature of conversion. His teaching on the Eucharist unfolds in the context of our relationship with Christ and is clearly evident in his devotional classic, *The Friendship of Christ* (1912).[1]

Benson's Theological Outlook

Friendship lies very near to the heart of Benson's theological outlook: "If there is anything clear in the Gospels it is this—that Jesus Christ first and foremost desires our friendship."[2] Such friendship is similar to what happens between two human beings but goes far beyond it: "Certainly it is a friendship between his soul and ours; but that soul of his is united to divinity. A single *individualistic* friendship with him therefore does not exhaust his capacities. He is man, but he is not merely a man: He is the son, rather than a son a man. He is the eternal word by whom all things were made and are sustained."[3]

For Benson, the friendship of Christ touches us both interiorly and exteriorly. Interiorly, Christ wishes to be admitted "not merely to the throne of the heart or to the tribunal

---

[1] For biographical profiles of Robert Hugh Benson, see Joseph Pearce, "R. H. Benson: Unsung Genius," *Catholic Authors*, http://www.catholicauthors.com/benson.html; Michael Keating, "Robert Hugh Benson (1871-1914)," *Crisis* (September 10, 2013), https://www.crisismagazine.com/2013/robert-hugh-benson-1871-1914.

[2] Robert Hugh Benson, *The Friendship of Christ* (Chicago: The Thomas More Press, 1984), 21.

[3] Ibid., 22.

of conscience, but to that inner secret chamber of the soul where a man is most himself, and therefore most utterly alone."[4] There, in that inner spiritual sanctum, "we pass from a knowledge about him to a knowledge of him."[5] We begin to see that eternal life impresses upon us in the present moment and consists a personal encounter with Jesus and, through him, an intimate knowledge of God, the Father. This interior friendship of Christ with the soul is possible not only for Catholics, but for all Christians, and potentially for the entire human family: "For our Lord is the 'light that enlightens every man,' it is his voice that speaks through conscience, however faulty that instrument may be; it is he, since he is the only absolute, who is the dim ideal figure discerned standing in the gloom of all hearts who desire him; it is he whom Marcus Aurelius and Gautama and Confucius and Mahomet, with all their sincere disciples, so far as they were true to themselves desired, even though they never heard his historical name of Jesus, or, having heard it, rejected him, so far as that rejection was without their own fault."[6] Benson tells the story of an old Hindu who, upon hearing one sermon about Christ, requested baptism at once. When asked how he could ask for it after hearing just one homily, he

---

[4] Ibid., 18-19.
[5] Ibid., 27.
[6] Ibid., 51.

replied: "But I have known him and have been seeking him all my life long."[7]

In addition to knowing him interiorly, Benson maintains that we must also encounter Christ in the myriad ways in which he comes to us in the external world: "He must be known (if his relation with us is to be that which he desires) in all those activities and manifestations in which he displays himself. One who knows him therefore solely as an interior companion and guide, however dear and adorable, but does not know him in the Blessed Sacrament—one whose heart burns as he walks with Jesus in the way, but whose eyes are held that he knows him not in the breaking of the bread, knows but one perfection out of ten thousand. And again, he who calls him friend in Communion, but whose devotion is so narrow and restricted that he does not recognize him in that mystical body in which he dwells and speaks on earth— one, in fact, who is a dévot, an individualist, and does not therefore understand that corporate religion which is the very essence of Catholicism; or, again, who knows him in all these ways, yet does not know him in his vicar, or in his priest, or in his mother— or again, who knows him in all these ways— (who is, in popular language, an "admirable Catholic")—but who does not recognize the right of the sinner to ask for mercy, or the beggar for alms, in his name: or again, who recognizes him under sensational circumstances,

---

[7] Ibid., 52.

but does not under dreary ones—who gives lavishly to the first beggar who pleads in Christ's name in the street, but fails to find him in the unappealing dullard—those, in short, who recognize Christ in one or two or three aspects, but not in all—(not, at least, in all those of which Christ himself has explicitly spoken)—can never rise to that height of intimacy and knowledge of that ideal friend which he himself desires, and has declared to be within our power to attain."[8]

Benson understands that Christ calls us to encounter him both interiorly and exteriorly, both "within us" and "in our midst." The kingdom of God is like a two-edged sword that cuts through the sinews of the soul and enables it to sense his palpable presence in the ordinary events of the day. Christ desires to be at the heart of all our human relationships. He gave us to Eucharist to unite us in a personal bond with him and with one another.

Benson's Teaching on the Eucharist

For Benson, the Eucharist is one of the primary ways by which we come to encounter Christ in our midst: "It is not enough to know Christ in one manner only: we are bound, if we desire to know him on his own terms and not on ours, to recognize him under every form which he chooses to use. It is not enough to say, 'Interiorly he is my friend, therefore I

---

[8] Ibid., 22-23.

need nothing else.' It is not loyal friendship to repudiate, for example, the Church or the sacraments as unnecessary, without first inquiring whether or not he has instituted these things as ways through which he designs to approach us. And, particularly, we must remember, in the Blessed Sacrament he actually conveys to us gifts which we cannot otherwise claim. He brings near to us, and unites to us, not only his divinity, but that same dear and adorable human nature which he assumed on earth for this very purpose."[9]

According to Benson, "Jesus Christ…dwells in our tabernacles today as surely as he dwelt in Nazareth, and in the very same human nature; and he dwells there, largely, for this very purpose—that he may make himself accessible to all who know him interiorly and desire to know him more perfectly."[10] This is an expression of Jesus' humility: "Could there be anything more characteristic of the Christ who dwells in the heart, than that he who is so simple interiorly, who lies patiently within the chamber of the soul, should lie also in the realm without, desiring us to acknowledge him not only in ourselves, but outside ourselves; not only in interior consciousness, but also, in a sense, in that very realm of space and time which so often leads to obscure his presence in the world?"[11] Christ's humility represents the seal of his

---

[9] Ibid., 52.
[10] Ibid., 54.
[11] Ibid., 55.

friendship: "It is in this manner, then, that he fulfills that essential of true friendship, which we call humility. He places himself at the mercy of the world that he desires to win for himself. He offers himself there in a poorer disguise even than 'in the days of his flesh,' yet, by faith and teachings of his Church, by the ceremonies with which she greets his presence, and by the recognition by his friends, he indicates to those who long to recognize him and who love him, and (though they may not know it), that it is he himself who is there, the desire of all nations and the lover of every soul."[12]

For Benson, Christ's humility, manifested in his presence in the tabernacle, was made possible by the deeper humility of his becoming present on the altar in the form of a victim: "In the sacrifice of the Mass he presents himself before the world, as well as before the eyes of the eternal Father, in the same significance as that in which he hug upon the cross, performing the same act which he did once for all, the same act by which he displayed that passion of friendship in whose name he claims our hearts, the climax of that greatest love of all by which he 'laid down his life for his friends.'"[13]

Benson points out, moreover, that the Eucharist embodies one last humiliation of Christ: "The tabernacle...presents Christ to us as friend; the altar presents him performing before our eyes that eternal act by which he wins in his

---

[12] Ibid., 55-56.
[13] Ibid., 56.

humanity the right to demand our friendship.... And yet there is one last step of humiliation, even deeper, down which he comes to us—that step by which our victim and friend descends to be our food. For, so great is his love to us that it is not enough for him to remain as an object of our adoration, not enough for him to lie there as our sin-bearer—not enough, above all, for him to dwell within our souls in an interior friendship in a mode apprehensible only to illuminated eyes. But, in Communion, he hurries down that very stairway of sense up which we so often seek to climb in vain. While we are 'yet a great way off' he runs to meet us; and there, flinging aside those poor signs of royalty with which we strive to honor him, leaving there the embroidery and the flowers and the lights, he not merely unites himself to us, soul to soul, in the intimacy of prayer, but body to body in the sensible form of his sacramental life."[14]

Jesus' humility reveals him as our "supreme friend."[15] He has humbled himself by being present to us in the tabernacle. He has taken our sins upon himself in the sacrifice of the Mass. He has united us to himself—in both body and soul—by giving us his own flesh and blood to eat and drink. Benson presents the Eucharist as the sacrament of Christ's friendship, and it is marked, he says, by these three humble expressions of his love. Through his hidden presence in the

---

[14] Ibid., 57.
[15] Ibid., 58.

tabernacle, Christ makes himself available to all people throughout history. In his sacrifice on the altar, he offers himself up for the sins of all humanity. In nourishing his followers with his body and blood, he unites them with his divinity and glorified humanity and enables them to enter the presence of the Father. We should learn something from Christ's sacramental humility. Like him, we too need to be present to others, give ourselves to them, and become nourishment for them. To bear the name Christian means that we seek to walk humbly with Jesus along the way of discipleship.

Some Further Insights

While the purpose the above description was to paint in broad strokes a picture of Benson's views on the Eucharist against the background of his overall spiritual outlook, the following remarks develop these insights in more detail to provide a better sense of the place of the sacrament in his life and thought.

To begin with, Benson treats the Eucharist from the perspective of Christ's presence in the external order. In doing so, he underscores Christ's rootedness in the real world and evades any temptation to limit him only to the subjective word of the believer. Although an interior knowledge of Christ is important, an authentic friendship must seek him in all the avenues that he has opened up to the believer. To ignore such in presence in the Church, in the sacraments, and especially in the Eucharist does not do justice to his universal Lordship. Limiting him merely to the interior realm can make the believer overly introspective and detach him or her from engaging the external world in constructive and meaningful ways.

Benson presents the Eucharist as the sacrament of Christ's friendship. It is the place where the internal and external orders meet and the means by which Christ draws the believer into a deeply personal and intimate relationship. Friendship with Christ, in other words, involves a mutual relationship with a Divine Person, characterized by a mutual indwelling of heart, mind, and soul. This friendship is centered on the love of the Father and results in our participation in the divine nature by means of our sharing in Christ's glorified humanity. In the Eucharist, Christ becomes our food so our humanity might mingle with his humanity and share in his divinity.

The Eucharist embodies Christ's humility, which Benson identifies as an essential mark of true friendship. In this sacrament, Christ empties himself and meets us where we are. He enters time and space and becomes present to us. He does so, in order to enter into communion with us and give us a share in the intimate love of the Trinity. This divine self-emptying reveals something of the very nature of God. "The Good is self-diffusive," we are told.[16] God does not desire to

---

[16] Pseudo-Dionysius, *The Divine Names*, chap. 4.

lord his divinity over us, but rather seeks to share it with as many people as possible. The Eucharist is the way he chose to be present to us through time by giving himself up for us and becoming for us our nourishment and source of hope.

Christ's real presence in the Blessed Sacrament is a perfect example of Christ's divine humility. His presence in the tabernacle is just as real as when he lived in Nazareth and walked the roads of Galilee. "The Word became flesh and made his dwelling among us" (John 1:14).[17] Jesus' hidden life in Nazareth is a foreshadowing of his hidden presence in the Blessed Sacrament. The God who humbled himself to dwell among men continues to humble himself to this day. His presence in the tabernacle points to his yearning to dwell in the tabernacle of our hearts. Because of his love for us, however, he will enter only when he is invited to enter there and rest his head.

Christ's divine humility is also present in the sacrifice of the altar. At the Eucharist, the one sacrifice of Calvary becomes present in a real, powerful (albeit unbloody) way. As Jesus himself reminds us, "No one has greater love than this, to lay down one's life for one's friends" (John 15:13). Jesus does not look upon us as his slaves or servants, but as his friends. At every Mass, the same Jesus who took our sins

---

[17] All quotations from Scripture come from *The Catholic Study Bible,* Second Edition. *The New American Bible, Revised Edition* (Oxford: Oxford University Press, 2011).

upon himself and offered himself on Golgotha in our stead some two thousand years ago, immerses us in that one timeless, redeeming event. At every Mass, Jesus comes to us as both priest and victim. He takes our sins upon himself, offers himself on our behalf, and washes us clean in his sacrificial blood.

At the Eucharist, Christ's humility is also manifest in his becoming food and nourishment for us. He emptied himself not only by becoming human in the mystery of the Incarnation, but continues to pour himself into bread and wine in the mystery of the Eucharist, transforming them into his glorified body and blood, so that he could enter not only into our souls, but also into our bodily existence. He does so out of his desire to enter into friendship with the entire person—body, soul, and spirit—and elevate us beyond our nature so that we might share in his divinity: "Whoever eats my flesh and drinks blood has eternal life, and I will raise him on the last day. For my flesh is true food, and my blood is true drink. Whoever eats my flesh and drinks my blood remains in me and I in him" (John 6:54-56).

Finally, Jesus is not content with befriending us only in our interior lives, but wishes to enter into intimate, personal contact with us on every level of our human makeup. The Eucharist is the primary means he uses to bridge in inner, subjective word of believers with the external world that he created and over which he too reigns as Lord. In this sacrament, he humbles himself by making himself present to us in the

Tabernacle, by laying his life down for us at the Altar, and by giving us his own body and blood as food to eat at his Table. These humble actions are not isolated, but intimately related parts of a single divine plan to win our friendship. If humility is an essential sign of true friendship, then the Eucharist is the sacrament par excellence of divine/human friendship. As friends of Jesus, we are called to follow in his footsteps by being present to others, by giving ourselves to others, and by becoming food and nourishment for them.

Conclusion

It has been more than a hundred years since Robert Hugh Benson died at the young age of forty-two, while preaching a mission in Salford, Greater Manchester. Although he was an important figure in the Catholic literary revival of his day, his memory has largely faded from today's Catholic consciousness, and his works do not attract as wide a readership as their quality deserve. A convert to Catholicism, he stands with men like John Henry Newman, Evelyn Waugh, and Ronald Knox for the depth of his learning and the passion with which he embraced his newfound faith.

A talented author with a wide range of literary interests, Benson was able to probe the teachings of the Catholic faith and help his readers discover things they had never seen before. The friendship of Christ is a case in point. He used the metaphor of friendship as a way of tying together both the subjective and objective world of his readers and did in a way that enabled these horizons to blend and exist in harmony. Friendship, he believed, was all that Christ wanted from us. It was the very secret of the saints, who in the early Church and the days of late antiquity were known as the "friends of God."[18]

The Eucharist, for Benson, is the seal of Christ's friendship. In it, Jesus undergoes a threefold humiliation by making himself present to us in the Tabernacle, by laying down his life for us at the Altar, and by offering his own body and blood for nourishment at the Table. Since humility lies at the heart of authentic friendship, the sacrament becomes, for him, the sacrament of Christ's friendship. Those who receive it are called to follow Christ by allowing him to become himself in them—and vice versa. They are called to listen to his words— and do likewise.

Reflection Questions

- What role does friendship play in your approach to life? Is it an essential *sine qua non*? A peripheral concern? A nice thing to have but not a necessity? How does friendship fit into your understanding of the movement of world history? How does it fit into your

---

[18] See Peter Brown, *The Making of Late Antiquity* (Cambridge. MA: Harvard University Press, 1978), 54-80.

religious and spiritual outlook? What is its relationship to your understanding of the Eucharist?

- How do you look upon Jesus? How does he look upon you? How do you relate to him? How does he relate to you? Do you look upon him as a judge? A distant, impersonal lord? Is he someone you can talk to and share your deepest concerns? Is he your closest friend, someone you can always turn to? What's keeping you from looking to Jesus as your supreme friend?

- What do you think the end of the world will be like? Do you ever think about it? Do you believe that Jesus is the Lord of history? Do you look upon him as the Alpha and the Omega, the beginning and the end? How does the Eucharist fit into God's plan for the world? Is it truly the sacrament of the New Creation? To what extent does it foreshadow the end of time and the beginning of a New Age, one that is already here, yet still to come?

Voice Three

G. K. Chesterton
The Ball and the Cross

Gilbert Keith Chesterton (1874-1936), a towering figure in Catholic thought of his day, wrote during the first third of the twentieth century and remains a relevant and influential voice to this day. Born in London, he attended St. Paul's School and the Slade School of Art at the University College London without finishing his degree. He married Frances Blogg in 1901, found his way back to the Anglican faith through her influence, and converted to Catholicism in 1922.

A journalist by trade, Chesterton wrote in a variety of literary genres: newspaper articles, poetry, novels, art and literary criticism, philosophical and theological essays—to name but a few. As a journalist, he wrote for *Daily News*, *The Illustrated London News*, and *G. K.'s Weekly,* and also gave a series of very popular radio talks for BBC from 1932 until his untimely death in 1936. His literary corpus is enormous, considering that he died at the relatively young age of sixty-two. Among his better-known works are *The Napoleon of Notting Hill* (1904), *Heretics* (1905), *Orthodoxy* (1908), *The Man Who Was Thursday* (1908), the *Father Brown* short stories (1910-36), *The Everlasting Man* (1925), *Thomas Aquinas*

(1933), and his *Autobiography* (1936). His complete works are available in a multi-volume series published by Ignatius Press.

Chesterton was close friends with Hilaire Belloc, another popular Catholic of the day and who with Chesterton, John Knox, and others, were major voices of the Catholic literary revival in England in the early twentieth century. He died of congestive heart failure at his home in Beaconsfield, Buckinghamshire and was buried from Westminster Cathedral, London. Knox preached at his funeral and spoke of the impact he had on a whole generation of the Catholic faithful.[1]

Chesterton's Spiritual Outlook

Although baptized into the Church of England shortly after his birth, Chesterton grew up in a non-practicing Unitarian household and had drifted away from faith in God in his early years. He eventually embraced the Anglican communion in his late twenties and finally converted to Catholicism at the age of forty-eight. By that time, he had already written a sizeable number of literary works and was well on his way to becoming a noted author and commentator in England and beyond. His conversion to Catholicism was the

---

[1] For more on Chesterton's life and literary corpus, see "G. K. Chesterton," *New World Encyclopedia*, https://www.newworldencyclopedia.org/entry/G._K._Chesterton.

culmination of a lifelong search for the truth about the ultimate questions of life and the world he lived in.

Chesterton considered himself an orthodox Catholic and was one of the great apologists of the faith. His book, *The Everlasting Man*, written only a few years after his conversion to Catholicism, has this to say about the authenticity of the faith:

> I attempt no apologetic about why the creed should be accepted. But in answer to the historical query of why it was accepted, and is accepted, I answer for millions of others in my reply; because it fits the lock; because it is like life. It is one among many stories, only it happens to be a true story. It is one among many philosophies; only it happens to be the truth. We accept it; and the ground is solid under our feet and the road is open before us. It does not imprison us in a dream of destiny or a consciousness of the universal delusion. It opens to us not only incredible heavens, but what seems to some an equally incredible earth, and makes it credible. This is the sort of truth that is hard to explain because it is a fact; but it is a fact to which we can call witnesses. We are Christians and Catholics not because we worship a key, but

because we have passed a door; and felt the wind that is the trumpet of liberty blow over the land of the living.[2]

Sometimes referred to as the "prince of paradox," Chesterton conveyed his thoughts in a popular style that used easily accessible images and metaphors that appealed to plain common sense.[3] He wrote in a style that left the truth hidden in plain sight, only to be revealed in a mounting literary and rhetorical flourish that would turn commonly held truths and aphorisms on their heads. This openly disarming treatment of the rationalist pundits of his day caused his readers to look beneath appearances so as to discover the deeper truths beneath what eyes could see. In dealing with his opponents, he reveals the inadequacy of their arguments by forcing them to take their reasoning to logical conclusions, thereby forcing them to admit the opposite from their own rational premises.

Along with Belloc and other well-known Catholic figures such as Dorothy Day and Peter Maurin, the founders of the Catholic Worker movement, Chesterton was a staunch defender of Distributism, a social theory that tried to steer a middle course between laissez-faire Capitalism and state-run

---

[2] G. K. Chesterton, *The Everlasting Man* (Garden City, NY: Image, 1955), 254.

[3] For Chesterton's literary output and style, see Jill Carattini, "Prince of Paradox," *RZIM*, https://www.rzim.org/read/a-slice-of-infinity/prince-of-paradox.

Communism. This social theory, he believed, was rooted in Catholic social principles which sought, at one and the same time, to preserve respect for both the individual and common good. It upheld such things as the right to private property, closeness to the land, distributing the means of production across a wide swathe of society rather than centralizing it in the state, and an embrace of the Catholic principles of subsidiarity and solidarity. He and Belloc were some of the earliest proponents of this social theory, which continues to be viewed as a viable alternative to those socio-economic theories that have dominated human history in recent centuries. Chesterton's embrace of this theory shows that, in addition to his concern for the integrity of the individual, his spiritual outlook involved an understanding of the social dimensions of human existence and the need to root humanity's well-being in a concern for both the dignity of the human person and the preservation of the common good. Much the same can be said for his views on the Eucharist.[4]

---

[4] For more on Chesterton's understanding of distributism see, "The Distributist," The Society of Gilbert Keith Chesterton: The Apostle of Common Sense, https://www.chesterton.org/category/discover-chesterton/chestertons-selected-works/the-distributist/.

Chesterton on the Eucharist

Regarding his view on the Eucharist, Chesterton believes in Jesus' Real Presence. Although he recognizes this presence in the world in a variety of other ways—in the poor, in the priest, in the worshiping community, wherever two or three are gathered in his name—he considers his presence in the sacrament to be qualitatively different from the others. It would be like saying: "The spirit of Jehovah pervades the universe" and saying, "Jesus Christ just walked into the room."[5] In his mind, Jesus's presence in the Eucharist falls under the latter category.

Chesterton also affirms the Catholic belief that the same Jesus who walked this earth some 2,000 years ago continues to enter our world daily in the sacrifice of the Mass and reposes in all the tabernacles of the world hidden in the consecrated bread which has been transformed into the glorified body and blood of the Risen Lord. In a certain sense, Jesus' presence in the Blessed Sacrament is even more real than when the Word of God took on human nature entered our world so long ago: the former represents Jesus' glorified presence, while the latter his earthly presence before he underwent his passion, death, and resurrection. As the first fruits of the New Creation, Jesus' presence in the Eucharist

---

[5] Cited in Mark P. Shea, "Are the Sacraments Narrow?" http://www.mark-shea.com/narrow.html.

Voice Three: G. K. Chesterton—*The Ball and the Cross*

points to his presence to humanity in a new and vital way. In an article published in *Good Housekeeping* in 1932, he has this to say about Jesus' nearness to his people:

> If I am to answer the question, 'How would Christ solve modern problems if He were on earth today', I must answer it plainly; and for those of my faith there is only one answer. Christ is on earth today; alive on a thousand altars; and He does solve people's problems exactly as He did when He was on earth in the more ordinary sense. That is, He solves the problems of the limited number of people who choose of their own free will to listen to Him.[6]

Jesus, for Chesterton, continues to enter our world today, but does so hidden beneath the appearances of bread and wine and in such a way that only those who believe in him can listen to the still small voice of his Spirit dwelling within their hearts. This hidden presence is deeper and even more real than when he was on earth, because he now not only enters our world but through the eyes of faith also enters the human heart. When we listen to him, Jesus shapes our minds and hearts and enables us to look at the problems of the world in a new and transformative way, one which

---

[6] G. K. Chesterton, "Our Tradition: If Christ Should Come," *Good Housekeeping* (April, 1932).

recognizes the dignity of the human person and the importance of working for the common good.

That is not to say that, even for those who believe in Jesus' Real Presence at Mass and in the Blessed Sacrament, that gathering for worship and prayer before the tabernacle does not at times seem boring and even tedious. "The Mass is very long and tiresome, he maintains, "unless one loves God."[7] Faith in Jesus' Real Presence must be complemented by hope and especially by love. These are the three things that last (1 Cor 13:13). All three are necessary for our earthly sojourn. In faith, we recognize Jesus' presence in the Eucharist; in hope we yearn for his coming and long to one day see him face to face; in love seek to live as he lived and reach out to others as he has done so to us.

A reflection of Chesterton's belief in the Real Presence also appears in his fiction. In his novel, *The Ball and the Cross* (1909), for instance, Chesterton turns the table on secular atheists by using their own arguments against them and showing that belief in Christ and his presence in the Eucharist represents a threat to their world view and a soothing balm to those blessed with simple childlike faith. One of the major themes of the novel is that those who seek to undermine the mystery of the cross by means of cold, rational arguments end up undermining everything else, even their

---

[7] G. K. Chesterton, *The Ball and Cross*, chap. 11 in The Essential G. K. Chesterton Collection e-book (original ed., 1909), 563.

Voice Three: G. K. Chesterton—*The Ball and the Cross*

own secular world view. In one scene, Turnbull, a die-hard atheist, has a conversation with Madeline, a young woman of faith to whom he feels a strong attraction. They represent two very different views of the world: one imbued with faith; the other, with cold logical argument. Their conversation goes like this:

> [Turnbull] finally says: "I am sure there is no God." "But there is," said Madeline, quite quietly, and rather with the air of one telling children about an elephant. "Why I touched His body only this morning." "You touched a bit of bread." said Turnbull, biting his knuckles. "Oh, I will say anything that can madden you!" "You think it is only a bit of bread," said the girl, and her lips tightened ever so little. "I know it is only a bit of bread," said Turnbull, with violence. She flung back her open face and smiled. "Then why did you refuse to eat it?" she said.[8]

Madeline uses Turnbull's own rational argument on its head to undermine his position. If he truly believed that the Eucharist was not what the Church says it is, he would have no hesitation eating it. After all, it is only a bit of bread. That Chesterton wrote these words more than a decade before his conversion to Catholicism indicates that his belief in the Real

---

[8] Ibid., 564

Presence was strong even when he was a member of the Church of England. His eventual journey into the Catholic fold would strengthen this conviction even further.

Some Further Insights

Although the above brief summary of Chesterton's views toward the Eucharist is by no way exhaustive, it offers an opportunity to delve a bit further into his staunch religious outlook and the challenge it makes to the secular world around him. What follows are some observations aimed at probing his understanding of the Eucharist in a little more depth.

To begin with, it is important to emphasize that Chesterton's belief in the Real Presence predates his conversion to Catholicism. For decades years prior to his conversion to the Catholic faith, he held fast to the tenets of Anglo-Catholicism (or High Anglicanism, as it is also called). According to this tradition, Christ is truly present in the Eucharist, although not in the same way that Catholics hold. Rather than the substances of the bread and wine actually being transformed into the body and blood of Christ (as in the Catholic doctrine of transubstantiation), it generally holds that the substance of the bread and wine coexist alongside the substance of the Risen Christ. There can be no doubt that the Anglo-Catholic tradition affirms Christ's Real Presence in the Eucharist and that Chesterton held this belief prior to his conversion to Catholicism. If we can infer that Madeline's belief in the incident cited above from *The Ball and Cross*, published when Chesterton was a member of the Church of England, reflects his own view on the matter (as it likely does), it is clear that his belief in the Real Presence was set long before his entrance into the Catholic faith.

According to Chesterton, the Catholic faith is one of many stories, but happens to be a true story. The Eucharist is not only a part, but a central part of that story. Without it, the Christian story loses its cohesive, unifying power. Known as the "sacrament of sacraments" and the "sacrament of unity," it is the primary means by which Christ remains in communion with the members of his body, the Church. Whenever we eat and drink of the body and blood of Christ, our humanity is mingled with his which, in turn, is intimately united to his divinity. As members of his body, we are thus able to enter into the presence of the Father and participate in the intimate communion of love that is shared by the Father, Son, and Holy Spirit. The human mind cannot fathom the mystery of this Triune God who, at one and the same time, is both one and three. This underlying paradox of the Catholic faith lies at the top of the hierarchy of truths, and the Eucharist is not far behind. Chesterton understands that his story and our own ultimately lead to an encounter with this divine mystery and that the Eucharist is the primary vehicle of that encounter.

Chesterton has been called the "prince of paradox" and writes in a style that displays his uncanny ability to come to a resolution by setting two seemingly contradictory statements side by side. The Eucharist, in many ways, is the "paradox of paradoxes" in that it claims God's obscure, hidden, yet very real presence in what, by all other counts and objective measurements, is nothing but a bit of bread and a sip of wine. Chesterton believed that Christ solved modern problems in much the same way he did when he walked the earth some 2,000 years ago. For those who believe, he is present every day on a thousand altars. Although not visible to the eye, this presence is just a real as his more ordinary earthly presence. All one needs to do is take time out to listen to him and hear what he has to say. Doing so requires faith that he is there to listen and that he empowers us to understand what he is saying. When seen in this light, the Eucharist represents a marriage between heaven and earth, between God and humanity, between our hunger and thirst for God and God's hunger and thirst for us.

Chesterton agrees that, if a person does not love God, the Mass can seem very long and tiresome. In this simple statement, he invites his readers to ask themselves why they bother to attend Mass in the first place. Do they attend out of a sense of obligation? Do they do so out of a sense of some cultural expectation, or because it is what is expected? Do they go because they are looking for what they can get out of it? Or do they go because they love God and desire to visit him and render him worship? Coupled with the whole question of intention is the whole question of understanding. Do

Voice Three: G. K. Chesterton—*The Ball and the Cross* 49

they really understand what is going on at Mass? Do they understand that it makes present in a mystical and unbloody way Jesus' bloody sacrifice on Calvary? Do they understand that the consecrated host they receive on their tongues is the body, blood, soul and divinity of the glorified and risen Lord? Do they understand that it is a meal and a foreshadowing of the messianic banquet? Chesterton packs a great deal in one simple, seemingly non-intrusive sentence, and leaves his reader with the task of unraveling his or her own reasons for attending Mass.

Finally, it bears noting that the underlying theme of The Ball and the Cross *has to do with the question of which has precedence: the world or the cross.* In other words, should the cross be planted on top of the world (as found on the top of many church steeples)—or vice versa? Chesterton's point in the novel is that, when the world tries to place itself over the cross, it usually ends up in a worse position than before. Jesus' cross was firmly planted in the earth. He was born in a cave and was laid to rest in a cave. He descended to the bowels of the earth to preach the triumph of the cross. While it is true that in our present historical circumstances, Catholics find themselves members of two cities—The City of God and the City of Man (to borrow some imagery from Augustine)—we view ourselves as a pilgrim people, whose destination is not the earth as we know it, but a new heaven and a new earth. Jesus' cross was planted in the earth in order to transform it. The Eucharist is the "sacrament of the New

Creation." The paradox of the cross is that, while it appears to be at odds with the world, it is really the means by which it will ultimately come to discover its full destiny. Jesus turned the cross, an instrument of unimaginable cruelty, into a symbol of love and redemption. In a similar way, he wishes to transform the world by dying on the cross and pouring out his blood upon it. The Eucharist is the means by which that turning point in history accompanies humanity down the corridors of time.

Conclusion

Chesterton was a larger than life figure, the kind one would expect to encounter in one of his novels. A man of large, portly stature, his physical presence rarely went unnoticed when he entered a room. He knew how to be serious, as well as to laugh at his opponents and even at himself. His writing was orthodox, opinionated, thought-out, paradoxical, humorous, sometimes outrageous, and at times even threatening. His enormous literary corpus covered a wide range of topics ranging from the political, religious, social, economic, and personal—to name but a few. He knew how to draw connections between a wide range of what otherwise might seem disparate, even disconnected, topics. He had an eye for paradox and knew how to find a middle way between opposing camps that kept the best of each and discarded whatever remained.

Voice Three: G. K. Chesterton—*The Ball and the Cross*

Chesterton's writing had an enormous impact on Catholic thought and continues to be a touchstone and point of reference for the adherents of Catholic orthodoxy to this day. A major voice of the Catholic literary revival, his spiritual and theological outlook was expansive and included a deep sensitivity for the common man and his typical commonsense approach to life. His style was easily accessible to a wide range of readers and was very much appreciated by the learned and unlearned alike. He loved to debate ideas but knew how to form solid relationships, even friendships, with those who disagreed with him. He had a deep sense of the sacredness of life and sought to instill it in his writing, even if the topic at hand was not particularly religious. He was a man who came from humble origins and who never lost sight of the humility we all must try to display before others and especially before our God.

Chesterton's view on the Eucharist falls within the mainstream of the Catholic faith and reflects his own love for paradox and the juxtaposition of opposites. He believed in Jesus' Real Presence in the Eucharist and understood this presence to be something very concrete and tangible. Being in the presence of the Blessed Sacrament was like being in the same room as Jesus himself. Jesus, he believed, comes to us on a thousand altars each and every day, because he loves us and wishes to journey with his people and help them navigate the various vicissitudes of life. He is ready to help us solve our problems, if only we have faith in him and are willing to listen to him. Chesterton understood that the Mass could seem dry and boring at times, but not for those who love God.

In addition to his many talents, Chesterton was also deeply aware of his own foibles and weaknesses, not the least of which was a propensity for hurtful and unwarranted ethnic prejudices. He looked to the Church and her sacraments as a healing balm that would heal him of his sins and weaknesses and allow him to stand with dignity before the judgement seat of God. The Eucharist, for him, was a sign of Christ's love not only for an abstract humanity, but for each individual, including himself. And for that he was ever grateful.

Reflection Questions

- Why do you believe? Have you ever not believed? Have you ever entertained the thought of not believing? Why do you believe in Christianity? Does it "fit the lock," as Chesterton was wont to say? Does it correspond to life? Do you agree with him that it is one of many stories but happens to be a true story? How would you explain the rational basis of your faith to an unbeliever?

- Do you believe in the Real Presence? If so, how and in what manner? Is Jesus present in the poor? Is he present in the priest? In the believing community? Is he present in the consecrated bread and wine? How is his presence in the Blessed Sacrament different from all the other ways in which he is present to his people? How is it different from when Jesus himself walked the earth?

- How would you explain the "paradox of the Eucharist?" How does Chesterton explain it? Can it be fully explained? What is it about the sacrament that eludes definition? How does the mystery of the sacrament continue to fascinate and prod the imagination? What role does the Eucharist play in Chesteron's novel, *The Ball and Cross*? Do you agree with Chesterton's depiction?

Voice Four

Georges Bernanos
A Diary of a Country Priest

Georges Bernanos (1888-48), a French writer and winner of the coveted *Grand prix du roman* of the French Academy in 1936, was born in Paris to a family of devout Catholic artisans. He grew up in the country village of Fressin, studied with the Jesuits at Vaugir, and continued his formal education at the Institute Catholique and the University of Paris, where he received licentiates in both law and letters. He married in 1917, served as a corporal in the French army during World War I, and received the *Croix de Guerre* for being severely wounded in battle. He was a member of the Action Française in his youth but broke with the movement in 1932. He lived in Majorca in 1936, moved back to France in 1937, emigrated to Paraguay and then Brazil in 1938 when political tensions were on the rise. During World War II, he lamented France's existential ennui and blamed its lack of spirit for the way Germany had overpowered it in 1940. An outspoken critic of the Vichy regime, he supported the Free French Forces led by Charles De Gaulle and was invited by him at the war's end to assume an active role in French politics, an offer he refused on account of his continued disillusionment with the lack of élan he experienced upon his return to

France. Many of his numerous works translated into English and include: *Under the Sun of Satan* (1926), *Joy* (1928), *The Crime* (1935), *The Diary of a Country Priest* (1936, his best known work for which he won the *Grand Prix*), *Mouchette* (1937), *A Diary of My Times* (1937), *The Open Mind* (1943), *The Fearless Heart 1943), Night Is Darkest* (1943), *Plea for Liberty* (1944), *Sanctity Will Out* (1947), *Tradition of Freedom* (posthumous, 1950), and *The Last Essays of George Bernanos* (posthumous, 1955). His views on the Eucharist are tied to his understanding of the priesthood and what Allan White calls "the transparency of grace."[1]

Bernanos's Spiritual Outlook

Bernanos was a simple (although not a naive, unquestioning) believer with a restless soul. Critical of the clericalism in the institutional Church that isolated itself from the needs of the people and relished instead in the allures of careerism and self-comfort, his heroes were often marginalized priests who were generally looked down upon by their colleagues and even by the people they served. The Curé of Ambricourt in Bernanos's masterpiece, *The Diary of a Country*

---

[1] For further biographical information on Bernanos, see Hans Urs von Balthasar, *Bernanos: An Ecclesial Existence*, trans. Erasma Leva-Merilakis (San Francisco: Ignatius Press, 1996). See also Allan White, "The Transparency of Grace: Bernanos and the Priesthood," *New Blackfriars* 79 (November, 1998): 464-73.

Priest and the abbé Donnissan in *Under the Sun of Satan* are two examples of priests who, despite being ostracized by the world and by their own people, understood that the true following of Christ involved a wisdom that could not be learned merely from books but involved something much deeper, a humility that acknowledged one's own frailty and insignificance before God, while also being open to the stirring of his grace in the human heart.[2]

Bernanos's restlessness in spirit also manifested itself in his wandering life. Born to a Spanish family that had emigrated to France that had already become entrenched in French culture long before his birth, he moved at various points in his life from France to Majorca, where he became disgusted with the brutality and petty violence Spanish Civil War, then back to France, then to Paraguay, then to Brazil in the years immediately preceding the outbreak of World War II, and finally back to France at the end of the war. This sense of restlessness is reflected in his novels and represents the hunger of a believing Christian disillusioned with the world's broken, fallen status and weary of waiting for the Lord's coming. In his novels, he depicts a world saddened by its inability to rise above the surrounding boredom, feigned

---

[2] See White, "The Transparency of Grace," 465.

civility, and subtle (and often open) hostility of one human being to another.³

Bernanos's response to this sad and depraved world is "the transparency of grace." The spirituality of St. Thérèse of Lisieux's "Little Way" lies behind this spiritual outlook and is evidenced by the emphasis on being faithful in carrying out the little things of day-to-day living, the joyful and willing abandonment to the defense of Truth, and the dying Curé's final words in *A Diary of A Country Priest*, "Grace is everywhere."⁴ What is more, according to Allan White, "The theological tone of Bernanos's treatment of the priestly vocation and its association with some themes in the writings of Thérèse of Lisieux can be traced to a common ancestor, Cardinal Pierre de Bérulle (1575-1618), a seminal figure in the French school of spirituality of the sixteenth and seventeenth centuries."⁵

Predominantly Augustinian in outlook, Bérulle's main concern was for the renewal of the Catholic priesthood. He hoped to bring this about through a focus on the Christological and Incarnational understanding of the Catholic priesthood and believed that Christ was present to humanity through the Eucharist and the priesthood. For this reason

---

³ See Matthew Hoen, "Georges Bernanos (1888-1946), http://www.catholicauthors.com/bernanos.html.

⁴ Georges Bernanos, *The Diary of a Country Priest*, trans. Pamela Morris (New York, Macmillan, 1937, 1965), 298.

⁵ See White, "The Transparency of Grace," 469.

the two are very intimately related. The purpose of the priesthood, Bérulle maintained, was for Christ to befriend and ultimately dwell in a priest so that God's grace would flow out to the faithful and make itself available to everyone down the corridors of time. When seen in this light, the priesthood is all about Eucharist—and vice versa.[6]

Bernanos on the Eucharist

In *The Diary of a Country Priest*, Bernanos brings out the close relationship between priesthood and Eucharist in a subtle and very inconspicuous way. Although nowhere in the novel does he present the Curé of Ambricourt actually celebrating Mass, it is clear by the numerous (almost offhand) references to the sacrament that it is part and parcel of his daily duties. It is a source of heartache for him that most (if not all) the members of his wayward flock treat it as a sterile routine that has lost any deep religious significance for them. In fact, much of the novel's action takes place after the Curé's daily celebration of Mass. His conversations with Mlle. Louis, M. le Comte, the meeting he announces after his celebration of High Mass, his care for ailing parishioners, with the Curé of Torcy, his encounter with Mlle Chantal are

---

[6] Ibid., 471.

all examples of how the Mass serves as a backdrop for the novel's unfolding action.[7]

One of the best examples of the great indifference and lack of respect the characters in the novel have for the Eucharist comes in a discussion Mlle Chantal has with the Curé immediately after Mass: "Now I'd like to tear her eyes out, I would! Yes, and stamp on them like that!" The Curé responds, "How can you say that within a few steps of the Blessed Sacrament? Have you no fear of God?"[8] The Curé's parishioners have no fear of God, because God no longer has an impact on the way they live their lives. The Catholic religion has become, for them, nothing but an empty shell of religious practice with little (if any) bearing on their daily lives. It gives them no sense of transcendence and has become nothing else but a part of the boring leprosy of their empty, bourgeoise existence.

Bernanos depicts the Curé of Ambricourt (the country priest) as a Christ figure, who suffers humiliation from every side: his fellow clergy, his parishioners, even the children who he had hoped to teach the beauties of the sacraments and Holy Communion. This humiliation reflects that of Christ himself, who was rejected by many and abandoned by his closest followers. The Curé's close configuration to

---

[7] See Bernanos, *The Diary of a Country Priest*, 25, 29, 84, 102, 128, 199f.).

[8] Ibid., 130.

Voice Four: Georges Bernanos—*A Diary of a Country Priest*

Christ also manifests itself in his diet and sickly demeanor, both of which point to the mystery of the Eucharist which, as a priest and *alter Christus*, he embodies in his own body and blood. The stomach cancer which haunts him throughout the novel is a symbol of Christ's cross. Although not fully aware of it, the Curé is slowly dying. Christ's passion and death is palpably present in his very bones and nothing can relieve it but the bit of dry bread and wine that he takes to soothe his gnawing pain.[9] This daily diet of dry bread and wine symbolizes the close configuration he has with the Eucharist. His parishioners' failure to appreciate the beauty of the sacrament spills over into their lack of respect (even ridicule) of their own priest. Since the Eucharist and priesthood are so closely tied to one another, it follows that a disregard for one would flow over into a similar lack of appreciation (even scorn) for the other. The Curé, we might say, embodies in his person both the passion and death of Christ and his Eucharistic body and blood. The intimate relationship between the sacrament and the sacrifice of Christ on Calvary plays itself out in this rural country priest. Although no one realizes it, he has become Eucharist both for himself and others. One example of this is he impact he has on the Mme. la Contesse through his simple, childlike words and demeanor

---

[9] Ibid., 32, 43, 127.

helps her to let go of her grief over the loss of her young son and open her heart to life, to others, and to God himself.[10]

Still, the deepest and most thorough conversion that takes place in the novel is in the life of the Curé himself. Coming from a poor peasant background, he has a low opinion of himself and feels very much out of place even in a country parish that lives in the shadow of a Chateau of lower nobility. He knows he is looked down upon with disdain by his fellow clergy and feels insecure in the presence of the village children, who tease him behind his back and play rude tricks on him.[11] As the novel unfolds, he gradually comes to the realization that even he is beloved by God and that that is all that matters. On his deathbed, when his stomach cancer has taken its course, he finds himself in the home of his good friend from his days in the seminary who has left the priesthood and is now living with a woman. Knowing he is near death he asks his friend to hear his confession. Although a priest has been sent for to give him Viaticum and the final consolations of the Church, the time of his earthly sojourn has come to an end. Told that the priest is on his way, his final words are, "Does it matter? Grace is everywhere...." (298).[12] At the end of his life, the Curé has been given the eyes to see what he has been struggling to see all his life. He

---

[10] Ibid., 146-74.
[11] Ibid., 26-28.
[12] Ibid., 298.

sees as Jesus sees. The grace of the sacrament has done its work.

Some Further Insights

This brief presentation of how the Eucharist appears in *The Diary of a Country Priest* reveals something of the "transparency of grace" that is a consistent theme in much of his other writing. The following remarks seek to go more deeply into the religious outlook that sustains this understanding of God's accessibility to man.

To begin with, when we look upon the Curé *of Ambricourt as a Christ figure, it becomes clear that the diary he has left behind is a testament of his life and work.* As such, it corresponds to the way in which the Scripture reveals the identity of Christ. The diary, we might say, is to the Curé as the Scriptures are to Christ. The words of the former point to the words of the latter—and vice versa. As the Curé becomes the bits dry bread and wine he consumes for his daily sustenance, his diary records the narrative of his inner spiritual struggle that ultimately leads him to the realization that "Everything is grace." When all is said and done, nothing else matters. Except for the concluding letter written by his friend to the Curé of Torcy, all we know about the Curé comes to us through his diary. His words, which were never meant for public consumption, stand as a monument to his spiritual martyrdom. They relate the *passio* of one willing to follow Christ wherever he leads. In this case, he carries his cross into the spiritual desert of the nominal, unbelieving Christians of a small twentieth-century French country village.

"Truly I tell you, unless you change and become like children, you will never enter the kingdom of heaven" (Mt 18:3; NRSV). The Curé's parishioners, steeped in a superficial bourgeois mentality causing everyone to live on the surface of life, are either incapable or unwilling of delving beneath appearances and experience others, let alone God, as they truly are. Even the children of the parish are infected by this crass, cynical mindset, as evidenced by the cruel tricks they play on their priest which bring nothing but upon ridicule and scorn upon him. Of all the characters in the novel, he alone possesses the innocent air of a child. His simple childlike character takes people off guard and elicits from an array of responses that range from scorn to ridicule to pity to disgust. His childlike demeanor eventually breaks through the defenses of Mme. la Contesse's bitterness towards God, her family, and everyone else over the premature death of her son and brings her back to herself and the land of the living just before she dies. The Curé himself dies realizing that grace abounds everywhere and that, when all is said and done, nothing else matters.

The contrast Bernanos creates between the Curé of Torcy, a priest from an older, more social-minded generation, and the sickly Curé of Ambricourt, who seems out of place in the society of clerics and laity alike, reveals a subtle shift in priestly identity and purpose that represents one of the underlying themes of the novel. While both priests celebrate Mass each day for their parishioners, the former does so from within their bourgeois mindset, while the latter resists being sucked into their empty, boorish wasteland. While the former has come to live with and accept the people he serves as they are without placing any undue demands on them, the latter frets over them and seeks to find ways of getting through the vapid bourgeois defenses that they have accumulated over generations of lukewarm, mediocre Catholic practice. Except for the change of heart in Mme la Contesse, the latter's efforts largely fail. Those very efforts, however, have effected a change in his own heart and have brought him further along the road to sanctity.

Bernanos sets up a similar contrast between the Curé of Ambricourt and his friend, the ex-priest, Monsieur Louis Dufréty. The two men became friends in the seminary and were very different in their approach to learning and its place in the following of Christ. Although they both steeped themselves in their studies, the former did so as a means to priestly ordination and understood that mere book-learning would have little effect on his priestly ministry if it were not complemented by a humble search for wisdom, while the latter sought learning for learning's sake, a quest that eventually led him away from his priestly duties to other, more mundane and worldly pursuits. That the Curé maintains the relationship with his friend even after he leaves the priesthood says something of the depth of the bonds he is willing to maintain and his willingness both to welcome him and be welcomed by him at a pivotal turning point in his life. That he asks the ex-priest to hear his confession shortly before his death, says a great deal about his understanding of the priesthood. Even though he was not able to receive Viaticum and the final comforts of the Church, the last hours of his life were spent in the presence of a friend, someone who shared his table with him, who heard his confession, and who heard the last words that came from his lips.

Finally, the contrast Bernanos makes between the Curé of Ambricourt *and Dr. Laville, the medical doctor who diagnoses him with stomach cancer near the end of the novel, represents considerably different approaches to life and its purpose.* The former is a man of faith who struggles with a poor self-image and a sense of failure on account of his inability to break through to the hearts of the people under his care. The latter, by way of contrast, is an avowed atheist, who deals with the underlying melancholy in life by fostering a cynical view toward religion and self-medicating himself with morphine. Still, he displays compassion toward the sickly priest by not revealing to him the seriousness of his illness and who does so only when the priest returns to retrieve his medical prescription. In one sense, the encounter between the two represents a certain reversal of roles. The doctor diagnoses the sickly priest with a death sentence. The disease has progressed to far and nothing can be done to allay its progress. The Curé's simple, childlike presence, in turn, pierces the doctor's cynicism and makes him aware of his own spiritual poverty. The doctor diagnoses the priest's physical ailment; the priest, in turn, by his weak, childlike presence does the same for the doctor's spiritual impoverishment.

Conclusion

Georges Bernanos is once noted for saying, "No, I'm not an 'author.' Had I been a real one, I never should have waited till I was forty before I published my first book."[13] Despite this humble assessment of his career, his literary corpus continues to shed light on a world that has lost sight of the sacred and views the practice of religion as nothing but empty ritual. A devout Catholic he was particularly concerned when he sensed the intrusion of the bourgeois mindset into the practice of the faith and the vapid effect it had on people's lives and the communities in which they lived.

Endowed with a simple (although not uncritical) faith, Bernanos had little patience for a Church that isolated itself from the lives of its people and hid behind the barriers of institutional structures, heady intellectualism, and clerical

---

[13] Hoen, "Georges Bernanos (1888-1946), http://www.catholicauthors.com/bernanos.html.

privilege. His was a faith rooted in the heart, grew in the soil of life's deepest, most existential questions, and was watered by the ever-present (yet ever-elusive) transparency of grace. The only barriers to the fruitful reception of this grace were those created by our own minds to keep us from recognizing the truth about ourselves. Only humility and a willingness to open one's heart to God with a simple, childlike faith can break through the walls of privilege, pride, cynicism, and distrust. Only another Christ, a marginalized and looked-down-upon figure like Bernanos's country priest, can help us see that, in the end, "Grace is everywhere...."

In *The Diary of a Country Priest*, the celebration of Eucharist forms a part of the Curé of Ambricourt's daily routine, so much so that it is merely mentioned as a matter of fact while the rest of the novel's narrative unfolds. It's impact, however, is strong and unmistakable. Bernanos's country priest embodies in himself the close relationship between Eucharist and priesthood: he suffers on the cross of cancer and nourishes himself daily on a bit of dry bread and wine. In doing so, he embodies in his life the person of Christ himself and has become a saint. At the novel's end, this sickly, melancholic priest, who is ridiculed, looked down upon, and scorned by so many, is able to see what so many others (even his fellow members of the clergy) fail to see: Grace is everywhere and there for the asking.

Voice Four: Georges Bernanos—*A Diary of a Country Priest*

Reflection Questions

- Have you ever felt as though those around you looked down on you because of your education, background, or appearance? If so, how did you deal with such prejudices? Did they hinder you from being yourself before them? Did they prevent you from sharing your faith with them? Were you able to see through them? Did they help you get in touch with what truly mattered in life?

- What is the relationship between the suffering in your life and Christ's paschal mystery? Do you see any connection? Little connection? A complete connection? How does our attitude toward suffering change when it is viewed through the eyes of faith? What is the relationship between suffering the cross of discipleship? What is the relationship between suffering and the Eucharist?

- Unless you become like a little child, you cannot enter the kingdom of heaven." What are the qualities of spiritual childhood? How does the Curé of Ambricourt display them? Do you see any of these qualities in your own life? If so, how could you foster them? What does it mean to view the world through the eyes of a child? Do you believe that everything is grace? What is the relationship between spiritual childhood and the Eucharist?

Voice Five

Charles Williams
The Principle of Coinherence

Charles Williams (1886-1945), a prolific lecturer, poet, playwright, novelist, biographer, literary critic, and lay theologian was born in London and studied at St. Albans School and University College, London. He joined the staff of Oxford University Press at the age of twenty-two first as a proofreader and later as an editor, remaining there for the rest of his life. A strong adherent of the Catholic wing of the Church of England, he was friends with such literary figures as T. S. Eliot, C.S. Lewis, J. R. R. Tolkien, and Dorothy L. Sayers. He was also a member of The Inklings, an informal literary club hosted by Lewis that met weekly on Tuesday mornings at The Eagle and the Child pub in Oxford. His rather extended literary corpus includes seven books of poetry, eighteen plays, seven novels, eight biographies, ten works of literary criticism, and six theological writings. His novels include: *War in Heaven* (1930), *Many Dimensions* (1930), *The Place of the Lion* (1931), *The Greater Trumps* (1932), *Shadows of Ecstasy* (1933), *Descent into Hell* (1937), and *All Hallows Eve* (1945). In his theological writings, he is best known for his work on the theology of romantic love and his theory of coinherence, both of which had a profound influence on his understanding of the Eucharist.[1]

Williams's Spiritual Outlook

Williams was a member of the High Anglican tradition, which is otherwise referred to as the Catholic wing of the Church of England. An eccentric and charismatic figure, he was traditionalist and conservative in his theological outlook, yet known to have dabbled in the occult other esoteric practices. Although his reputation somewhat waned after his death in 1945, it has undergone a resurgence in recent years, in part because of his association with C. S. Lewis, J. R. R. Tolkien, and The Inklings, and also because of recent biographies on him.[2] In his theological writings, he made two important contributions that deeply influenced his spiritual outlook: his development of the theology of romantic love and the notion of coinherence.

Williams developed his theology of romantic love from his musings on Dante's feminine muse, Beatrice, who leads the poet through the stages of the spiritual journey in the *Divine Comedy*. "The basic principles of Romantic Theology,"

---

[1] For more on the life of Charles Williams, see "About Charles Williams," in *The Charles Williams Society*, https://www.charleswilliamssociety.org.uk/about/ .

[2] See, for example, Grevel Lindop, *Charles Williams: The Third Inkling* (Oxford: Oxford University Press, 2015).

he states, "can be reduced to a single formula: which is, the identification of love with Jesus Christ, and of marriage with His life."[3] According to Grevel Lindop, from this basic principle Williams goes on "to find analogies or 'correspondences' between the experiences of love and marriage and the life of Christ."[4] The narrative of the life of Christ, for Williams, is the interpretative pattern for understanding marriage. Jesus' birth corresponds to the birth of love between husband and wife; his baptism, to the marriage ceremony; his temptation in the desert, to those that a couple undergoes when they are tempted to think that the sufferings of married life can be magically turned around. In time, love will also undergo a crucifixion, a resurrection, as well as an experience of the indwelling grace of the Spirit. Williams, in effect, was trying to establish a new branch of theology, one that gave erotic love its due as an authentic way to holiness rooted in the Gospels and the way of the Lord Jesus. Called to see the beloved through the eyes of God, each lover would see their relationship as patterned after the love of God, the Word-made-flesh.[5]

Williams's theory of coinherence, in turn, is a development of the patristic concept of *perichoresis* (or circumincession), a doctrine that explains the interpenetration of the

---

[3] Charles Williams, *Outlines of Romantic Theology* (Berkeley, CA: The Apocryphile Press, 2005), 14.

[4] Lindop, *Charles Williams*, 110.

[5] Ibid., 110-11.

relationships among the three persons of the Blessed Trinity, as well as that between the divine and human natures in Christ. It explains the unity of the one and the many by showing how, even though the various persons of the Trinity or natures of Christ penetrate one another, they still maintain their distinct and proper boundaries. Williams takes this concept and extends it to the Body of Christ and the New Creation. Jesus, he maintains, divinizes humanity, "not by conversion of Godhead into flesh, but by taking of the manhood into God."[6] Faith in Christ, moreover, also immerses us in a web of relationships: with Christ himself and, through him, with the Father and the Spirit, as well as with the communion of saints, and with all of creation. Our individual identities, while distinct and with clear boundaries, thus cannot be separated from this intricate web of relationships, which thus highlights the social character of human existence. Salvation, when seen in this light, is not an isolated affair between the individual and God but a communal enterprise with ramifications for the human community as a whole and for each of us as individuals: "The principle is one of the open secrets of the saints; we might draw the smallest step nearer sanctity if we used it. Substitution in love, exchanges in love, are a part of it; 'oneself' and 'others' are only

---

[6] Charles Hefling, ed. *Charles Williams: Essential Writings in Spirituality and Theology* (Cambridge, MA: Cowley Publications, 1993), 147.

specialized terms of its technique."⁷ We are saved primarily as a people and only secondarily as individuals. Williams's theology of romantic love and his concept of coinherence permeates his entire spiritual outlook and have great importance for his understanding of the sacraments of the Church.

Williams on the Eucharist

Williams's explanation of the Eucharist is a case in point. The theology of romantic love, he maintains, embodies the same love present in the sacrament through the conjugal love of husband and wife. The sacrament also represents the fullness of coinherence, since a union of separate ontological entities takes place with no confusion of substances. Jesus lives in us and we in him. These two concepts—the theology of romantic love and the principle of coinherence— work together to bring a very creative understanding of what takes place at the Eucharist.

When applied to the Eucharist, for example, Williams's theology of romantic love draws a close connection between the sacrament and the marriage bed: "In that intercourse which is usually referred to as the consummation of

---

⁷ Charles Williams, *The Descent of the Dove: A Short History of the Holy Spirit in the Church* (London: Faber and Faber, 1939), 236.

marriage the presence of Love, that is, of Christ, is sacramentally imparted by each to the other. If this act is not capable of being a sacrament, then it is difficult to see in what way marriage itself is more sacramental than any other occupation; … the Christ of the Eucharist and the Love of the marriage-night are indeed not two but one."[8] In this instance, the marriage bed points to the sacrament of the Eucharist and even participates in the Love that Christ seeks to communicate to his Church. The work of sanctification takes place in the love of husband and wife, especially in the intimate bodily and spiritual exchange that takes place in sexual intercourse. The body of the Risen Lord, who is present in the consecrated species "may already be shaped and nourished throughout the sacred bodies of the lovers."[9]

In a similar way, the principle of coinherence underscores how the Incarnation of Christ continues in and through the Eucharist. In the Incarnation, divinity weds itself to humanity in a way that unifies them while at the same time keeping them distinct. Whenever Mass is celebrated, the same union-in-separation takes place in the Eucharistic elements: Jesus body, blood, soul and divinity become one with the bread and wine, while remaining distinct. As Mary McDermott Shideler notes "…it is the sacrament [the

---

[8] Williams, *Outlines of Romantic Theology*, 44-45; Lindop, *Charles Williams*, 111.

[9] Williams, *Outlines of Romantic Theology*, 45.

Eucharist] that most directly involves the body: the communicant eats and drinks; the stomach digests the elements; the physical flesh is nourished and renewed. Man gave his flesh to Christ; and receives Christ's flesh back from him in a mystery of mutual exchange, so that the acts of exchange operate not only through minds, hearts, and wills, but also physically."[10] The coinherence of Jesus' glorified body with the Eucharistic elements of bread and wine facilitates a similar coinherence between him and the communicant: the two become one body yet remain distinct; the communicant also becomes one with the entire communion of saints, all of whom are distinct members of the one mystical Body of Christ.

For Williams, the theology of romantic love and the principle of coinherence shed new light the meaning of the Eucharist. In seeking to highlight the spiritual significance of erotic love, he shows that, because "Jesus Christ is Love," marital intercourse is an authentic manifestation of what takes place at the Eucharist: the love of God that is really present in the consecrated species is also present in the mutual love of husband and wife, and especially in the marriage bed. In like manner, the principle of coinherence, operating within the immanent Godhead of the Most Holy Trinity,

---

[10] Mary McDermott Shideler, *The Theology of Romantic Love: A Study in the Writings of Charles Williams* (Eugene, OR: Wipf & Stock, 2005), 200-1.

extends itself to every level of God's actions in creation: in the mystery of the Incarnation, in the mystery of Christ's spousal relationship to the Church, in his presence through the sacraments, and especially in his presence in the Eucharist, the sacrament of sacraments.

Some Further Insights

Although these examples of Williams's views on the Eucharist do not exhaust his understanding of what takes place in the sacrament, they provide the general contours within which a fuller presentation of his beliefs can unfold. The remarks that follow seek to delve a bit more deeply into his attitude toward the Eucharist.

Although Williams's application of the principle of coinherence to the Eucharist may coincide with his Anglo-Catholic belief in that it affirms the corporeal presence of Jesus in the Eucharist, it would be difficult to reconcile it with the Catholic doctrine of transubstantiation, which maintains that the substance of the bread and wine are transformed into (not merely penetrated by) the body and blood of Christ. Coinherence of the Christ body and blood with the bread and wine actually resembles more the doctrine of consubstantiation (held by some Anglicans), which maintains that that the substance of Christ's corporeal being exists alongside of the substance of bread and wine. The main difference between William's notion of coinherence and consubstantiation is that in the former the two substances interpenetrate one another while remaining distinct, while in the latter they merely coexist side-by-side. In any case, it would be difficult to reconcile coinherence with transubstantiation, since the latter says that the substance of the bread and wine no longer exist but are themselves not mere penetrated by but actually transformed into the body and blood of the Risen Christ.

When we understand that the Eucharist is the sacrament of the New Creation and that the Holy Spirit is invoked over the elements of bread and wine at the epiclesis of the Mass, it becomes clear that, for Williams, the interpenetration of Christ with the bread and wine also points to a similar coinherence with all of creation and therefore all of history. His book, *The Descent of the Dove* (1939), which was originally going to be entitled, *A History of Christendom*, is a reflection of the presence of the Spirit in the history of the Church. This coinherence of the Holy Spirit with the movement of history represents the next stage in God's providential plan for humanity. If God, the Father, created the world, and God the Son, redeemed the world, the Holy Spirit sanctifies the world. God, in other words, not only created the world, but penetrated human nature by virtue of the Incarnation and now penetrates the whole of creation and the movement of history by virtue of the sanctifying coinherence of the Holy Spirt. Williams also deals with this theme in his novel, *Descent into Hell* (1937), his theological work, *He Came Down from Heaven* (1938), and his book of poems, *Taliessin through Logres* (1938).

Williams bases his interpretation of the Eucharist on the premise that "Jesus Christ our Lord" is also "Jesus Christ Our Love."[11] If the Eucharist is the "Sacrament of Love," it follows that it finds itself wherever authentic love exists. Since the physical love between husband and wife represents the most intimate exchange of mutual love and sharing to be found on earth, it follows that their actual physical embrace, that is to say, their mutual coinherence of persons made visible and very concrete in their conjugal love for one another, reflects the coinherence of the Three Persons of the Blessed Trinity, the coinherence of the human and divine natures in Christ, and especially the coinherence of Jesus' body and blood with the Eucharistic elements. When seen in this light, Williams's theology of romantic love is a precursor of John Paul II's Theology of the Body. The two approaches to marriage have very much in common, not the least of which is the understanding that the intimate sharing of authentic sexual love images Christ's spousal love for the Church and makes it present to the world in a very visible and concrete way.

That said, Williams himself was aware that his theology of romantic love presented some dangers, among which number ingenuity and sentimentality. Closely related, each of

---

[11] Williams, *Outlines of Romantic Theology*, 48; Lindop, *Charles Williams*, 111.

these focuses more on the means toward arriving at the living principle rather than on the end. They differ in that the first is intellectual and the second emotional. Ingenuity arises from delight in the intellectualization of romantic love, looking to its symbolic meaning rather than its ultimate purpose. It substitutes appearances for reality and can easily lead the person into a dream world that is out of touch with daily life. Sentimentality, in turn, arises from the passions and allows them to blur one's vision of the actual status a loving relationship. These dangers, according to Williams, are offset by the skepticism and devotion. Although they do not always work together very easily, when they do, these remedies provide important safeguards to a distortion of romantic love. Skepticism offsets an over intellectualization of romantic love; devotion, in turn, prevent the emotions from completely taking over one's senses in the way a person relates to others. When applied to the Eucharist, Jesus Our Love must be neither overly intellectualized nor overly sentimentalized. As an expression of authentic Eucharistic love, both husband and wife must look to the heavens but have both feet firmly planted on the ground.[12]

One of the strengths of Williams's concept of coinherence is the continuity it brings to every level of the reality. Coinherence, the interpenetration of separate entities, exists in the Holy Trinity, in the union of the human and divine in Christ,

---

[12] Williams, *Outlines of Romantic Theology*ˆ, 49-54.

in the Church and her sacraments, and in all of creation. It is important to point out, however, that this interpenetration is not univocal, but takes place in varying degrees and intensities, depending on which level of reality we are dealing with. The *perichoresis* (or interpenetration) of the three persons of the Blessed Trinity, for example, is qualitatively different from that which takes place between the divine and human natures in Christ, or between Christ and his Church, or between the communicant and the sacrament of the Eucharist. Coinherence, in other words, is an analogous concept that, despite the likeness and difference within the concept itself, offers us a way of seeing a unifying concept in all of reality, including both uncreated and created realms of existence. What is more, it makes sense that the unifying principle within the Godhead is that which holds together every other aspect of reality. When seen in this light, the principle of coinherence gives us another insight into how vestiges of God are present within his creation.

Williams's concept of "coinherence" also offers new insights into the meaning of the Neoplatonic notion of "participation," which theologians have adapted to explain how human beings can come to share in the divine nature. It does so by emphasizing the kind of sharing that takes place, a penetration of two separate entities that brings about a single ontological union while at the same time maintaining the distinctions among them. When seen in this light, human beings share in the divine nature in a way that is similar (although not identical) to the interpenetration of the Divine Persons themselves. In the former case, the distinction between the creator and his creation remains, while in the latter the distinction makes no sense. The benefit of Williams's notion of "coinherence" is that it helps us to unpack a basic theological concept and gives us a clear indication of what it might mean. It also gives us a deeper understanding of Christian discipleship and Jesus's exhortation that his followers remain in him so that he might remain in them (Jn 15:4).

Finally, although Williams's theology of romantic love fills a lacuna in the contemporary theological discourse of his day, it must be remembered that eros *(i.e., romantic love) must be complemented by the other loves of* storge *(natural affection),* philia *(friendship), and* agape (divine love).[13] As evidenced in the Bible, the phrase "God is Love" applies to all of these loves. Since we refer to God as "Father, Spouse, Friend, and Suffering Servant, it would be wrong to attribute his love for humanity solely in terms of romantic love. If Williams elevated romantic love to a deserving place in theological discourse, we must remember that it too must be complemented by these other loves. While each of these loves exist separately in human experience and can, at times,

---

[13] For a treatment of these loves and how they interrelate, see C. S. Lewis, *The Four Loves* (New York, 19600.Harcourt, Brace, Jovanovich

interpenetrate one another (as in the case of a married couple who have become close, intimate friends), within the Godhead, they themselves coinhere, while at the same time remaining distinct. When seen in this light, the concept of coinherence enables us to appreciate the meaning of romantic love while also recognizing its distinct limitations.

Conclusion

Charles Williams was a creative and influential force in the literary world of his day and wrote across a wide range of literary genres. Along with C. S. Lewis, J. R. R. Tolkien and other well-known literary figures, he was regular member of The Inklings literary club, a prolific writer, and probably best known for his imaginative novels that have the supernatural penetrating the everyday life. Known for his ideas about the theology of romantic love and the principle of coinherence, he was devout member of the Catholic wing of the Church of England and saw the purpose of his writing as bringing sound doctrine to others without them being aware of it.

Williams's spiritual outlook was deeply influenced by his ideas about the nature of romantic love and coinherence. In the former, he saw an intrinsic link between love and Jesus Christ and looked to his life to draw out the profound meaning of the marital bond. In the latter, he looked to the interpenetration of the Persons of the Trinity as a way of understanding how the supernatural penetrated the created world.

These two concepts are themselves intimately related, since the whole idea behind the theology of romantic love is that the life of Jesus has penetrated the marriage bed and that the love between husband and wife reveals in a very concrete and palpable way God's love for humanity and all the world. Same holds true for the Eucharist.

This sacrament is the fullest expression of Christ's love for the Church and humanity. In this most physical of the sacraments, the body of the Risen Lord penetrates the bread and wine in such a way that they become totally one with him, while at the same time remaining distinct and separate entities. When eating the bread and drinking the consecrated bread and wine, the communicant receives the body and blood of Christ into himself or herself and the ongoing process of interpenetration continues. This coinherence of the believer with Christ is a manifestation of God's committed and unbreakable spousal love for the Church, a reality which the marriage itself both points to and makes visible. When seen in this light, Williams's understanding of the sacrament, if not in complete compliance with Catholic doctrine, seeks to find a way of showing how vestiges of the Trinity are present on every level of the spectrum of creation. In doing so, it provides a very creative (albeit alternative) way of understanding how the actions of God, all of which are actions of love, flow from his very being and are hardwired into the very nature of the created world.

Reflection Questions

- How would you describe Williams's principle of coinherence? How does it resemble the traditional Christian concept of *perichoresis* (or circumincession)? How does it differ from it? How does he apply this concept to the Eucharist? In what ways does his application coincide with the traditional Catholic doctrine on the Real Presence? How does it differ?

- How would you describe Williams's theology of romantic love? What are its main characteristics? How does it complement the traditional Christian understanding of *agapic* love? What are its major strengths? What are its limitations? How does he apply this theology to the Eucharist?

- Do you think Williams's principle of coinherence can explain the fullness of the mystery of the Eucharist? Can it stand alone? Does it need to be used in conjunction with other models? What are its strengths? What are its weaknesses? What dangers does it present to our understanding of the sacrament? How does it contrast with the Catholic doctrine of transubstantiation?

Voice Six

J. R. R. Tolkien
A Letter to His Son

John Ronald Reuel Tolkien (1892–1973) was professor of Anglo Saxon at the University of Oxford and the author of such popular and widely read works of fantasy fiction such as *The Hobbit* (1937) and *The Lord of the Rings* (1954-55). He was also a founding member of an Oxford literary group called "The Inklings," among whom were numbered Owen Barfield, Charles Williams, C. S. Lewis, and others.

Born of British parents in 1892 in Bloemfontein, South Africa, he settled the Midlands of England with his mother and younger brother after his father's death in 1896. In 1900, his mother Mabel converted to Catholicism and raised her sons in the faith. She died of diabetes in 1904, leaving her two sons orphaned. At that point, Father Francis Morgan, the priest who ministered to Tolkien's mother, looked after the two boys' material and spiritual needs. He attended King Edward's School in Birmingham and in 1911 matriculated at Exeter College, Oxford, eventually focused on English Language and Literature, and graduated in 1915.

With the outbreak of World War I, he enlisted as a second lieutenant in the Lancashire Fusiliers, married in 1916, and went to fight on the Western Front soon thereafter.

After four months in the trenches, he developed trench fever and was sent back to England to recuperate. After the war, he was employed for a brief time as assistant lexicographer for the New English Dictionary, before accepting a position in 1920 as senior reader at the University of Leeds. He remained in that post until 1925 when he became the Rawlinson and Bosworth Professor of Anglo Saxon at Oxford. In 1945 he became the Merton Professor of English Language and Literature and remained in that position until his retirement in 1959. He died on September 2, 1973 and is buried with his wife in Wolvercote cemetery just north of Oxford.[1]

Tolkien's Spiritual Outlook

Tolkien once described himself as a Hobbit "in all but size:" "I like gardens, trees, and unmechanized farmlands; I smoke a pipe, and like good plain food (unrefrigerated), but detest French cooking; I like, and even dare to wear in these dull days, ornamental waistcoats. I am fond of mushrooms (out of a field); have a very simple sense of humor (which even my appreciative critics find tiresome); I go to bed late

---

[1] This biographical information comes from David Doughan, "J. R. R. Tolkien: A Biographical Sketch," The Tolkien Society, https://www.tolkiensociety.org/author/biography/.

and get up late (when possible). I do not travel much."² He had a deep appreciation of the natural world and lamented its destruction at the hands of man living in a mechanized age. If he had lived in Middle Earth, the world where his epic fantasy takes place, he would have resided in the Shire.

In one of his letters he writes: ". . . there are a few basics, which however drily expressed, are really significant. For instance, I was born in 1892 and lived for my early years in 'the Shire' in a pre-mechanical age. Or more important, I am a Christian (which can be deduced from my stories), and in fact a Roman Catholic. The latter 'fact' perhaps cannot be deduced."³ Tolkien believed one's writing should speak for itself and objected to the trend in literary criticism that sought to find reflections of an author's life hidden in the text. Doing so, he believed, turned attention away from the work itself: "But only one's guardian Angel, or indeed God Himself, could unravel the real relationship between personal facts and an author's works. Not the author himself (though he knows more than any investigator), and certainly not so-called 'psychologists.'"⁴ Middle Earth, the world in which his fiction unfolds, comes from the Old English word, "Middangeard," "an ancient expression for the everyday

---

² Humphrey Carpenter, ed., with the assistance of Christopher Tolkien, *The Letters of J. R. R. Tolkien* (Boston: Houghton Mifflin Harcourt, 2000), 288-89.
³ Ibid., 288.
⁴ Ibid.

world between Heaven above and Hell below."[5] Tolkien's fiction takes place in Middle Earth during "the Third Age," an earlier time in earth's history, before the "Age of Man" had begun.

A devout Catholic, Tolkien's outlook on the world was shaped by his strong religious convictions. He believed in all the tenets of the faith: The Trinity, Creation, the Fall, the Incarnation, the Resurrection of Christ, Redemption in Christ, the Church, and the sacraments. He believed in the four last things: death, judgment, heaven, and hell. He had a strong devotion to the Blessed Mother, believed in the communion of saints, and awaited Christ's second coming. As might be expected, the Eucharist was also very dear to his heart.

Tolkien on the Eucharist

One of Tolkien's most beautiful passages on the Eucharist comes in a letter he wrote to his son Michael, dated March 6-8, 1941. Writing on the subject of marriage and relations between the sexes, he observes that we live a fallen world and concludes that "[t]he dislocation of the sex-instinct is one of the chief symptoms of the Fall."[6] A bit later in the letter, he writes:

---

[5] Doughan, "J. R. R. Tolkien," https://www.tolkiensociety.org/author/biography/.

[6] Carpenter, ed., *The Letters*, 48.

> Out of the darkness of my life, so much frustrated, I put before you the one great thing to love on earth: the Blessed Sacrament . . . . There you will find romance, glory, honour, fidelity, and the true way of all your loves on earth, and more than that: Death: by the divine paradox, that which ends life, and demands the surrender of all, and yet, by the taste (or foretaste) of which alone can what you seek in your earthly relationships (love, faithfulness, joy) be maintained, or take on that complexion of reality, of eternal endurance, which every man's heart desires.[7]

The Eucharist, Tolkien reminds his son, helps us to integrate all our human loves and orient them toward our final end in God. It gives our lives on earth a foretaste of things to come by drawing us into the eternal and making our earthly lives deeper and more authentic. By making the Blessed Sacrament the one great love of our lives, all our other loves become focused and fall into place.

In another letter to his son, Michael, dated November 1, 1963, he speaks of how the Eucharist strengthens those weak in faith:

---

[7] Ibid., 53-54.

The only cure for sagging or fainting faith is Communion. Though always Itself, perfect and complete and inviolate, the Blessed Sacrament does not operate completely and once for all in any of us. Like the act of Faith it must be continuous and grow by exercise. Frequency is of the highest effect. Seven times a week is more nourishing than seven times at intervals.[8]

Tolkien was a firm believer in frequent communion because, like the act of faith, it grows by means of constant practice. He even identified St. Pius X's promotion of frequent, even daily, communion as "the greatest reform of our time" and wonders "what state the Church would be but for it."[9]

Later in the same letter, Tolkien tells his son of the difficulties he had early in life: "I witnessed (half-comprehending) the heroic sufferings and early death in extreme poverty of my mother who brought me into the Church; and received the astonishing charity of Father Morgan."[10] He goes on to write of his deep love for the Eucharist and laments his lack of faithfulness and failure to pass on his faith in this blessed and wonderful gift:

---

[8] Ibid., 338-39.
[9] Ibid., 339.
[10] Ibid., 340.

But I fell in love with the Blessed Sacrament from the beginning—and by the mercy of God never have fallen out again: but alas! I indeed did not live up to it. I brought you all up ill and talked to you too little. Out of wickedness and sloth I almost ceased to practice my religion—especially at Leeds, and at 22 Northmoore Road. Not for me the Hound of Heaven, but the never-ceasing silent appeal of Tabernacle, and the sense of starving hunger. I regret those days bitterly (and suffer for them with such patience as I have been given); most of all because I failed as a father. Now I pray for you all, unceasingly, that the Healer (the *Hælend* as the Saviour was usually called in Old English) shall heal my defects, and that none of you shall ever cease to cry *Benedictus qui venit in nomine Domini*.[11]

Tolkien loved the Eucharist very much and deeply regretted those times when he had fallen out of the practice of receiving it, as well as his failure to pass on love of the sacrament to his children. Despite his failings in such matters, his love for the sacrament perdured.

Although Tolkien wrote that the fact that he was a Roman Catholic "perhaps cannot be deduced from his writing,"[12] he recognized critics who thought otherwise:

---

[11] Ibid.
[12] Ibid., 288

...one critic (by letter) asserted that the invocations of Elbereth, and the character of Galadriel were clearly related to Catholic devotion to Mary. Another saw in waybread (lembas)=viaticum and the reference to its feeding the *will* . . . and being more potent when fasting, a derivation from the Eucharist. (That is: far greater things may colour the mind in dealing with the lesser things of a fairy-story.)[13]

Although he was reticent about drawing such outright comparisons, there can be little doubt that Tolkien's beliefs served as a backdrop against which the world of Middle Earth sprang from his imagination and into the minds of his readers. The Eucharistic overtones of the *lembas* bread are a case in point.

Some Further Insights

Although these examples of Tolkien's views on the Eucharist do not exhaust the richness of his love for and devotion to the sacrament, they provide a general context within which a deeper understanding of his beliefs can unfold.

To begin with, Tolkien's deep attachment to the Eucharist and his Catholic faith throughout his life was likely influenced

---

[13] Ibid.

by the loss of his mother at such an early age. Her conversion to Catholicism in 1900 left her estranged from both sides of the Tolkien family, who were very much against it. Bringing Tolkien and his brother into the faith was a gift she had bequeathed to them. Her Catholic faith, in other words, was a piece of herself that she had left behind. When seen in this light, it makes perfect sense that Tolkien would feel close to her by loving the faith she loved and suffered for so much. Receiving communion was a way of being united with Christ and the members of his body (and thus his mother).

For Tolkien, the Eucharist was "the one great thing to love on earth." Although he knew the world was fallen, he was also deeply aware that Jesus entered it and came to redeem it. The Eucharist, for him, was the sacramental means of bringing Christ's sacrificial death into the present so that all people could benefit from its redemptive fruits. It does so by putting all other loves in perspective taming them over time, and orienting them toward God, the one thing that matters. Because of this sacrament, Death would lose the stranglehold it had on our souls and be defeated by the power of love poured out on the cross and in the empty tomb.

For Tolkien, the effect the Eucharist has on a person takes place not in a single instance but over a lifetime of continuous practice. Holy Communion means "union with" (in this case, "with Christ") and has to do with fostering a personal relationship with him. We do so by spending time with him over the course of our lifetimes. Receiving him at Mass, serving him at Mass, adoring him before the Blessed Sacrament: Tolkien did all these things during his lifetime. Although he regretted those moments in his life when he slacked off in his practice of the faith, the silent draw of the Tabernacle was always there ready to lure him back.

Tolkien regrets that he has failed as a father by not passing on a love for the Eucharist to his children. He laments his lack of initiative in that regard and wishes he had overcome his selfishness and sloth and done something about it. This failure to act, spurred him on later in life to pray for all his children unceasingly. He prayed to Jesus, our Savior, to heal his defects and to kindle in his children a love for both prayer and the sacrament. The awareness of his own flaws, however, did not keep him from renewing his love for the Blessed Sacrament and hoping and praying that they would never stop crying out, "Blessed is he who comes in the name of the Lord."

The Church, Tolkien writes, "was not intended to be static or remain in perpetual childhood; but to be a living organism (likened to a plant), which develops and changes in externals by the interaction of its bequeathed divine life and history—the particular circumstances of the world into which it is set."[14] It was for this reason that he opposed the "'protestant' search backwards for 'simplicity' and directness."[15] The seed of the

---

[14] Ibid., 394.
[15] Ibid.

Church planted by Christ some 2,000 years ago no longer exists. It would be a mistake for the keepers of the Tree to try to capture primitive Christianity and discard all the doctrinal and liturgical developments that happened over time. The Church's deepening understanding of the profound mystery of the Eucharist over time was a case in point.

Tolkien says that his Catholic faith probably could not be deduced from his fiction and that he would hesitate to draw a one-to-one correspondence between certain characters or events in his writing, on the one hand, and Catholic teaching (e.g., Galadriel=Mary; Lembas Bread=Eucharist), on the other. Although we must be careful to avoid a strictly allegorical interpretation of his saga, there are moments in his writing when the sun breaks through the darkened sky above and a particular reference to his Catholic faith shines forth. The clearest example of this comes at the end of *The Lord of the Rings* when Frodo and Sam destroy the ring and Sauron's hold over Middle Earth, doing so on the twenty-fifth of March, the day in the Catholic liturgical calendar is the feast of the Annunciation and the day when Christ assumed human flesh in the womb of the Virgin Mary.[16] The mystery of the Incarnation makes that of the Eucharist possible: both reveal the Body of Christ to the world and are thus deeply intertwined.

---

[16] J. R. R. Tolkien, *The Lord of the Rings*, vol. 3, *The Return of the King* (Boston: Houghton Mifflin, 1965), 283.

Finally, because of his Catholic faith, Tolkien saw an intimate connection between the Eucharist, the Church, and the papacy. In a letter to his son, Michael, he writes: "I myself am convinced by the Petrine claims, nor looking around the world does there seem much doubt which (if Christianity is true) is the True Church, the temple of the Spirit dying but living, corrupt but holy, self-reforming an rearising."[17] He goes on to note that the pope, as the head of the Church on earth, has ever defended the Blessed Sacrament: "'Feed my sheep' was His last charge to St. Peter; and since His words are always first to be understood literally, I suppose them to refer primarily to the Bread of Life."[18] Tolkien's words should bring comfort to Catholics today who themselves, living through a period of corruption and needed reform, must turn to the Eucharist for healing and renewal.

Conclusion

By the time of his death in 1973, Tolkien had become famous for the world of Middle Earth he had created with such careful attention to accuracy and minute detail. The capstone of his work, *The Lord of the Rings*, a trilogy of epic proportions dealing with the struggle between good and evil, was widely read and translated into many languages. A

---

[17] Carpenter, ed., *The Letters*, 339.
[18] Ibid.

popular British poll once designated this work the greatest book of the twentieth century, while his good friend, C. S. Lewis, even nominated him for the Nobel Prize in Literature.

Tolkien's vivid imagination and creative literary powers were surpassed only by his deep, heartfelt faith. He loved the Catholic Church and saw it as a living organism that, like a tree, was rooted in the earth but soared upwards toward the sky. The Church, for him, was both human and divine, a home to sinners and saints, a place for fellowship and worship. The sacraments, for him, were actions of Christ given to the members of his body as signposts on their pilgrim journey through life, into death, and beyond.

The Eucharist, for Tolkien, was food for this journey. He loved the Blessed Sacrament and believed it was the most important love a person could have in life. It gave nourishment to the faithful, strength to the faint of heart and, most importantly, communion with Christ and his Church to those who received it. It was the means chosen by Christ to be present to his people through time. This presence was a Real Presence. At each Mass, Christ himself entered the world anew, to create it anew, making all things new.

Reflection Questions

- What impact did Tolkien's Catholic faith have on his writing? Why does he say that his being a Christian can likely be deduced from his writing but not his being Roman Catholic? What is it about his notion of being a sub-creator that prevents him from drawing too close a correspondence between his personal faith and his fiction?

- How does Tolkien's Catholic faith shine through in his letter to his son, Michael? Why is it that he feels free to express his Catholic faith, and in particular his belief in the Blessed Sacrament and Real Presence in a personal letter to his son and not in his writing geared toward a wider audience? Does he neglect his faith completely in his fiction or does he embed it deep in the worldview that sustains it?

- In what sense does Tolkien view the Eucharist as food for the journey? Why does he say it is the most important love a person can have in this life? Do you have such a love for the Eucharist? Would you like to? What concrete steps could you take to place the Eucharist at the center of your life? How can you make it the source and summit of your Christian life?

Voice Seven

Catherine de Hueck Doherty
"Poustinia" and "Sobornost"

Catherine Kolyschkine (1896-1985) was born in Nizhny-Novgorod, Russia and raised in an aristocratic family. At the age fifteen, she married her cousin Baron Boris de Hueck. The couple served on the Russian Front during World War I, lived through the Russian Revolution, and barely escaped the hands of the Bolsheviks. As refugees, they fled first to England and then to Canada in 1921, where their son, George, was born. In their early years in Canada, the couple's marriage became strained and was later annulled. After some successful years on the lecture circuit across North America, she felt drawn to live entirely for Christ by selling all of her possessions and giving them to the poor. In 1930, she made provisions for her son, dedicated herself to Christ with the blessings of Archbishop Neil McNeil of Toronto, and began her apostolate as a lay apostle by living the hidden life of Nazareth among the poor in the slums of Toronto. In the years of the Great Depression, she founded Friendship House, a lay apostolate in Toronto which, following the spirit of St. Francis of Assisi, begged for food and clothing in order to give to those in need. Internal tensions and misunderstandings led to the closing of this apostolate in 1936 and its relocation in Harlem, New York in 1938 where she championed the cause of black civil rights. She married journalist Eddie Doherty in 1943 and went with him to Combermere, Ontario in 1947, where they edited a newspaper and later, in 1954, founded Madonna House, a house of hospitality, whose members professed the evangelical counsels of poverty, chastity and obedience. In 1955, she and her husband made a promise to live as celibates for the remainder of their years. The Eucharist, as we can we imagine, held a prominent place in her spiritual vision.[1]

Doherty's Spiritual Outlook

In large part, Doherty's spiritual outlook was shaped by her experience of the Russian revolution. Being a member of the aristocratic class, she lost many family members during this tragic upheaval in Russian society and barley escaped death herself. She believed the revolution was caused by the society's failure instill authentic Christian values into the fabric of ordinary life. The purpose of Christianity, she believed, was not to oppress, but to serve. The revolt of the poor against the established structures of the day was a symptom of the moral collapse of a Christian society. To follow Christ

---

[1] This and more information on Doherty's life, writings, and related publications, see "Catherine Doherty," http://www.catherinedoherty.org.

meant to live in service of others, especially the poor. It was hypocritical, she believed, to profess the Christian faith and to live for oneself rather than for others. Doherty dedicated her life to living Gospel values by serving those who lived on the fringes of society.[2]

Doherty sought to restore Christian values in a heavily secularized world. With that view in mind, she started a newspaper with her husband entitled, *Restoration*. Her vision was to rebuild Christian culture from the ground up. Everything could and should be done for the glory of God. One of the ways she sought to do this was to bring the mystical vision of the Christian East to Western ears with the hope that it would bring back a sense of the transcendent in the ordinary events of daily life. She became widely known for this attempt to bring the spiritual sensitivities of Eastern Christianity to the Western world. Eastern spirituality, she believed could serve as a leaven that would awaken the spiritual sensitivities of the Christian West and bring about a renewal of the universal Church.[3]

One Eastern Christian concept that she brought to the West was that of "poustinia," the Russian word for "desert." Her book, *Poustinia: Christian Spirituality of the East for Western Man* (1975) describes this concept in this way: "The word to the Russian means much more than a geographical

---

[2] Ibid.
[3] Ibid.

place. It means a quiet, lonely place that people wish to enter, to find God who dwells within them. It also means truly isolated lonely places to which specially called people would go as hermits, and would seek God in solitude, silence and prayer for the rest of their lives."[4] Modern man, she believed, needed silence and solitude in order to understand his place in the word and rediscover the pull of God tugging at his heart. Such a place does not need to be completely withdrawn from human society. It could also be a simple cell or corner of a room to which a person turns in order to wash oneself in the waters of solitude. Ultimately, the goal is to enter the poustinia of one's own heart and to be able to bring solitude of heart with one wherever one goes.

Another Eastern Christian concept popularized by Doherty was the "sobornost," a Russian word for the unity of mind and heart made possible by the action of the Holy Trinity in one's life. Such unity was beyond our natural human capacities and was made possible by the gratuitous gift of God himself. The unity within God pours itself into the human heart and brings about a deep unity between the individual and God and among all the faithful. The unity of the Church is a reflection of "sobornost" and offsets the tendency toward isolation and individualism so rampant in

---

[4] Catherine de Hueck Doherty, *Poustinia: Christian Spirituality of the East for Western Man* (Notre Dame, IN: Ave Maria Press, 1975), 30-31.

Western society. In her book, *Sobornost: Eastern Unity of Mind and Heart for Western Man* (1977), she describes the concept thus: "People can be united on political and economic unity or policy, but the word 'sobornost' goes much deeper than all that. It means a unity that has passed through the gospel as a 'gathering factor'—for in Russian, 'sobornost' means 'gathering.'"[5] For Doherty, both "poustinia" and "sobornost" have very much to do with the Eucharist. This sacrament is, at one and the same time, both a "desert" and a "gathering." It brings us solitude of heart and gathers us together into one body.

Doherty's Teaching on the Eucharist

One way of approaching Doherty's understanding of the Eucharist is to look at some of her prayers from her diaries. One in particular stands out. Dated December 8, 1935, the Solemnity of the Immaculate Conception, it reads: "At Mass, a flood of joy! I will never forget this Mass—the closeness of God, a feeling of profound union, a vivid and terrifying realization of my unworthiness, a sense of joy and reverence for being chosen to do His work, a realization of the privilege. I received a thousand glimpses into my reality. I thought I was

---

[5] Catherine de Hueck Doherty, *Sobornost: Eastern Unity of Mind and Heart for Western Man* (Notre Dame, IN: Ave Maria Press, 1977), 11.

in heaven: all my sorrows, all my burdens lifted, just my soul and Him remaining—a lifetime in an hour!"[6] In this single prayer the themes of both "poustinia" and "sobornost" converge. On the one hand, the Eucharist is a deserted place where Doherty could encounter God in the solitude of her own heart ("poustinia"): "…just my soul and Him remaining."[7] On the other hand, it was also a place where she experienced a deep sense of unity with God ("sobornost"): "the closeness of God, a feeling of profound union."[8] The Eucharist, for Doherty, nourished her internally in the quiet solitude of her heart, imparted a deep sense of oneness with God, and gave her a deep reverence and respect for the privilege of being chosen to do His work.

The Eucharist, for Doherty, was the primary source for the restoration of Christianity in a secularized world. In an earlier prayer, dated November 13, 1933, she writes: "O God, I went to Mass today. How full of beauty is the Church—eternal, glorious beauty. What a privilege is the Roman Catholic Church. It is a gem beyond any understanding. A lover beyond comparison."[9] The Eucharist, for her, was the treasure in the field or the pearl of great price that one should seek

---

[6] Catherine de Hueck Doherty, *Jesus: Prayers from the Diaries of Catherine de Hueck Doherty* (Combermere, ON: Madona House Publications, 1996), 107.

[7] Ibid.

[8] Ibid.

[9] Ibid., 19.

to possess at all costs (Mt 13:44-46). It inspired her to take the words of Jesus to heart: "What profit would there be for one to gain the whole world and forfeit his life?" (Mt 16:26). The Mass brought transcendence into the here-and-now, making it incarnate, even immanent. It carried her to the threshold of the sacred into an encounter with the divinizing and transforming grace of God's Spirit. If Doherty dedicated her life to bringing the spirituality of the Christian East to the West, the Eucharist was the place par excellence where East and West met. At Eucharist, heaven comes to earth, and earth touches heaven: "God became man so that man might become divine."[10] These words of St. Athanasius of Alexandria resonated in Doherty's heart and lies at the very heart of her Eucharistic spirituality.

The Eucharist, for Doherty, also has both a purifying and fortifying effect on the soul. On the one hand, it cleanses us of sins committed after Baptism: "The sacrament of the Eucharist washes our sins away, for we come to it no matter how holy we may be, with the dust of the world upon our holiness. Few of us are really holy but the sacrament of the Eucharist itself takes away our sins. True, some of the sins we have to confess, but if there is contrition the sacrament of the Eucharist will wash the dust away. Yes, it will."[11] On the other hand, it strengthens the soul and makes us capable of

---

[10] Athanasius of Alexandria, *On the Incarnation*, 54.3.
[11] Doherty, *Sobornost*, 78.

doing great things for God: "Incredible as it might seem, you and I have the strength of God, for God is in us and he has said, 'Amen, amen I say to you, he who believes in me, the works that I do he shall also do, ad greater than these he shall do…' (Jn 14:12). Now the road to sobornost is yours for you are penetrated with God. Now nothing is impossible to the prayer of faith, and to you. Now sobornost becomes a reality. It is truly closed with flesh—the flesh of Jesus Christ."[12] The Eucharist, for Doherty, brings Christ's presence into the world and enables him to act through the members of his body. It immerses us in the saving action of Christ's paschal mystery and continues his redeeming presence in the world through the body of the believers.

Some Further Insights

If the purpose the above description was to paint in broad strokes a picture of **Doherty's** views on the Eucharist against the background of her overall spiritual outlook, the following remarks develop these insights in more detail to provide a better sense of the place of the sacrament in her life and thought.

To begin with, the traumatic effect of the Russian Revolution on Doherty's life led to her determined effort to counteract Communism by means of a reinvigorated Christianity by

---

[12] Ibid.

introducing the insights of the Christian East to the secularized Western society. By bringing together the insights of both East and West, she sought to combat the extreme individualism that had crept into Western society and that threatened to erode its very foundations. Her attempt at renewing the Christian culture upon which the West was founded had its roots in the breakdown in Russia society occasioned by the Communist revolution. This collapse stemmed from the failure of Christian society to be faithful to the Gospel values manifested in the beatitudes and a life of service to the poor. The Eucharist, she believed, embodied these values and lies at the very heart at any authentic Christian renewal of mind and heart.

Doherty introduced the Russian concept of "poustinia" (or "desert") to the West, because she believed the problems of the Western soul could only be resolved by an encounter with silence and solitude, which ultimately could be found on in the deepest recesses of the human heart. She spoke of this "desert" both as a physical place, such as a hermitage far removed from human society, and as a metaphor for the "poustinia" within the human heart, which one could live in even in the hustle and bustle of the marketplace. The Eucharist, she believed, let the soul into these deserted places with the heart and enable it to encounter the stillness, solitude, and peace of Christ. For this reason, it was often filled with "a fear and incredible joy at his nearness."[13]

Doherty also emphasized the importance of the Russian concept of "sobornost" (or "unity") for the renewal of society. This "unity" was not the superficial unity based on ideology or policy, but was something that went beyond the capacities of human nature and was made possible only by the divinizing action of the Hoy Trinity. The unity within the Trinity, in other words, penetrates the human heart and transforms it to create deep bonds of unity with God, with the Church community, with the rest of humanity, and indeed, with all of creation. For Doherty, the Eucharist represents the deepest form of this Trinitarian unity, since it gives glory to the Father, through Christ, with Christ, and in Christ and does so in the unity of the Holy Spirit, along with the entire community of the faithful gather together in worship.

Doherty emphasizes the cathartic, purgative effects of the Eucharist, saying how it cleanses those who gather for it of the sins committed since Baptism. This purgative dimension reveals the mercy of God to his children and prepares them for the spiritual journey ahead of them. Detachment and purgation from all created things is an essential first-step in everyone's journey to God. The penitential rite of the sacrament affirms that we are all sinners in need of God's mercy and that we must humbly ask his forgiveness for our sins. While

---

[13] Doherty, *Jesus*, 107.

she recognizes that, because of their seriousness, some sins must be confessed through sacramental reconciliation, she does not understate the purgative roe of the Eucharist itself. As the "sacrament of sacraments," she also recognizes that it is the sacrament of God's love and tender mercy.

Doherty also emphasizes the fortifying dimension of the Eucharist. This sacrament empowers us to perform actions in the name of Jesus Christ. It puts us in touch with the living Christ and enables him to act through us. It clothes us with his living, glorified flesh and strengthens us to do things far beyond our natural capacities. Because of the Eucharist, our humanity is united with Christ's humanity and elevated in such a way so as to touch his divinity. This participation in the divine life deepens our faith and enables us to call on the power of God to act through our humble humanity. The Eucharist, for Doherty, channels God's grace into the hearts and minds of the faithful and inspires them to do great things for the glory of God. For her, "[t]he most holy sacrament of the Eucharist penetrates the faithful beyond our ken."[14]

Doherty draws a close connection between the unity wrought by the Eucharist and service to the poor. It is through the Eucharist that Jesus enters today's world and actualizes his redeeming mission through the members of his body, the Church. Doherty was at the forefront of the development of the lay apostolate and was deeply convinced that the work of

---

[14] Doherty, *Sobornost*, 78.

the Gospel was meant not merely for clergy and religious, but for all believers. Her commitment to the poor and marginalized was rooted in her deep faith in Jesus and his beloved Mother. With them at her side, she believed it was possible to do great things for God. And that she did.

Finally, Pope St. John Paul II once said that the Church breathes with the two lungs of the Christian East and the Christian West.[15] Doherty's life is a perfect example of how the two traditions can meet to form a vital spiritual organism that is emphasizes both spiritual growth and apostolic outreach. Although she lived most of her life in North America, she never lost touch with her Russian roots and used concepts from Eastern Christian spirituality to revitalize an increasingly secularized Christian West. For Doherty, the Eucharist was the place where the Christian East and West could meet, interact, and be mutually nourished in desert solitude ("poustinia") and profound God-centered unity ("sobornost").

Conclusion

Catherine de Hueck Doherty dedicated her life to Christ by serving society's poor and marginalized. She did so by

---

[15] John Paul II, *Ut unum sint* (Encyclical Letter "On Commitment to Ecumenism," May 25, 1995), no. 54 in "The Holy See," http://w2.vatican.va/content/john-paul-ii/en/ encyclicals/documents/hf_jp-ii_enc_25051995_ut-unum-sint.html.

living the hidden life of Nazareth in their midst and trying to bring an ounce of love, hospitality, and compassion to their lives. She tried to imitate Christ by giving not from her surplus, but from her need. She was a forerunner of the lay apostolate at a time when the laity were often viewed as passive onlookers rather than active participants in the Church's missionary activity. She wanted to change that impression of the laity. First at Friendship House and later Madonna House, she sought to bring the face of Christ to society's poor and faceless in an active and zealous way.

Doherty believed that the West had become increasingly secularized and was desperately in need of a spiritual renewal. She sought a reconstruction of the foundations of Western society by injecting into it some key concepts from Eastern Christian spirituality, particularly "poustinia," (Russian for "desert") and "sobornost" (Russian for "unity"). For her, the reconstruction of the West would happen only with an inward quest for solitude and a corresponding outward search for unity.

The Eucharist, Doherty believed, had an important role to play in the spiritual renewal of society. On the one hand, it nourished people's souls with the body and blood of Christ, thereby uniting his humanity with theirs and enabling them to participate in his divinity. On the other hand, it empowered them to go forth and spread the Good News of Christ's redeeming love for humanity, especially the poor and marginalized. Her love for the Eucharist was rooted in her love for Christ and Christ's love for the poor. In her eyes, the three were all so very closely intertwined.

Reflection Questions

- How would you describe de Hueck Doherty's concept of *poustinia*? What does it mean to enter into the desert of the world? Have you ever done so? What does it mean to enter into the desert of one's heart? Have you ever done so? What does it mean to enter into the desert of another person? Have you ever done so? If not, where should you begin?

- How would you describe de Hueck Doherty's concept of *sobernost*? How does the action of the Trinity bring unity into one's inner life? How does it bring unity into one's relationships? Into one's community? What is the relationship between *sobernost* and the spirituality of communion?

- How do the concepts of *poustinia* and *sobernost* affect de Hueck Doherty's understanding of the Eucharist? Do you agree with her that the sacrament has both **a purifying and fortifying effect on the soul?** Have you experienced these effects in your own life? What role does the Eucharist play in the spiritual renewal of society?

Voice Eight

Myles Connolly
Mr. Blue

Myles Connolly (1897-1964), an Academy Award nominated motion picture writer and producer, was also a popular author best known for his religious novel, *Mr. Blue* (1928). He was born in Roxbury, Massachusetts and was a graduate of both Boston Latin High School and Boston College. After his graduation in 1918, he served in the U. S. Navy for the remainder of World War I and then as a journalist for *The Boston Post*. A devout Catholic, he married Agnes Bevington in 1929 and was editor for a time of *Columbia*, the magazine of The Knights of Columbus. He also served on the first board of directors of The Catholic Book Club. In 1929, he went to Hollywood to pursue a career in films, where for more than two decades he wrote screenplays and/or served as an associate producer for over forty films. He received an Academy Award nomination for his screenplay for *Music for Millions* (1944), shared a Hugo Award nomination for best dramatic presentation for *Harvey* (1951), and a nomination for the best written American musical for *Here Comes the Groom* (1952). In addition to *Mr. Blue*, his other novels include *The Bump on Brannigan's Head* (1950), *Dan and the Noonday Devil* (1951), *The Reason for Ann* (1953), and *Three*

Who Ventured (1958). His Catholic faith shaped much of his literary output, the best example of which is *Mr. Blue*, a novel that remains in print to this day.[1]

Connolly's Spiritual Outlook

Connolly and his wife were devout Catholics and had members on both sides of their immediate and extended families enter the priesthood and religious life. Their spiritual outlook was shaped by Catholic teaching and the way it permeated all aspects of life. In their view, nothing was barred from the influence of Christ and his Mystical Body, the Church, who with Christ as its head seeks to bring about a transformation of world and inaugurate the beginning of a New Creation.

Connolly's spiritual outlook resonates deeply with Jesus' exhortation to his disciples in the Gospel of Matthew: "If any want to become my followers, let them deny themselves and take up their cross and follow me" (Mt 16: 24). The way of discipleship, he believes, requires a total self-emptying of self

---

[1] For biographical details, see "Myles Connolly: Screenwriter, Writer, Film Producer," Prabok, https://prabook.com/web/myles.connolly/2090510 ; "Myles Connolly: A Film Writer, 66," *New York Times* (July 17, 1964), https://prabook.com/web/myles.connolly/2090510. For a brief history of *Mr. Blue*, see Stephen Mirarchi, "Introduction," in Myles. Connolly, *Mr. Blue: A Novel* (Providence, RI: Cluny Media, 2015), vii-xvii.

in a life of service. This way of life involves a gradual process of giving oneself to God and others that results in deeper and deeper experiences of communion with them. What is more, God calls all people, indeed, all of creation to participate in this grand and glorious experience of communion with God.[2] Of his many disciples, Jesus' closest was his own mother, Mary, who followed him from his birth, during his hidden life, his public life, the cross, the tomb, and beyond. Connolly believes this, as does Blue.

Although care should be taken not to confuse Connolly's views with those of his title character too closely, it seems clear that the novel's hero represents everything that is both holy and inspirational about the Catholic faith. Being a devout Catholic himself, Connolly would identify deeply with Blue's desire to give his entire being over to the love of God. Such was the case with Jesus' mother, Mary. Through Mr. Blue, he depicts her as a real person, unlike any painting or statue ever seen before: "I have no clear conception of you. Yet you are more real to me than the people around me. Oh, much more real than they. A thousand times, a thousand

---

[2] See Sean Salai, "The Annotated 'Mr. Blue' by Myles Connolly: Q&A with Dr. Stephen Mirarchi," *America* (May 18, 2016), https://www.americamagazine.org/content/all-things/annotated-mr-blue-myles-connolly-10-questions-dr-stephen-mirarchi?gclid=CjwKCAjw4rf6BRAvEiwAn2Q76ghCQmt4FLwIY1y7LW3Z-E2N7N8Xuy3KK_DyILns2c8w7p9lf23R8xoCKegQAvD_BwE.

times more real than they."[3] Blue sees Mary not as the theologians do, but as a simple woman, small in stature who can identify with the many other mothers who have suffered their own Calvaries and have paid the price of great love.[4] In his imagination, he pictures her sometimes as a mother with hair of gray whose face is lined with sorry and at other times as "a young mother, robust, active, with smiling eyes."[5] Our Lady looms large in Blue's faith. Through him, Connolly give us a vision of how the way of holiness manifests itself in the ordinary and simple circumstances of daily life. Mary, Jesus' first and closest disciple, has a simple childlike faith that Blue seeks to emulate and that Connolly holds up as the epitome of a saintly life.

Connolly's spiritual outlook is perhaps best seen in one of Blue's letters, where the saintly *poverello* describes the day when all fellow travelers will make merry at the Tavern at the end of the World:

> When the day comes that the sky is emptied of stars, and the sun is black, and the distraught winds have only the void for their lament, I am sure that somewhere men will be merry together, somewhere good hearts will greet good hearts, and somewhere our dreams of unbroken love and good talk and laughter will have come true. This

---

[3] Connolly, *Mr. Blue*, 88.
[4] Ibid., 89.
[5] Ibid.

is a glorious Somewhere, and it is far nearer to us than the stars. There Our Lady talks of children to unknown mothers who taught their many children the love of her single Son. There Saint Joseph is a man among peasants. There Xavier is home from his wars, and there Suarez and Aquinas have their arguments out. There Thomas More swaps jests with the older Teresa, while the younger Theresa gathers her roses. There Saint George boasts of his conquest of the dragon, and mayhap the Good Thief listens, or mayhap he hears little saint Francis singing his songs. It is a good place, this Somewhere. It has been called Paradise. It has been called the Tavern at the End of the World. And it has been called Home. It is only Catholicism that would ever allow the like of me to hope someday to be there.[6]

Mr. Blue speaks for everyman, and Connolly, who wrote these words, is one of them. In this brief passage, he puts his finger on a hope deeply rooted in the hearts of all men and women. It is a hope for home, a sense of belonging, a yearning for a place where, in the midst of the heartache of the many vicissitudes of Life, all men and women of good will can gather in fellowship around the simple joys being human. God will not allow the looming darkness to overwhelm the human heart. Created in his image, humanity is

---

[6] Ibid., 75.

hardwired for joy. Paradise, Heaven, The Tavern at the End of the World, Home—whatever you call it —our destiny is to live in intimate communion with God and one another. Everyone is called to holiness, not merely a select few. At the end of the world, beyond the pale of death, good hearts, both large and small, will continue greet one another as they did while they walked the earth, the main difference being that it will involve an even deeper cause for joy and merriment, for they will have arrived at their true home, their final destination. For Connolly, as for Blue, the Eucharist has a great deal with heralding in this New Creation.

Connolly on the Eucharist

If Mr. Blue represents that part of Catholic faith that both humbles and inspires, Connolly is more like the novel's anonymous narrator who, while fascinated by his friend, knows all too well that most people cannot and are not called to live as he lived. Like Blue, the words of St. John Vianney resonate in the narrator's heart: "The cross is the gift that Good gives to his friends."[7] The narrator is also touched by the words that Blue himself says would like to be remembered by: "Never was there a worse sinner, and never was God kinder to one."[8] As we draw closer to God, we become

---

[7] Ibid., 105.
[8] Ibid., 92.

more keenly aware of our own sinfulness and unworthiness of God's love. Blue's joy in life springs from his understanding that suffering is a sign of God's friendship and that no one is worthy of such a great gift. The Eucharist, for Blue, is a concrete, visible sign of this great gift.

At one point in the novel, Blue shares with the narrator the plot of a movie he thought up about the end of the world. Since Connolly himself eventually became a successful motion picture writer, it would not be too far a stretch to think that Blue's fascination with movies reflects, at least on some level, Connolly's own professional and career aspirations. (Note that he left for Hollywood the very year that he published the novel.) For this reason, it seems highly relevant that the Eucharist plays such a central role in Blue's story about a dystopic secular world where the International Government of the World (IGW) has lost all sight of the sacred, boasts that it has stamped out all traces of Christianity, suppresses all signs of individual initiative, and values people only for the work they do. As the plot unfolds, prisoner 2,757,311 enters the scene, a loner who keeps to himself and who likes to take quiet walks beyond distant hills where he can escape surveillance and carry out his plan to bring God back to the world. As it turns out, this prisoner, whose real name is White, is a priest who, over an extended period time, tends a small patch of wheat that he has sown and cared for during his many walks beyond the hills.⁹

In time, White secretly harvests the wheat, makes flour from its grain, and brings back to the highly guarded compound a small package of thin white wafers. Then, early one morning before the break of dawn, he puts his plan of bringing God back into the world into action. He climbs a tall, dark tower making sure he could not be followed and stopped. When he reaches the top, this last Christian on earth, a priest of God, sets up a makeshift altar, and begins to celebrate Mass. When the authorities realize what is happening, they mobilize their forces, surround him by air, and are about to drop a bomb to obliterate him and his intentions. It is too late, however, since White is now well into the celebration and cannot be stopped.¹⁰ The scene unfolds thus:

> "And now the priest comes to the words that shall bring Christ too earth again. His head almost touches his altar: *Hoc est enim corpus meum. . . .*" Blue was whispering. I think he was shivering. "The bomb did not drop. No. No. There was a moment of awful silence. Then, a burst of light beside which day itself is dusk. Then, a trumpet peal, a single trumpet peal that shook the universe. Then, the sun blew up like a bubble. The stars and planets

---

⁹ Ibid., 46-55.
¹⁰ Ibid., 55-61.

vanished like sparks. The earth burst asunder. . . . And through this unspeakably luminous new day, through the vault of the sky ribbed with lightning came Christ as He had come after the Resurrection. It was the end of the world!"[11]

The Eucharist, for Blue, brings the presence of the risen and glorified Christ to the world. This central doctrine of the Catholic faith was held by Connolly and is present in what, in effect, is the first story for a motion picture he would ever write. If the plot seems a little too far-fetched by Hollywood standards, it reflects a deeply held truth that is professed by devout Catholics to this very day.

Some Further Insights

One of the aims of this article is to suggest that Connolly's views toward the Eucharist are closely related to those expressed by the title character of *Mr. Blue*. The argument, here, is that the latter figure represents an aspect of the Catholic faith that Connolly found to be mysterious, inspirational, challenging, yet difficult to comprehend. What follows are some further insights into the Eucharist as Connolly presents it through Blue's eyes and how it reveals some of the

---

[11] Ibid., 61.

unique characteristics of the Catholic faith that Connolly held so dear.

To begin with, care must be taken not to identify Connolly's views too closely with those of Blue. At the same time, Blue is a creation of his author's imagination and it would be a disservice to both to deny any connection whatsoever. A more subtle way of viewing the connection would be to see Connolly's views as rooted in the dynamic tension between the novel's anonymous narrator and its saintly protagonist. Both say something very important about the Catholic vision. The former is prudent and practical with both feet planted on the ground, while the latter is dreamy, starry-eyed mystic with his head in the clouds. One represents the concrete reality of a believer living in the world, while the other stands for one living life with a deep consciousness of the reality that is to come and, in some fashion, is already here. The friendship between Blue and the narrator represents the need for both aspects of the Catholic vision and the manner in which they complement each other. The Eucharist is the place where both aspects of this Catholic vision can meet and enrich one another.

It is also important to note that Connolly, who was both a novelist and an author of movie screenplays, allocates one of these very distinct avocations to each of the novel's two main characters. In relating a few episodes of Blues' latter years, the anonymous narrator produces a small novella of this unique figure in American life. He uses words to capture the joy with which Blue embraced life with all its vigor, suffering, defeats, and challenges. Although he recognizes his own inability to fully capture the incredible innocence, joy, and childlike faith in God that motivated Blue and propelled him to turn simple, ordinary acts of kindness into heroic tasks of saintly courage, he does so with a deep desire to conserve the memory of his dear friend, who was taken from this life at such an early age. Blue, by way of contrast, distrusts the written word and believes that images and pictures are what will capture the imagination of the people of his day. His sharing of his screenplay about the end of the world that culminates in the celebration of the Eucharist with the narrator represents a thoroughly Catholic and sacramental view of the world. When seen in this light, the narrator and Blue not only represent two dimensions of Connolly's own variegated personality, but also the dynamic relation between Word and Sacrament that forms such an integral part of the Catholic faith and vision.

Blue and the anonymous narrator also represent two very different kinds of Catholic believers. The former is a mystic and a dreamer; the latter, a realist and pragmatist. One looks to the heavens; the other has two feet planted firmly on the earth. One is so captivated by the message of Jesus that he is willing to forego ordinary comforts in order to place himself in and identify with the plight of the poor. The other loves the ordinary daily pleasures of a roof over one's head, warm clothing in the cold winter months, and a good meal. The friendship struck between the two characters points the universal nature of Catholicism and the wide range of people drawn to uphold its tenets. Just as Jesus called a variety of people from different walks of life to follow him in the way of discipleship, so too the Church has within its fold members from very different backgrounds and mindsets. It is also important to note that Catholic believers will tend to approach the Eucharist with different mental and spiritual dispositions. Some are imbued with a deep appreciation of the mystery of the sacrament and do not feel the need to reflect upon through the lens of philosophical and theological categories that might make its mystery more understandable to the inquiring mind. Others resort to such categories in an attempt to defend the faith from error and make it more intellectually palatable to the faithful.

Blue, it bears noting, seeks to love what, by all other appearances, seems unlovable, and it is for this reason that he has been likened to a modern-day St. Francis, a poverello willing to give up everything to see Christ in all people, especially the poor and downtrodden. The narrator admires Blue for doing so, yet recognizes his own inability to take this aspect of Gospel so readily to heart. Toward the end of the novel, Blue sees his true vocation as "going to pledge himself to poverty and live among the poor."[12] He sees himself as a member of a great army of disciples who, like Christ himself,

---

[12] Ibid., 111.

would reach out to the derelicts of modern civilization and befriend them by simply being with them and entering into their lives. He would call this army of good-hearted souls the "Spies of God," people who sought nothing more than to bring the presence of Christ in the midst of those who needed it the most. By reaching out to these derelicts, he believed he would find Christ himself in them and in the love they shared with one another. By entering into a holy communion with these outcasts, by hearing their stories, breaking bread with them, living with them, and even dying for them, he believed he would enter more deeply into the same passion, death, and resurrection of Jesus celebrated whenever the Church gathers for Eucharist.[13]

Finally, Blue's movie plot incorporates a number of important themes for understanding the Catholic understanding of the Eucharist. For example, having the end of the world heralded in when the last Christian on earth, a priest, is celebrating Mass brings out the eschatological dimension of the sacrament. The Eucharist is a foretaste of the heavenly banquet and thus looks to the end of the world as that moment will what it points towards will become a reality. What is more, that the priest plants and tends the wheat to be used for the final Mass on earth underscores the Eucharist as being both "fruit of the earth and work of human hands" and the inauguration of the New Creation that will be realized

---

[13] Ibid., 112-13.

with Christ's Second Coming. Notice, too, the intimate relationship between the Eucharist and its minister. The priesthood, according to Catholic doctrine, is intrinsically oriented toward the Eucharist—and vice versa. Only a priest can celebrate Mass. Only he can bring God back to the earth again. Only he, acting as an *alter Christus*, can bring Christ's passion, death, and resurrection into the world, even though it is separated by some 2,000 years from the actual historical event. These fundamental doctrinal aspects of Catholic doctrine are woven into the fabric of the Blue's narrative. Given Connolly's deep Catholic devotion and the numerous other parallels between him, Blue, and the novel's anonymous narrator, one cannot help but think that he gives the Eucharist such a central role in the screenplay (and in the entire novel), because of his own personal adherence to the Catholic faith and an awareness of its vast importance for humanity's redemption.

Conclusion

Although Myles Connolly was a successful Hollywood motion picture screenplay writer and producer for more for more than two decades, he is most remembered for his short religious novel, *Mr. Blue*. Written when he was in his early thirties, this short novel about a young modern-day St. Francis has over time quietly made its way into the Catholic imagination. The book remains in print to this day and promises to remain so for some time.

As mentioned earlier, one way of understanding the novel is to look at its two main characters as representing two facets of Connolly's own variegated personality. Blue is a whimsical troubadour of Life who takes his Catholic faith to heart and believes that it alone has given him hope of one day finding his way to heaven. The anonymous narrator, by way of contrast, is fascinated by Blue's zest for Life, impressed with the young man's desire to reach out to the poor and marginalized, and decides to keep a record of the exploits of his later years as a memorial to his untimely death. Connolly, the novelist and aspiring screenplay writer, speaks, on the one hand, through Blue, a man enamored of images and pictures and who himself has a story for a motion picture about the end of the world and, on the other hand, through the anonymous narrator, a writer who represents the more down-to-earth and pragmatic side of ordinary, everyday life and Catholic practice. The friendship between these two very different characters reveals something about how Connolly integrated the novelist and the screenplay writer, the editor and the movie producer, the whimsical dreamer and the realistic pragmatist in his own life.

The Eucharist plays a central role both in Blue's motion picture story and in the novel itself. The movie plot without the Eucharist would not be quite the same. Everything in it hinges on the last priest on earth bringing God back to the world through his celebration of the sacrament. The same can be said for the novel without the screenplay. Without it, much of Blue's spirit and mindset would be lost. The narrator himself says that Blue's movie plot gives a better insight into Blue's mind that anything else he knows.[14] Although Connolly, himself a devout Catholic, admits through the eyes of the narrator that Blue's story would have little appeal to a wide audience and would likely never be made,[15] he clearly presents Blue as a Christ figure willing to lay down his life for the marginalized and forgotten derelicts of the world. The novel ends with Blue pushing one of them out of the way of a speeding car, taking the hit himself, and dying in a hospital a few days later. This saintly figure, in the narrator's (and Connolly's) mind, represents the best Catholicism has to offer: the Eucharist. Blue took the meaning of this sacrament to heart by giving up his body and blood for a friend. The closing words of the novel could well have been said of Christ himself, who instituted the sacrament: "It can't be so. No one so brave, so heroic, so glorious, so immensely above the rest of us, can leave us so suddenly like that. He can't have gone,—Blue and his Spies of God. No. Say what you will. Do what you will. You can't make me believe that Blue is dead."[16]

---

[14] Ibid., 62.
[15] Ibid.
[16] Ibid., 125.

Reflection Questions

- How would you describe the relationship between Mr. Blue and the anonymous narrator in Connolly's novel? Cordial? Mutually beneficial? A deep friendship? Why does Blue fascinate the narrator so much? To what extent does he challenge the narrator's assumptions about the things that matter in life? To what extent does he challenge his faith? To what extent does Mr. Blue challenge your own faith?

- Have you ever met anyone like Blue? Have you ever met someone so penetrated with the love of God that nothing else in life seems really important? To what extent is Blue a Christ figure? What impact has he had on your life? Does he challenge you? Does he make you feel uncomfortable? Would you like to be like him?

- How would you describe Blue's views toward the Eucharist? Why does it hold such a central place in his movie script? Why does it hold such a central place in the novel as a whole? Do you share his views towards the sacrament? Do you believe it will herald in the Second Coming? To what extent is Christ already present in those like Blue who give up their lives before the fullest realization of the kingdom?

Voice Nine

C. S. Lewis
Letters to Malcom

Clive Staples Lewis (1898-1963) was a British scholar and lay theologian known for his studies in Medieval and Renaissance literature, his popular expositions of the Christian faith, his *Perelandra* space trilogy, and his famous Narnia tales. Born in Belfast, Northern Ireland, his early education consisted of private tutors and time spent at Wynyard School, Campbell College, and Malvern College. He entered Oxford University in 1917 but was there only a short while before he entered officer school for the British army to fight for his country during the First World War. After his training, he was commissioned as a second lieutenant and sent into trench warfare on the front lines in the Somme Valley in France, where he injured and eventually sent back to England to convalesce. Upon his discharge from the army in 1918, he resumed his studies at Oxford University, where he received Firsts in Greek and Latin Literature (1920), Philosophy and Ancient History (1922), and English (1924). In 1924, he became a tutor in philosophy at University College, Oxford and in 1925 was elected Fellow and Tutor in English at Magdalen College, Oxford, where he remained until accepting a chair in Mediaeval and Renaissance Literature at

Magdalen College, Cambridge in 1954. In 1956, he married Joy Davidman Gresham in a civil ceremony, and the two remained together until her death from cancer in 1960. Although he was baptized into the Church of Ireland as an infant, he became an atheist at the age of fifteen and converted to Christianity at the age of thirty-two through the influence of his friend, J. R. R. Tolkien. Along with Tolkien, he was a member of the informal literary club known as "The Inklings," which met regularly at The Eagle and Child pub in Oxford and in Lewis's rooms at Magdalen College. A prolific author, his scholarly works include: *The Allegory of Love* (1936), *English Literature in the Sixteenth Century [Excluding Drama]* (1954), and *The Discarded Image: An Introduction to Medieval and Renaissance Literature* (1964). Listed among his popular Christian writings are such works as *The Problem of Pain* (1940), *The Abolition of Man* (1943), *Miracles* (1947), *Mere Christianity* (1952) *Surprised by Joy* (1955), *The Four Loves* (1960), and *A Grief Observed* (1960). Among his works of fiction are his space trilogy—*Out of the Silent Planet* (1938), *Perelandra* (1943), *That Hideous Strength* (1945)—his popular children's books, *The Chronicles of Narnia* (1950-56), and *Till We Have Faces* (1956), a retelling of the myth of Cupid and Psyche.[1]

---

[1] For a timeline of C. S. Lewis's life, see *C. S. Lewis Foundation: Living the Legacy of C. S. Lewis*, http://www.cslewis.org/resource/chronocsl/ .

Lewis's Spiritual Outlook

Although he was raised in a religious family, Lewis disavowed any belief in God in his teenage years and was an atheist for most of his young adulthood. His newfound faith, first in God's existence and later in the Christian God, came through his friendship with J. R. R. Tolkien and Hugo Dyson when, during a long evening walk, they discussed the idea that Christianity was a myth that had become fact. The mythologies of Ancient Greco-Roman civilization and of the Norsemen, he came to see, were nothing but faint glimpses of a deeper reality that would manifest itself through God's gradual self-revelation to the Hebrew people and ultimately reach its fullness in the person of Jesus Christ, the God-man and Word-become-flesh.[2]

Lewis's conversion affected him deeply and changed the way he viewed himself and his relationship to others, and the world. God, for him, was not a distant, impersonal force who created the world and then left it to fend for itself, but a supra-personal reality who does not merely embody the reality of Love but actually *is* Love itself. Since Love, by its very nature, is other-oriented, this otherness must exist within the Godhead and is expressed in Christian doctrine through the

---

[2] See Colin Duriez, *Tolkien and C.S. Lewis: The Gift of Friendship* (Mahwah, NJ: HiddenSpring, 2003), 50-55; see also, C. S. Lewis, *God in the Dock*, (Grand Rapids, MI: William B. Eerdmans, 1970), 63-67.

belief in a Triune God of Father (God-transcendent), Son (God-incarnate), and Holy Spirit (God- immanent). Lewis's Christian apologetics flows from the fundamental insight that the God of love expresses himself through the three loving actions of Creation, Redemption, and Sanctification. Although God is One and always acts as One, each of these actions is typically associated with one of the Persons of the Blessed Trinity: Creation with the Father; Redemption with the Son; and humanity's sanctification and the transformation of the world with the Holy Spirit. In his Christian writings, Lewis employed a simple, popular style to show that these and other basic doctrines of the Christian faith (what he called "mere Christianity") were not mere imaginary well-wishing, but beliefs that could be rationally explained and verbally defended. Belief, in his mind, was not contrary to reason, but something that enlightened reason and enabled it to peer more deeply into the mystery of things.[3]

Lewis himself admitted that he vehemently resisted coming to a belief in the Christian God but ultimately came to see that his objections could not withstand the various counter-arguments showing that such beliefs were, in the very least, plausible— and even appealing.[4] He sought to show

---

[3] See C. S. Lewis, *Mere Christianity* (New York: Macmillan, 1952), 140-45.

[4] See Duriez, *Tolkien and C.S. Lewis*, 45-46.

through his writings that belief in Christianity was credible and that educated persons should not simply dismiss its doctrines as wishful ("pie-in-the-sky") thinking. A devout member of the Catholic wing of the Church of England, he believed that worship should be God-centered and embrace rituals that helped the faithful give God his due as Creator, Redeemer, and Sanctifier. Instituted by Christ at the Last Supper, he believed that the Eucharist was the appropriate place where such homage should take place.[5]

Lewis's Teaching on the Eucharist

Lewis did not write at length about the Eucharist. This conscious decision on his part was due, in part, to his focus on the basics upon which all Christians could agree. He was well aware that the meaning of the Eucharist differed across the various denominations and that this "sacrament of unity" had, in many respects, become a source of division among believers. He was also well aware that he was not a trained theologian and that he was not privy to the rarified distinctions commonly made by those better equipped to deal with the subject.

---

[5] For more on Lewis's ideas concerning worship, see Justin Taylor, "C. S. Lewis on the Theology and Practice of Worship," https://www.thegospelcoalition.org/blogs/justin-taylor/c-s-lewis-on-the-theology-and-practice-of-worship/ .

As a member of the High Anglican tradition, Lewis believed that, along with Baptism, the Eucharist was one of the two sacraments instituted by Christ. As a member of that tradition, he also believed in Jesus' Real Presence in the sacrament, although he hesitated to explore the nature of that presence in any great detail, preferring to leave it to the realm of mystery and the power of Divine Providence. In "The Weight of Glory," a sermon he preached on June 8, 1942 at St. Mary the Virgin Church in Oxford, he closes with the words: "Next to the Blessed Sacrament itself, your neighbor is the holiest object presented to your senses. If he is your Christian neighbor he is holy in almost the same way, for in him also Christ *vere latitat*—the glorifier and the glorified, Glory Himself, is truly hidden."[6] Jesus, he believed, was truly present, yet hidden, in the Eucharist. His glory is a hidden one, something that speaks of his humility in entering our world and taking on the burden and the weight of human flesh.

One place where Lewis chooses to treat the Eucharist is in chapter nineteen of his posthumous work, *Letters to Malcom: Chiefly on Prayer* (1964).[7] There he explicitly states that one reason why he has never written very much about Holy Communion is because he is "not good enough at

---

[6] C. S. Lewis, "The Weight of Glory," http://www.wheelersburg.net/Downloads/ Lewis%20Glory.pdf.

[7] C. S. Lewis, *Letters to Malcom: Chiefly on Prayer* (New York: Harcourt, Brace, Jovanovich, 1964).

Theology."[8] His general silence on the matter is not that he doesn't welcome the sacrament, but that he does not wish to unsettle people's minds: "…the very last thing I want to do is to unsettle in the mind of any Christian, whatever his denomination, the concepts—for him traditional—by which he finds it profitable to represent to himself what is happening when he receives the bread and wine. I could wish that no definitions had ever been felt necessary; and still more, that none had been allowed to make divisions between churches."[9] He understands that people have devised different theories about what takes place during the consecration of the bread and wine but wonders what the disciples themselves thought was happening. He finds it hard to fathom the Catholic doctrine of transubstantiation, saying that he finds it difficult to imagine what it is: "…I find 'substance' (in Aristotle's sense), when stripped of its own accidents and endowed with the accidents of some other substance, an Object I cannot think. My effort to do so produces mere nursery-thinking—a picture of something like very rarefied plasticine."[10] At the same time, he is not satisfied with merely saying that the bread and wine are symbols of Christ's body and blood: "I get on no better with those who tell me that the elements are mere bread and mere wine, used symbolically to

---

[8] Ibid., 101.
[9] Ibid., 101-2.
[10] Ibid., 102.

remind me of the death of Christ. They are, on the natural level, such a very odd symbol of *that*."[11] What is more, why were bread and wine chosen, since Lewis could think of a hundred other things that would remind him of Christ's death.[12] He does not wish to say that anyone's explanation of what takes place at the Eucharist is wrong, but simply states that every explanation does not exhaust its mystery. Lewis much prefers putting aside the various attempts to explain what takes place in this sacrament and simply accept it as such: "…I find no difficulty in believing that the veil between the worlds, nowhere else (for me) so opaque to the intellect, is nowhere else so thin and permeable to divine operation."[13] Lewis believed in the Real Presence but decided to leave explaining what happens there to mystery: "The command, after all, was Take, eat; not Take, understand."[14] He preferred to preserve what he called the "magical" element in Christianity which puts us in touch with the Divine Other. Theological explanations of the Eucharist, however refined and accurate they may be, will never exhaust the mystery it embodies.

Some Further Insights

---

[11] Ibid., 102
[12] Ibid., 102
[13] Ibid., 103.
[14] Ibid., 104.

Lewis's views on the Eucharist reflect his interest in highlighting what Christians have in common rather than what divides them. Although he believed in the Real Presence, he was hesitant to delve too deeply into the explanations concerning what actually happens to the bread and wine during the celebration of the sacrament, preferring instead to allow the mystery of the sacrament speak for itself. The following remarks seek to delve a bit more deeply into Lewis's view on the sacrament.

To begin with, Lewis's approach to the Eucharist must be understood within the context of his understanding of the purpose of Christian worship as a whole. He believed that such worship should be God-centered and universal in scope. A conservative and traditionalist by nature, he was against innovation for innovation's sake yet understood the importance of rendering praise and glory to God with the best that we have to offer him. Although what that might mean may vary from culture to culture, he was a strong advocate for constancy in worship: "My whole point," he claims, "was that any form will do me if only I'm given time to get used to it."[15] The repetitious nature of Christian ritual calmed the soul and was more likely to carry the community to the threshold of the sacred. Worship, moreover, was to be carried out regardless of what one was feeling at the time. It allows us to leave the ordinary run-a-day circumstances of our

---

[15] Ibid.

lives and enter into the realm of *Kairos* (sacred time). Instituted by Christ as a memorial to his sacrificial death and resurrection, the Eucharist, he believed, was especially suited to leading the Christian into the sphere of the sacred. Jesus' Real Presence in the sacrament guaranteed that, regardless of our private and communal failures at authentic worship, he would always be in our midst taking our humble offering into his hands and offering them to his Father in heaven.

Lewis does not wish to denigrate any attempts to formulate explanations of what takes place at the Eucharist. He merely is pointing out their inherent limitations. He finds them all unsatisfactory, because, despite however good they may seem, they all fall short of expressing the fullness of its mystery. While he believes in the Real Presence, the nature of that presence will always remain hidden, and he prefers to have it that way. He wishes to preserve the element of mystery and awe around this sacrament (what he like to call "magic"). Because of its inherent limitations, language hides and much as it reveals. For him, the hidden nature of Christ in the Eucharist represents its deepest, truest meaning. Attempts to define what happens during its celebration can take away from this sense of mystery rather than promoting it. They appear like sawdust to him, because, in the end, they lose sight of a mystery that no words (however finely tuned) can exhaust.[16]

---

[16] Ibid., 103-4.

Lewis believes that "the veil between the worlds" thins at times and the union of heaven and earth becomes almost palpable.[17] For him, the Eucharist is the place *par excellence* where this "thinning" takes place. Closely connected to Jesus' passion, death, and resurrection, it represents the nearness of God's presence to humanity made possible by Christ's suffering and death on the cross. At the moment of Jesus' death, the veil in the temple before the Holy of Holies was rent in two, and the power of God was unleashed upon the world (Mt 27:51). In a similar way, the boundaries between heaven and earth dissipate at the celebration of the Eucharist. We are given heavenly food to eat and digest and to make a part of ourselves so that God can give us a share in his divine life. Holy Communion represents the sacred bond, the New Covenant, between God and man made possible by Jesus' paschal mystery and memorialized in the sacrament.

After the Eucharist, the other place where the veil between heaven and earth grows thin most clearly is in one's neighbor. "Next to the Blessed Sacrament itself," Lewis claims, "your neighbor is the holiest object presented to your senses."[18] For him, the bond between the Eucharist and our neighbor is very close. Holy Communion refers to communion not merely with God but also with all those who believe in him

---

[17] Ibid., 103.

[18] C. S. Lewis, "The Weight of Glory," ," http://www.wheelersburg.net/Downloads/ Lewis%20Glory.pdf.

and, ultimately with all of humanity. After all, Jesus himself said, "I assure you as often as you did it for one of my least brothers, you did it for me" (Mt 25:40).[19] When seen in this light, the celebration of the Eucharist is a celebration of the new humanity. Jesus is the New Man, and we are members of his body. The mystery of the Eucharist, for Lewis, pours into the mystery of our communion with each other. It is the "sacrament of love," the sacrament of God's love for humanity, and of our love for God and one another.

For Lewis, understanding is secondary to following Jesus' commands. He understands that there are some things that our finite minds will never fully fathom. Few (if any) of us completely understand the process of digestion, yet we take food each day for nourishment, nonetheless. In a similar way, Jesus said, "Take, eat: not Take, understand."[20] Here, Lewis is not denigrating our desire to understand the nature and meaning of our faith, only that we must recognize our limitations and work within those boundaries. He is worried that placing understanding before action will lead us into a paralyzing inaction and the kind of Gnosticism that has haunted Christianity since its earliest years. Jesus said, "I give you a new commandment: Love one another. Such as my love has been for you, so must your love be for each other"

---

[19] All Scripture references come from *The New American Bible* (New York: Catholic Book Publishing, 1979).

[20] Lewis, *Letters to Malcolm*, 104.

(Jn 13:34). People, Lewis affirms, will know we are Jesus' disciples by the way we love one another, not by our level of understanding.

When Lewis speaks of the magical element of the Eucharist, he is not thinking of any cheap, paltry, hocus-pocus attempts to control the forces of nature, but to a sense of awe and enchantment that embodies a sacred (as opposed to secular) view of the world. Much of today's world has lost its sense of the sacred. The sacrament, he maintains, preserves this sense of awe and wonder at the heart of all reality. It does so by preserving a sense of mystery at the very heart of existence itself. In his mind, there is much more to reality than what meets the eye, much more than what the empirical sciences can detect and measure. A world that has lost its sense of the "magical" (i.e., the "sacred") deprives itself of the opportunity to peer beneath the appearances of things and come to an encounter with the source of all Being. As a sacrament, the Eucharist preserves this sense of the sacred and enables us to find meaning in the objective order and meaning in our place in it. It forces us to encounter Mystery outside of our own subjective awareness of things and to recognize that we are not the ultimate measure of things.

Finally, something should be said about Lewis's relationship to the Catholic Church. Although his conversion to Christianity was very much influenced by his close friendship with J.R.R. Tolkien, a devout Catholic and fellow Inkling, Lewis never became a Catholic, even though many of his ideas resonated with the truths of the Catholic faith. He seems to have had a suspicion of Catholicism (some might even call it a prejudice), which was partly due to his upbringing in the Protestant section of Northern Ireland and partly due his distaste for the kind of theological reflection that tried to explain too much and not giving the mystery of the faith its due. He found the Catholic doctrine of transubstantiation, for example, to be not only somewhat contrived and difficult to imagine, but also something that, when all is said and done, did not fully satisfy the imagination. It remains a moot point as to whether Lewis would, if he had lived longer, eventually have become a Catholic. It is well known that his friendship with Tolkien waned in his later years and, even though he believed in the Real Presence, confessed his sins regularly, and was against the theological and liturgical innovations arising with Anglicanism at the time, it seems that his decision to focus on "mere Christianity" (i.e., what all Christians share in common) would have led him to remain where he was, a committed member of the Catholic wing of the Church of England.[21]

---

[21] See Joseph Pearce, "C. S. Lewis and the Catholic Church," in *Catholic New Agency*, https://www.catholicnewsagency.com/column/c-s-lewis-and-the-catholic-church-3085

Conclusion

C. S. Lewis was fascinated by the human imagination and was one of those rare individuals who could harness its powers to produce a body of fiction that would withstand the test of time and both educate and entertain his readers for generations to come. This love of the imagination is evidenced, however, not only in his fiction, but in his scholarly works as well. One need only read his classic works, *The Allegory of Love: A Study in Medieval Tradition* and *The Discarded Image: An Introduction to Medieval and Renaissance Literature* to see the hand of an intellectual giant and a poetic genius combine to produce works of lasting import for the field of Medieval and Renaissance studies. His space trilogy and his seven-volume children's series, *The Chronicles of Narnia*, show how he applied the powers of the imagination to various other fields and genres.

Lewis was raised in a religious family, baptized into the Church of Ireland, became an avowed atheist, and, at the age of thirty-two finally converted to Christianity, becoming a member of the Catholic wing of the Church of England. From that moment on, he adopted the Christian world view as his own and, in addition to his own scholarly writings in English literature, proceeded to defend and promote it through numerous apologetic and fictional works that would impact thousands (if not millions) of believers in his own generation and many generations to come. His is widely viewed (and deservedly so) as one of the most influential Christian authors of the twentieth century. Very few would question the impact of his writings on the Christian imagination at a time when it was being seriously challenged by the forces of secularism and atheism.

Although Lewis believed in the Real Presence and loved the sacrament, he wrote very little about it, because he sensed that the various explanations given it were more often than not the cause of division and dissension within the Christian denominations. His emphasis on "mere Christianity" led him to concentrate on what united Christians in their battle against the despiritualizing forces that presented themselves in his world. That said, it is clear that he saw the Eucharist as a sacrament instituted by Christ that thinned the separation between the natural and supernatural worlds and brought the worshiper evermore closer to the threshold of the sacred. The Eucharist, for him, was a concrete, objective reality of God's ongoing presence with his people, a reality that began with the mystery of the Incarnation and continued in the mystery of the breaking of the bread. The Eucharist, in his mind, was all about the mystery of God's love for humanity. It was not necessary to understand this mystery or explain it. All that was necessary was for the believer to take, eat, and allow the Spirit of the Lord to enter into one's mind and heart— and allow him to accomplish his work.

Reflection Questions

- Do you understand why Lewis purposely chose not to write a great deal about the Eucharist, because he believed this this "sacrament of unity" had, in many respects, become a source of division among believers? Do you agree with his assessment of the situation? What could be done to make the sacrament more a source of unity rather than division among Christians?

- Although Lewis believed in the Real Presence, he had a difficult time fathoming the significance of the Catholic doctrine of transubstantiation. Do you believe in the Real Presence? Do you understand the Catholic doctrine of transubstantiation? Do you believe in it? Do you believe in the doctrine of transubstantiation? If so, how would you explain it to someone who shared Lewis's difficulties in understanding? Does the doctrine exhaust the mystery of the sacrament? Can other models be used in conjunction with it?

- What does Lewis mean by the "magical element" of the Eucharist? How does it cultivate a sense of awe and enchantment that embodies a sacred (as opposed to secular) view of the world? Have you ever experienced this "magical element?" Has the sacrament fostered a sense of awe and wonder in your own life? Has it given you a deeper appreciation of the sacredness of life and, indeed, of all creation?

Voice Ten

Caryll Houselander
A Rocking Horse Catholic

Frances Caryll Houselander (1901-1954), a British Catholic author, artist, poet, visionary, and mystic, wrote a number of popular books during her lifetime that had a deep impact on the popular Catholic spirituality of her day. Born in Bath, England, she was baptized into the Catholic faith at the age of six. After her parents separated, she was sent to a convent school and returned home in her teens to help her mother run a boarding house. She left the Catholic Church during her teens and returned in 1925 due to some mystical experiences that convinced her of Christ's deep love for all human beings and the call to see him in all people. A prolific author, she authored more than fifteen books and is most remembered for *This War is the Passion* (1943), *The Reed of God* (1944), *The Flowering Tree* (1945), her posthumous autobiography, *A Rocking Horse Catholic* (1955), and *The Risen Christ* (1958). Sickly for most of her life, she succumbed to breast cancer and died at the early age of fifty-three. Deeply devout, she had a way of explaining the faith that was, at one and the same time, both profound and easy to understand. Her teaching on the Eucharist is no exception. It flows from her deep Catholic faith and the conviction that the Risen

Lord has given us the sacrament to impart to impart his divine life to all who believe.[1]

Houselander's Spiritual Outlook

Much of Houselander's spirituality can be gleaned from her autobiography, *A Rocking Horse Catholic*, a story that chronicles her entrance into the Church, the difficulties that led up to her leaving it, and her final embrace of it in her mid-twenties. She uses the image of the "rocking horse" to distinguish herself from so-called "cradle" Catholics, many of whom never manage to delve beneath the externals of Catholic practice and fail to probe the deeper meaning of their faith. As her own experience would attest, a rocking horse Catholic is someone baptized not at birth, but at an early age in childhood, when rocking horses and other playthings occupy a child's growing imagination. Houselander's back and forth (one might say "rocky") relationship with Catholicism is also captured in the book's title. A rocking horse moves back and forth, giving the impression that one is on a

---

[1] This biographical information comes from Caryll Houselander, *A Rocking Horse Catholic* (New York: Sheed and Ward, 1955). See Internet Archive, https://archive. org/stream/rockinghorsecath008000mbp/rockinghorsecath008000mbp_djvu.txt. See also Karen Lynn Krugh, "Seeing Christ in All People," *Catholic Culture*, https://www.catholicculture.org/culture/library/view.cfm?recnum=528.

Voice Ten: Caryll Houselander—*A Rocking Horse Catholic*

journey when, all the while, one remains in the same place. In a similar way, at various times in her life, Houselander found herself outside of the Church, then in it, then out again, then in again. In the end, she found herself in the same place, but with a much deeper appreciation of her faith and the impact it has had on her life.

Houselander was not born into the faith, but was baptized at the age of six when her mother converted to Catholicism. As a teenager, she left the church on account of a scandal that arose from her mother accepting a derelict priest as a resident in her boarding house, an action that was looked down upon at the time and treated with great suspicion. Houselander herself saw nothing wrong in the arrangement, since her mother was known to be someone who would fly in the face of convention. The malicious gossip and outright cruelty resulting from this situation, however, made her examine her allegiance to the faith. One incident in particular stands out:

> One morning, quite by chance, I knelt at Holy Communion side by side with two people, a husband and wife, who had in the past been acquainted with my mother and the priest she now harbored. They were highly respected Catholics. After Mass I greeted them in the church porch. They ignored my greeting and turned away. From that moment I made up my mind to seek for some other religion. I did not doubt the Real Presence in

the Blessed Sacrament, but it seemed to me that Christ was a prisoner in the hands of hard and relentless people, people without compassion. I began to hope that there might be some other Church in which there would also be the Real Presence, but in which one could approach and receive Christ, not among respectable people, not among censorious people, but among those who were despised, who were failures, who were sinners, but who loved one another.[2]

Attracted by the Liturgy's beauty and the drawing power of the Blessed Sacrament, she continued attending Mass, since its mystery was the only thing that brought beauty and light to her otherwise drab existence. In time she began to wonder, however, if the powerful hold the Liturgy had on her prevented her from seeing clearly and judging things accordingly. Was this fascination with the Mass a help or a hindrance? Was it a phase that she must pass through or a reality she must embrace?

As it turned out, something happened one day that even turned her against Catholic worship itself. At the time, there still existed churches where the better seats were reserved for a price. On entering one of those churches one Sunday morning and finding no free seats, available, she sat in one of those that cost. With not a penny in her pocket, she felt

---

[2] Ibid., 106.

humiliated when an usher asked her for payment. When she protested that there were no seats available in the open section, the usher still demanded payment. Embarrassed and upset, she got up and started to leave the church. When a priest in the back aisle saw what happened and asked if she was leaving, she responded, "Yes, I am, and I will never come to Mass again."[3]

After experimenting with various churches— High Anglican, Methodist, and Russian Orthodox—she eventually found her way back to the Church, due to the influence of the Catholic Evidence Guild and its charismatic founder, Frank Sheed. At first, she was skeptical about this fledgling movement on account of her past experiences with Catholicism. In time, however, she realized that it was not a crank religion, but the real thing: "gradually I realized that it was nothing of the sort. It was the Catholic Church but it was the Catholic Church being Christ; not waiting for the people to come in, but coming out to the people . . . Christ following His lost sheep of whom I was one."[4] This experience brought Houselander back to Catholicism and to what was arguably the central insight of her spiritual outlook—the Mystical Body of Christ:

---

[3] Ibid., 105.
[4] Ibid., 132-33.

> For me, the greatest joy in being once again in full communion with the Catholic Church has been, and is now, the ever-growing reassurance given by the doctrine of the Mystical Body of Christ, with its teaching that we are the Church, and that "Christ and His Church are one" and that because Christ and His Church are one, the world's sorrow, with which I have always been obsessed, and which is a common obsession in these tragic years, is only the shadow cast by the spread arms of the crucified King to shelter us until the morning of resurrection from the blaze of everlasting love.[5]

The doctrine of the Mystical Body of Christ permeates Houselander's entire spiritual outlook and has much to do with her teaching on the Eucharist.

Houselander's Teaching on the Eucharist

In a certain sense, the Eucharist had as much to do with drawing Houselander away from the Church as much as it had with bringing her back to it. It was only when she came to a realization that she was just as unworthy of receiving Holy Communion as everyone else that she finally realized that she was called to see Jesus' presence in all people, even

---

[5] Ibid., 141.

those whom she disliked and believed had a very superficial understanding of their faith:

> Nevertheless, I longed for the Blessed Sacrament and the beauty of the liturgy of the Church, and this longing was made bitter to me by the perverse idea I had fostered, that the Blessed Sacrament had been put out of my reach because it had been put into the hands of the hard and righteous people in whom I felt I could have no part. It did not dawn on me that in condemning others wholesale as Pharisees, I myself was a Pharisee.[6]

The realization her own self-righteousness helped her to see that the Eucharist was not something to be exploited at the expense of others, but a gift meant to help her become her deepest, truest self, that is, someone molded after the image of Christ himself and capable of sensing his presence in all people. This insight enabled her to accept all of the Church's members as they were, regardless of where they were in their spiritual journey.

This insight brought Houselander to discover the secret of surrendering. In her book, *The Reed of God*, she views the body as "the means by which we can give ourselves wholly."[7]

---

[6] Ibid., 236.

[7] Caryll Houselander, *The Reed of God* (New York: Sheed and Ward, 1944), 84.

"We surrender our intimacy, the secret of ourselves," she states, "with the giving of our body; and we cannot give it *without* our will, our thoughts, our minds, and our souls."[8] By giving us his body, Christ imparted the secret of himself to each of us: "In Holy Communion this surrender of the secret of Himself goes on."[9] Christ, she asserts, longed for the moment when he would surrender himself in this way to each of us: "He waited thirty-three years in time for the Last Supper; two thousand years for me."[10]

According to Houselander, this act of self-surrender, involves not only the pain and privations so commonly associated with the act of our redemption, but also an imparting of joy: "Not only did He take our sorrows to Himself, but He gave the delight, that happiness that He *is*, to our humanness. No man ever enjoyed life as He did. He gathered up the color, sound, touch, meaning of everything about Him and united it all to the most exquisite sensitiveness, the most pure capacity for delight."[11] When receiving Holy Communion, we thus participate in Christ's humble surrendering of self: "The gift of Christ's Body makes everyone a priest; because everyone can offer the Body of Christ on the altar of his own life."[12] The Eucharist, for Houselander, is a sharing in

---

[8] Ibid.
[9] Ibid., 85.
[10] Ibid.
[11] Ibid., 86.
[12] Ibid., 90.

Christ's kenotic self-emptying: "Every gesture in life can be one with the gesture of the priest in Mass. It is not in making our flesh unfeeling that we hallow God's name on earth but in offering it to God burning with the flame of life. Everything can be put into the fire that Christ came to kindle; and whether it be the bitter wood of sorrow or the substance of joy, it will burn upwards with the same splendor of light."[13]

In her book, *The Risen Christ*, Houselander goes on to draw an intimate connection between the Eucharist and the prayer of Christ's Mystical Body: "The Liturgy is the expression of Christ's love, his prayer in his Mystical Body, into which our own prayer is gathered and integrated."[14] The Mass does not depend on our personal moods and feelings: "It never fails, day after day from the rising of the sun to its setting, in age after age, to adore God, to express sorrow for sin, to praise and thank God, to offer sacrifice, to petition for peace. It is the perfect expression of every individual, the voice of the inarticulate lifted in a hymn of love. At the same time it is the chorus of the whole human race made one in communion with Christ."[15] The simplicity of the Mass is meant to overflow into life itself: "In its simplest terms the way to restore our souls in this prayer of the Body is to slow down our pace to the pace of the Liturgy, to prune our minds

---

[13] Ibid.

[14] Caryll Houselander, *The Risen Christ* (New York: Sheed and Ward, 1958), 68.

[15] Ibid.

to its huge simplicities."[16] In this way, we turn life itself into a liturgy. All of our sorrows and heartaches are united to Christ's suffering and death: "Every day the suffering of the Lord's body is shown in the breaking of the bread."[17] For Houselander, as members of Christ's Mystical Body, we participate in Christ's paschal mystery: "This is the breaking of the bread, the supreme moment in the prayer of the body, the end of the liturgy of our mortal lives, when we are broken for and in the communion of Christ's love to the whole world."[18] There is no end to the prayer of Christ's body. "Even our dust," she says, "pays homage to God, until the endless morning of resurrection wakens our body, glorified."[19]

Some Further Insights

Although the above summary of Houselander's teaching on the Eucharist does not exhaust the richness of her appreciation of the sacrament, it provides a solid backdrop against which the following observations come to light.

To begin with, Houselander's autobiography offers some key insights into both the attraction the Eucharist had for her and a deep aversion to it due to the Pharisaical attitude of

---

[16] Ibid., 71.
[17] Ibid., 73.
[18] Ibid., 73-74.
[19] Ibid., 74.

many who participated in it. It was only when she saw her own self-righteous attitude toward these people that she came to recognize that the sacrament was not meant to be used as a means of judging others, but as a gift given to us by God to help us see Christ in other people. The Catholic faith is "universal," because it recognizes the presence of Christ in all people: "Truly I tell you, just as you did it to one of the least of these who are members of my family, you did it to me." (Mt 25:40).

Houselander's belief in the Mystical Body underlies her understanding of the Eucharist. The glorified body of the risen Christ that has ascended into heaven is really present in the consecrated bread and wine, which provides nourishment for the members of his body, the Church. Christ, moreover, continues to live his paschal mystery in and through the members of his body. The breaking of the bread represents the breaking of his body happened not merely 2,000 years ago when he died on the cross but continues in the suffering of his people.

The Eucharist, for Houselander, is also the sacrament of surrendering. Christ laid down his life for the salvation of the world and instituted the sacrament as a way of continuing that self-offering through the members of his body. When we break bread together, we share in the sacrificial offering of Christ and profess to live our lives accordingly. Just as Christ surrenders the secret of his life in his death on the cross and sacramentalizes it in the breaking of the bread, so do the members of his body, the Church, offer their lives through him as a living sacrifice of praise and glory to the Father.

For Houselander, Christ's action of self-surrender involves not only the pain and suffering typically associated with his sacrificial death, but also the imparting of delight to our humanity. Life in Christ, in other words, enables us to take delight in the gift of life and to share in the happiness of who Jesus is and who we are by virtue of being members of his body. Such joy is possible, because Jesus is the New Adam, someone fully alive to the Father and fully at home in the created world. By sharing in his life, we are able to delve beneath the appearances of things and appreciate the gift of life in an entirely new and different way.

For this reason, the Eucharist offers believers the opportunity to transform their very lives into a continuous liturgy. Worship does not end with the conclusion of Mass, but issues forth into the liturgy of life. Houselander offers many examples in her writings of how the Eucharist is designed to transform the ordinary circumstances of daily life. When seen in this light, it is the sacrament of the world's transformation that heralds in the new creation through the power of the Risen Lord who has come "to make all things new" (Rev 21:5).

By making us members of his body, Christ also offers us a share in his priesthood. When we break open our lives and unite everything with Christ's offering to God, we share in his priesthood. Everyone is a priest when they celebrate the liturgy of life. While this priesthood is not the same as the sacramental priesthood, it is nevertheless a real participation in the Christ's priesthood in which all the members of Christ's body share. For Houselander, this insight is not a mere metaphor but recognition of the deep significance of what it means to be a member of Christ's Mystical Body.

Finally, the Eucharist, for Houselander, enables us to view life through the eyes of faith and see things the way Jesus would see them. Doing so means viewing everyone as a child of God with the dignity of a son or daughter of the Father. The sacrament brings about a transformation of the human person by casting out the darkness from our minds, strengthening our resolve, and taming our emotions. It enables us to see Christ in others by first allowing us to encounter Christ within ourselves. This personal encounter with Christ within oneself is one of the deepest joys a person can have in life. Being able to recognize him in others intensifies that joy and makes the intimate unity of his Mystical Body palpable. Houselander experienced both in her life and was deeply grateful for the way the Lord had gifted her.

Conclusion

Caryll Houselander was a popular Catholic spiritual writer whose influence extended far beyond her lifetime. If she was not as popular as some of the other notable Catholic authors of her day, she is still widely read (many of her books are still in print) and her body of work has a noteworthy place in Catholic spiritual writing. Her insights into the Catholic faith maintain their freshness and are poetically conveyed. It is not unusual for those who read her to want to read more of her. It is unfortunate that, having died so young, her body of writing is relatively small when compared with other Catholic authors of her day.

Houselander's teaching on the Eucharist flows from her understanding of Christ's Mystical Body. The sacrament, for her, was the means used by Christ to surrender himself wholly to the will of the Father. Broken on the cross of Calvary, his body is broken again each time his followers gather for the breaking of the bread. By sharing his body with us, he gathers us into himself and offers this mystical union of bodies and souls to his Father in heaven. This intimate union of Christ and his Church cannot be undone. The Eucharist is the glue that holds it together. It conforms us onto Christ and makes us fully alive in him. It enables us to share in Christ's priesthood by allowing us to offer our lives up with his in the liturgy of daily life. It enables us to unite all our disappointments and triumphs, sorrows and joys, heartaches and delights with Christ's humble offering of himself to the Father.

Houselander's spirituality was thoroughly Eucharistic. Deeply attracted to the beauty of the Mass, she gave the sacrament a central place in her writings. The reason for this is clear. Her belief in the Real Presence was just as central to her spiritual outlook as her belief in the Mystical Body of Christ. She saw a deep continuity between Christ's risen body, his presence in the sacrament, and his presence in the members of his body. She saw the sacrament as a way each individual believer could unite his or her life to the life of Christ—and vice versa.

Reflection Questions

- Have you ever had a rocky relationship with the Church? If so, what were the details that brought it about? Was it the way you were treated by other Catholics? Was it because you were you made to feel unwelcome because you were of a different ethnic, economic or social background? Did you ever think of leaving the Church? If so, why? If not, what made you decide to stay?

- Do you consider yourself unworthy to receive the Eucharist? Do you consider yourself just as unworthy as those who have treated you poorly? Do you believe that the Eucharist is a manifestation of Jesus' love for all humanity? Do you see it as a manifestation of his love for you? Do you believe that Jesus is really present in the Blessed sacrament? Do you sense his presence in other people?

- What is the relationship between the Eucharist and Christ's Mystical Body? Do you consider yourself a member of that body? If so, how is this membership manifested in your life? If so, how is it manifested in your attitude toward the Eucharist? If you are a member of Christ' mystical body, to what extent is the Eucharist a part of your own body—and vice versa?

Voice Eleven

Evelyn Waugh
Brideshead Revisited

Evelyn Waugh (1903-66), born in Hampstead and educated first at Lancing and later at Hertford College, Oxford, was one of the most prolific English authors of the twentieth century. Known for his style, wit, comic genius, complex characters, and reverence for the past, his literary corpus is impressive, considering the fact that he died at the relatively young age of sixty-two. The wide range of literary genres in his resume include novels, biographies, travel logs, newspaper articles, and book reviews. He converted to Catholicism in 1930, a moment which proved to be a turning point in his life. During the Second World War, he served first with the Royal Marines and later as a Commando with the Royal Horse Guard. The biographer of artist and poet Dante Gabriel Rosetti (1828-82) and the Catholic English martyr Edmund Campion (1540-81), he was world traveler, who also wrote a number of well-received travel books. His novels, both comic and serious, include such works as *Decline and Fall* (1928), *Vile Bodies* (1930), *Black Mischief* 1932), *A Handful of Dust* (1934), *Scoop* (1938), *Work Suspended* (1939), *Put Out More Flags* (1942), *Brideshead Revisited* (1945), *The Loved One* (1948), *Helena* (1950), *Men at Arms*

(1952), *Love Among the Ruins* (1953), *Officers and Gentlemen* (1955), *The Ordeal of Gilbert Pinfold* (1957), *Unconditional Surrender* (1961), and *Sword of Honour* trilogy (1965). As his celebrity waned in the 1950s, he struggled financially and suffered from deteriorating health, so much so that in 1954 he began hearing voices and hallucinating. Although it seemed he was having a mental breakdown, it was later discovered that he was suffering from bromide poisoning, a complication from his many medications. A vocal critic of the reforms of the Second Vatican Council, he died as the liturgical changes were being introduced into the Church. Many of his letters and diary entries reveal his disillusionment with the direction the Church was taking. Be that as it may, the Eucharist was precious and dear to his heart right to the very end.[1]

Waugh's Religious Outlook

Waugh believed that the modern world had become a "wasteland" and that spiritual solace needed to be found elsewhere. The source of his religious outlook stemmed from a complete rejection of the modern world, belief that the twentieth century was "a decaying corpse," and a nostalgia

---

[1] For more on his biography of and a complete listing of his works, see *The Evelyn Waugh Society*, https://evelynwaughsociety.org .

for the medieval worldview.[2] His conversion to Catholicism in 1930 was a highpoint in his life, one that changed the way he viewed the world around him and his relationships with others. It helped him see that God was the underlying cause and center of all things and that the great divide between the human and the divine, the earthly and the spiritual, was bridged by Christ and the Church he founded that continued his presence on earth through the sacraments. This sensitivity to the way in which the sacraments mediated divine grace to humanity in the present historical moment was central to his religious outlook and appeared in much of his fiction, which often contained characters who had different attitudes toward God, religion, Catholicism, and ultimately the sacraments themselves.

In his later years, Waugh was disappointed (even disillusioned) with the liturgical reforms of the Second Vatican Council. He felt that they had lost sight of the transcendent, God-oriented nature of Catholic worship at a time when, because of the secularizing tendencies going on in the world, the Church should have now more than ever be highlighting this dimension of rather than downplaying it. Dialogue with the world, he believed, should not be done on the world's

---

[2] For the impact of this outlook on Waugh's fiction see, Charles J. Rolo, "Evelyn Waugh: The Best and the Worst," *The Atlantic Monthly* (October, 1954), https://www.theatlantic.com/past/docs/issues/54oct/rolo.htm .

terms, but on God's.[3] Although he remained a devout Catholic until his death, he believed that the reforms were undermining centuries of the West's cultural and spiritual heritage, something that could not be easily retrieved once it was lost. Because of the changing spiritual landscape, he was detecting within the Church, he was gradually becoming a liturgical minimalist, that is, someone who sought to do the least that was required of him without falling out of favor with the Church. His death in 1966 took place at a time when the Church's liturgical reforms had not yet been fully implemented. It remains to be seen how he would have reacted if he had lived to see them fully come to term.

Waugh's outlook focused more on the individual's rather than community's relationship to God. It was difficult for him to shift from this individualized piety that had attracted him to the faith in the first place to one that focused more on the communal dimension of Christian existence. While he believed in the Mystical Body of Christ and that he was a member of the threefold mystery of Church militant, purgative, and triumphant, his experience of divine worship was deeply personal. The Eucharist, for him, was the means by which God entered a person's soul and sanctified it. It was a sacrament of sacrifice and presence more than one of

---

[3] For Waugh's disillusionment with the liturgical reforms of the Second Vatican Council, see Alcuin Reid, ed. *A Bitter Trial: Everly Waugh and John Carmel Cardinal Heenan on the Liturgical Changes, Expanded Edition* (San Francisco: Ignatius, 2000).

banquet and celebration. It was more a sacrament of personal rather than communal thanksgiving. Although he was, at times, thought to be detached, aloof, and arrogant, as well as lacking in humility, compassion, and love,[4] he was very clear about what he professed to be true and the doctrines of the Catholic faith lay at the very heart of his belief system, especially those concerning the celebration of the Eucharist.

Waugh on the Eucharist

Perhaps one of the best ways of understanding Waugh's views toward the Eucharist is to look at the eulogy delivered in his memory by Fr. Philip Caraman, S. J. at the Latin requiem Mass celebrated at Westminster Cathedral on April 21, 1966: "The Mass mattered for him [Waugh] most in his world. During the greater part of his lifetime it remained as it had done for centuries, the same and everywhere recognizable, when all else was threatened with change. He was sad when he read of churches in which the old altar was taken down and a table substituted, or of side altars abolished as private masses were held to be unliturgical or unnecessary. With all who know something of the pattern of history, he was perturbed."[5] As someone steeped in the

---

[4] Rolo, "Evelyn Waugh," https://www.theatlantic.com/past/docs/issues/54oct/rolo.htm.

[5] Reid, ed. *A Bitter Trial*, 101. The full text of the panegyric appears in the *Tablet* (April 30, 1966): 318.

history of Western civilization, Waugh himself openly avowed, "… the Vatican Council weighs heavily on my spirits."[6] Even if the changes in the liturgy were nearer to the practice of primitive Christianity, he wondered if, "…the Church rejoices in the development of dogma; why does it not also admit the development of liturgy."[7] He brings out a very good point here. If it is true that *lex orandi, lex credendi* ("the law of what is to be prayed [is] the law of what is to be believed"), it follows that development of doctrine should presuppose developments in the liturgy—not vice versa. Despite these troubling events, he had no doubt that, in time, Truth would prevail.[8]

Waugh's sacramental view of life appears in much of his fiction. In *Brideshead Revisited* (1945),[9] for example, the narrator, Captain Charles Ryder of the British Army arrives at Brideshead with his company in the early 1940s to establish a new camp. Most of the novel is a flashback to the 1920s when he visited the manor, the home of a prominent

---

[6] Ibid., 67 ("Letter to Lady Diana Cooper, November 1, 1964)

[7] Ibid., 37 ("The Same Again, Please," *The Spectator*, November 23, 1962, 785-88).

[8] Ibid., 67 Ibid., 67 ("Letter to Lady Diana Cooper," November 1, 1964).

[9] Evelyn Waugh, *Brideshead Revisited* (London: Chapman & Hall, 1945). See also Dr. Albert Marie Surmanski, "Sacraments in Brideshead Revisited," *Homiletic and Pastoral Review* (June 12, 2017), https://www.hprweb.com/2017/06/sacraments-in-brideshead-revisited/ .

Catholic family, as a result of his friendship with Sebastian, one of the sons, and his eventual engagement to the woman he loves, Julia, one of the daughters.

Toward the end of the novel, Lord Marchmain, the head of the family who has been estranged from them and from the Church for years, returns to his manor from Italy with his mistress, Cora, to die. In remembering these events, Ryder, an atheist who by the end of the novel comes to a certain understanding of the faith, witnesses the powerful forces at play in the family as their father nears death, and they debate whether they should call in a priest to administer the last rites. Ryder does not understand the reason for this discussion and openly questions the efficacy of such an action.

As the story unfolds, the priest is called in and soon turned away by Lord Marchmain himself, who is in denial about his approaching death. When called in a second time, the priest starts to anoint the dying man, who is now unconscious or at least semi-conscious. At that moment, Ryder asks for a sign for the sake of the family and especially for Julia, the woman he loves. At the conclusion of the anointing, Lord Marchmain raises his right hand to his forehead and blesses himself with the sign of the cross. Having witnessed this change of heart in her father at his dying moments, Julia tells Ryder that she cannot marry him, because she would have to give up God if she did, and regardless of how she lived her life in the future she could never cut herself off from God's mercy.

When the flashback ends, Captain Ryder has gone through the manor, finds himself in the chapel, and is saddened by "the fierce little human tragedy"[10] that had taken place at this manor. Downcast because he sees himself as childless, middle-aged, and homeless,[11] he leaves with renewed hope and a cheerful demeanor when he sees the red sanctuary lamp burning beside the tabernacle, a sign of God's continuing presence in the midst of a world's looming darkness.

A similar theme occurs in Waugh's earlier short story, "Out of Depth" (1933),[12] which tells the story of Rip (aka Van Winkle), a lapsed Catholic who has veered into the ways of hard drinking and womanizing, goes to a party in London hosted by Lady Metroland and meets there a Dr. Kakophilos, a magician and dabbler in black magic and whose motto is, "Do what thou wilt shall be the whole of the law."[13]

As the plot unfolds, Rip gets drunk and offers the doctor a ride to his apartment, along with drunken companion, Sir Alistair Trumptington. While in the flat, the magician, disgusted with the two drunks, makes an incantation that transports them some 500 years into the future. There, Rip finds

---

[10] Waugh, *Brideshead Revisited*, 315.

[11] Ibid., 314.

[12] Evelyn Waugh, "Out of Depth," in *The Complete Stories of Evelyn Waugh* (New York: Little, Brown and Company, 1998), 146-56.

[13] Ibid., 147.

a London that has been reduced to ruins along with the rest of Western civilization. As he makes his way through the mud huts and white savages, in the midst of the chaos, he finally comes across something familiar to him. A black man dressed as a Dominican friar has gathered a small group of believers in a log-built church and is celebrating Mass. This was "[s]omething being done that Rip knew; something that twenty-five centuries had not altered; of his own childhood which survived the age of the world."[14]

The story concludes when, some days later, when Rip wakes up in a hospital, and is told that he and his companion had been in an accident with a mail van. Not convinced that his dream had nothing to do with reality, he asks for the priest who, as he was told, had been with him after the accident, asks if he could go to confession, and says, "Father...I have experimented in black art..."[15] Once again, the Eucharist represents the one point of continuity in the midst of the world's chaos and uncertainty.

Some Further Insights

Although these examples of Waugh's views on the Eucharist do not exhaust the richness of his love for and devotion to the sacrament, they provide a general context within

---

[14] Ibid., 156.
[15] Ibid.

which a deeper understanding of his beliefs can unfold. The remarks that follow seek to delve a bit more deeply into his attitude toward the Eucharist and the liturgical changes brought about Vatican II that displeased him so much.

To begin with, Waugh views the Eucharist as a point of continuity in the midst of the vicissitudes of life. Change, on whatever level, although inevitable, is never easy to deal with. In Waugh's view, as the Church travels down the corridors of time, the one constant has been its Liturgy, especially its celebration of the Eucharist. As a novelist and a believer, he looks to the sacrifice of the Mass and Jesus' presence in the Blessed Sacrament as points of stillness in a fragmented world undergoing constant change. While he recognizes the necessity of change for the life of the Church (as for any living organism), he also believes that the Latin Mass has achieved a sacrosanct status within the Church's worship and belief that renders it untouchable. He is upset by the liturgical changes brought about by the Second Vatican Council, because he feels that the authorities in question—bishops and theologians alike—do not fully appreciate the significance the traditional Latin Mass has for Western civilization as a whole. If he fails to recognize that many of the unquestioned assumptions of the past were themselves once questioned and open to doubt, it may be because of his own cultural-historical vantage point has blinded him to certain considerations.¹⁶

Waugh's point that the Church's teaching on the development of doctrine should also allow for a development in the liturgy is very well taken. If the law of prayer points to (and ultimately defines) the law of belief, it makes perfect sense that developments in the later should be preceded by developments in the former. Not to allow any developments in the liturgy undermines the fundamental notion that doctrine flows from how the Church worships. Development of doctrine, in other words, does not occur in a vacuum, but out of the living faith of the worshiping community. Since the Church is a supernatural organism that exists historically and develops over time, it follows that Waugh's intuition here is fundamentally sound. Rather than trying to return to the form of worship of early Christianity (as the liturgical reformers of the Council were wont to do), Waugh makes the insightful observation that theologians and liturgists should instead be spending their time demonstrating how developments in Catholic doctrine sprouted from developments in the Church's Eucharistic worship.¹⁷

Waugh maintains that the Church's love of diversity should move it to allow Latin to coexist alongside the

---

[16] Reid, ed. *A Bitter Trial*, 18-19.

[17] Ibid., 37 ("The Same Again, Please," *The Spectator*, November 23, 1962, 785-88).

vernacular. He states: "All the tongues of Babel are to be employed save only Latin, the language of the Church since the mission of St. Augustine."[18] Here, he overlooks the fact the liturgical reforms of Vatican II did not disallow the revised rite to be celebrated in Latin. What he really has in mind is the establishment of parallel Latin rite. He points out that the Church's love of variety is already expressed in the various Catholic rites (e.g., Byzantine, Maronite, Syro-Malabar, etc.). In the name of variety, he appeals to the Holy See for the erection of a Uniate Latin Church that would observe all the rites as they existed during the pontificate of Pius XI.[19] Although it does not go quite that far, perhaps the rehabilitation of the Extraordinary Form of the Latin Mass according to pastoral need under the Pontificate of Benedict XVI in 2007 would have met, at least in part, Waugh's request for variety.

Waugh is very much aware that, when responding to the liturgical reforms of the Second Vatican Council, his voice is very much in the minority. This knowledge, however, does not quiet (let alone mute) his objections. He is deeply convinced that the artist's "inspiration" involves more than a mere passive reception of a hierarchical authority but a vital influence on how the Church should conduct herself. He believes that Church teaching develops along artistic lines: The

---

[18] Ibid., 83 ("Letter to the Editor," *Tablet*, July 17, 1965, 792-93).

[19] Ibid., 47 ("Letter to the Editor," *Tablet*, March 16, 1963).

Church's inspired decisions, he maintains, "... are not revealed by a sudden clear voice from heaven. Human arguments are the means by which the truth eventually emerges. It is not really impertinent to insinuate one more human argument into the lofty deliberations"[20] Waugh believes that his minority opinion would eventually be heard, and that Truth would prevail.

Waugh is concerned that, in addition to the aesthetic changes brought on by the liturgical reforms, there are also going to be suggested changes in faith and morals. He detects a new kind of anti-clericalism in the description of the Mass as a "social meal" celebrated by the "people of God" because it downplays the unique sacramental role of the priest.[21] Here, he overlooks the fact that the Eucharist as meal does not seek to marginalize its sacrificial dimension but complement it. The priest, in other words, is the main celebrant of the sacrificial meal that Jesus ate the night before he died. When seen in this light, the Council was not making changes in faith and morals, but merely highlighting elements of the Mass that were already there but themselves been marginalized and, by many, long since forgotten.

Lying behind Waugh's dissatisfaction with the liturgical reforms of the Council are an understanding of the priest that

---

[20] Ibid., 41 ("The Same Again, Please," *The Spectator*, November 23, 1962, 785-88).

[21] Ibid., 79 (Michael Davie, ed., *The Diaries of Evelyn Waugh*, Boston: Little, Brown and Company, 1976, 789).

highlights his sacred craft to the exclusion of the faithful. He writes: "When I first came into the Church I was drawn, not by splendid ceremonies but by the spectacle of the priest as a craftsman. He had an important job to do which none but he was qualified for. He and his apprentice stumped up to the altar with their tools and set to work without a glance to those behind them, still less with any intention to make a personal impression on them."[22] "Participation," in such a view, does not involve taking part in the work itself, but appreciating it from afar, as one would a work of a great artist. The priest, in Waugh's eyes, performs a specific work for the faithful that they benefit from but cannot do themselves.

Finally, in Waugh's fiction the Eucharist provides the world with a sense of changeless continuity in the midst of life's uncertainties. Although his characters react to it differently—some with sincere faith, others with tepid approval, still others with doubt and disbelief—it remains a steady point of contact with the transcendent in a world that has lost its bearings and become highly secularized. Part of the reason why he is upset by the liturgical reforms of the Council is that he feels that this sense of the sacred would be lost and replaced by nothing of equal aesthetic value. The bland Church architecture and art in the immediate post-Vatican II years demonstrates that his intuition was not entirely off base. Although in the minority, his reaction to the Council

---

[22] Michael Davie, ed., *The Diaries of Evelyn Waugh*, 788-89.

was shared by many who regretted what they had lost and found it difficult to adjust to what had been put in its place. Although Waugh's faith remained firm, it was badly shaken. As he himself remarked the month before he died, "The Vatican Council has knocked the guts out of me."[23]

Conclusion

In his later years Waugh was known to be ill-tempered and cantankerous, due in part to his declining popularity, ill health, and disillusionment with the changes in the liturgy. His fiction reflects his own personal interests and reveals a sensitive artistic temperament that focused a complexity of atmosphere, character, and plot that has made him one of the most widely acclaimed authors of his generation. His many novels, short stories, travel books, reviews, letters, journal entries, and newspaper articles also make him one of the most prolific and highly regarded authors of his day.

The Catholic faith was very dear to Waugh, and it enters his fiction in various ways. Sometimes it forms a part of the religious backdrop against which his plot unfolds. At other times, it moves to the foreground and becomes a central theme of the novel or short story. At still other times, it forms a part of the mindset of his character and motivates him or

---

[23] Reid, ed. *A Bitter Trial*, 95 ("Letter to Lady Diana Mosley," March 9, 1966).

her in nuanced and, at times, even unconscious ways. Whenever he incorporated it into his fiction, he did so in a way that highlighted its sacred character and ability to address the ultimate questions of life such as the existence of God, the question of the afterlife, the conflict between good and evil, and the extent of divine mercy. Given the Church's nature, it should come as no surprise that the sacraments play a prominent role in his stories.

For Waugh, the Eucharist represented the embodiment of Christ's sacrificial death on the cross for the salvation of souls and the Real Presence of his body, blood, soul, and divinity in the consecrated species. More than a mere sign of God's love for humanity, it was the very sacrifice and love of God himself that made itself present through the ages by the actions of the priest when he celebrated Mass. Waugh saw the priest as a craftsman of the sacred whose job was to administer the Eucharist and other sacraments properly so that Christ could continue to rest in the tabernacle and live among his people. As such, the Eucharist represented the presence of the eternal in the midst of time, the changeless mystery of the divine floating in a sea of historical change. He embraced this belief with all his heart and promoted this understanding in his fiction. His difficulties with the liturgical changes made by the Second Vatical Council stem from his intuition that the sacrament would be looked upon more and more as a celebratory meal and that, even with the best of intentions to do otherwise, its sacrificial nature and the doctrine of the Real Presence would be marginalized and moved to the periphery of the believer's awareness. Given the findings of a recent Pew Research study that less than one third of American Catholics believe in the Real Presence and the doctrine of transubstantiation, it may very well be that his intuition was correct—and perhaps even prophetic.[24]

Reflection Questions

- What does it mean to have a sacramental view of life? In what ways does God reveal himself through his creation? In what ways does he reveal himself through the circumstances of daily life? Do you have a sacramental view of life? If so, how does God reveal himself you through your words, thoughts, and actions?

- Do you agree with Waugh the Church's teaching on the development of doctrine should also allow for a development in its liturgical worship? Does it make sense to you that if the law of prayer points to (and ultimately defines) the law of belief, then developments in the later should be preceded by

---

[24] See Pew Research Center, https://www.pewresearch.org/fact-tank/2019/08/05/ transubstantiation-eucharist-us-catholics/ .

developments in the former? Why did Waugh have such a difficult time with the liturgical changes brought in by the Second Vatican Council? Do you share any of his difficulties?

- Does the Mass matter to you? Is it the most important thing in the world to you? Do you look forward to attending it? Do you look upon it as a time when you can render glory, praise, and honor to God? Do you look upon it as an obligation or a privilege? Why is it that the Mass seems to matter so little to so many people (even Catholics) in the world today?

Voice Twelve

Graham Greene
The Power and the Glory

Graham Greene (1904-91), one of the leading English novelists of his generation, was born in Berkhamsted, Hertfordshire, studied at Berkhamsted School, where his father taught and later became headmaster, and went on to graduate from Balliol College, Oxford in 1925 with a degree in history. Upon graduation, he worked as a journalist for the *Nottingham Journal* and later for *The Times*. An agnostic in his early life, he converted to Catholicism in 1926 and remained a member of the Church for the rest of his life. Recruited by British intelligence and stationed in Sierra Leone during the Second World War, many of his novels were spy thrillers and what he sometimes liked to refer to as "entertainments." Although he disliked being called a "Catholic novelist,"[1] he authored some twenty-five novels, many of which dealt with themes revolving around the Catholic faith. Nominated twice for the Novel Prize in Literature, his books were widely acclaimed for their character development, atmosphere, plot, and wide popular appeal. His most popular works

---

[1] See, for example, Bernard Bergonzi, "The Catholic Novel: Is There Any Such Thing?" *Commonweal* April 30, 2007), https://www.commonwealmagazine.org/catholic-novel.

include *Brighton Rock* (1938), *The Confidential Agent* (1939), *The Power and the Glory,* (1940) *The Heart of the Matter* (1948), *The End of the Affair* (1951), *The Quiet American* (1955), *Our Man in Havana* (1958), *The Human Factor* (1978), and *Monsignor Quixote* (1982).[2]

Greene's Religious Outlook

Many of Greene's novels contain religious themes dealing with some of the most basic questions of human existence: the meaning of life, the struggle between good and evil, the seemingly irresistible allure of sin, the need for hope and redemption—to name but a few. His characters, many of whom reflect his own personal struggles, have complex inner lives that, haunted by deep-seated conflicting voices, lead them into compromising circumstances with no clear way of determining the right path to take. Unconscious forces, mixed intentions, and unruly passions move them to peer more deeply into themselves, look beneath the masks they hide behind, and get a glimpse of what is really there. What they see is often frightening. The inability to change what they wish to change about themselves leads them either to hope or despair. Sometimes the two are strangely mixed.

---

[2] For more bibliographical information on Graham Greene, see "Greeneland: The World of Graham Greene," http://greeneland.tripod.com/bio.htm.

Redemption and damnation, sin and grace, hope and despair overlap in the lives of his characters and, as can well be imagined, also in the lives of his readers.

Greene's religious sensibilities changed during the course of his life. An avowed agnostic in his younger years, he was a member of the Communist party for a short while, before converting to Catholicism. His struggles with some of the doctrines of Catholic orthodoxy are sometimes reflected in his novels. The whiskey priest's drunken perseverance in *The Power and the Glory* and Scobie's dreaded fear of damnation in *The Heart of the Matter* are but two examples of how a strange mixture of good and evil, sin and grace, virtue and vice can exist side-by-side in life's daily circumstances. The characters who inhabit, "Greeneland," as the landscape his characters inhabit is sometimes called,[3] have at one and the same time both saintly aspirations and demonic obsessions that help to shape their identities and guide their faith experiences (or lack thereof). Greene's own struggles with Catholicism led him later in life to describe himself as a "Catholic agnostic," someone who believes but does not believe, who identifies with a particular religious tradition but is uncertain about its truthfulness and the extent of his own allegiance to it tenets.[4] His turn toward humanism in his

---

[3] Ibid.

[4] See, for example, Chilton Williamson, Jr, "Musings of a 'Catholic Agnostic,'" *Crisis* (February 11, 2020), https://www.crisismagazine.com/2020/musings-of-a-catholic-agnostic. See also,

later fiction demonstrates his disillusionment with some of the principles of Catholic orthodoxy, possibly brought on by his marital problems, separation from his family, drinking, numerous extramarital affairs, and inability to get a divorce from his wife due to Catholic teaching.[5]

Catholicism, for Graham, became deeply embedded in his psyche and thus in his writing. He uses its principles to draft the main contours of the religious world his characters inhabit. He also uses them as a way of crafting some of his thoughts on the nature of language and its impact on human experience.[6] Although Greene may not have liked being called a "Catholic novelist," it is clear that, at least in his early fiction, he used the novel form to explore the mystery of belief and unbelief from within the mindset of the believer and, in doing so, set the standard for the genre for years to come. Because the Eucharist is so central to the practice of the

---

Joseph Pearce, "Graham Greene: Doubter Par Excellence," *Catholic Authors*, http://www.catholicauthors.com/ greene.html.

[5] For a treatment of Greene's personal problems, see Michael Thornton, "The Decadent World of Graham Greene—The High Priest of Darkness," *Daily Mail* (March 19, 2008), https://www.dailymail.co.uk/news/article-539011/The-decadent-world-Graham-Greene--high-priest-darkness.html.

[6] See Emily R. Brower, "'If I Were in a Book:' Language and Sacrament in Graham Greene's *The Heart of the Matter,*" *Renascence: Essays on Value in Literature* 69/4(Fall, 2017): 240-53,73, https://search.proquest.com/docview/2085067284?pq-origsite=gscholar .

Catholic faith, it should not be surprising that it plays a prominent role in much of his fiction.

Greene on the Eucharist

The Eucharist plays a prominent role in several of Greene's stories. In *The Power and the Glory* (1940),[7] for example, a nameless priest, a drunkard who has also fathered a child, misses his chance to leave the secularized Mexican state because of his love of brandy and his sense of priestly duty. Angered by the very people he serves and who cause him to miss his chance of escape, he must keep on hiding from the government authorities, who have outlawed the priesthood under penalty of death.

The whiskey priest, as he sometimes refers to himself, is torn between his fear of being captured and his sense of duty, since he is the only remaining "ministering" priest in the entire country. He has dedicated his life to both the bottle and the chalice—and reverences both. He is well aware of his unworthiness to celebrate Mass yet does so out of the recognition that the people, though themselves unworthy, are desperately in need of it.

In the end, the whiskey priest is betrayed by his own sense of priestly duty. His face, for example, is known only

---

[7] Graham Green, *The Power and the Glory* (London: W. Heinemann, 1940).

because a photograph of him at a First Communion celebration is posted by the police on their wanted board. Despite his reluctance to celebrate Mass for the people, on account of his own sinfulness and fear of being caught, he does so because he understands that he alone can give them what they so deeply desire. He alone in all of Mexico can give them the Eucharist, which even he, despite his sins, still recognizes as a conduit for God's grace. The inner struggle he has between his desire to flee and his sense of priestly duty is heightened by the scarcity of wine that is needed to celebrate Mass and the availability of brandy, the cause of his priestly downfall.

As the novel unfolds, the whiskey priest becomes a hesitant penitent and a reluctant martyr, totally unlike the sentimental martyrs presented in the popular hagiography of the day. Although the people refuse to disclose his whereabouts to the authorities, he is betrayed by a crafty *mestizo*, who sets a trap by asking him to hear the confession of a dying criminal. The priest agrees even though he distrusts the *mestizo* and suspects a betrayal, yet embraces his fate, goes to hear the outlaw's confession, and accepts the consequences of his actions. Unable to receive the last rites for himself at the novel's end, he confesses his sins into the air with a strange mixture of sincerity and pure formality before going to his death by firing squad.

Some Further Insights

Although this brief presentation of how the Eucharist appears in *The Power and the Glory* does not do justice to the role it plays in Greene's fiction as a whole, it does point to some of the general themes he develops in some of his later works. The following remarks seek to identify some of these themes that help form the religious atmosphere in which much of his fiction would eventually unfold.

To begin with, Greene is not so much interested in the Catholic teaching on the Eucharist itself as in the impact it has on the inner world of his characters. In *The Power and the Glory*, the sacrament's hold over the whiskey priest is so strong that it has penetrated his own identity and self-understanding. Despite his many sins and human frailties (of which he is keenly aware), he recognizes that he has been given the power to confect the Eucharist, something relatively few others can do (and now, except for him, no one at all in all of Mexico). This knowledge of the power of the priesthood is deeply embedded in his psyche and pushes him to do things that he himself otherwise would seek to avoid. In many ways, he embodies the words of the Apostle Paul who said, "I will boast all the more gladly of my weaknesses, so that the power of Christ may dwell in me therefore I am content with weaknesses, insults, hardships, persecutions, and calamities for the sake of Christ; for whenever I am weak, then I am strong" (2Cor 9-11).

Throughout the novel, Greene sets up an interesting parallel between the wine needed to celebrate Mass and the brandy that has played such a large role in his soiled reputation. Although wine is always scarce, he always seems to get his hands on a ready supply of brandy. This parallel resembles that made by the Apostle between a life lived according to the Spirit and one lived according to the flesh (Gal 5:16-26). The difference between these two potent and intoxicating beverages is that one has been specifically ordered by God to be part the sacramental matter of the Eucharist, while the other is not. One points to the realm of grace; the other, to the realm of nature (the implication being *fallen* nature). Together, the wine and brandy point to the struggle going on within his own soul. Although this struggle is never fully resolved, the novel ends with the priest confessing sins, even though he knew he would likely succumb to again if the opportunity arose.

Another interesting parallel is the one Greene sets up between the whiskey priest and Padre José, a priest who has sold out to the government, renounced his priesthood, and no longer exercises his ministry. The whiskey priest readily admits that Padre José was always the better priest. Such an admission stems from his deep awareness of his own sinfulness and unworthiness to celebrate the sacraments. The difference between the two of them is stark. Before the suppression of the Church and its ministers, Padre José was a model priest, someone who made no waves, played by the rules, and was generally well-liked by the people. When the circumstances changed, however, and when it was no longer easy to profess the faith, let alone exercise the powers of the priesthood, the most important of which was to celebrate Mass and bring the Eucharist to the faithful, he recanted his faith, got married, refused to administer the sacraments, and even denied hearing the confession of the whiskey priest before his execution. The whiskey priest, by way of contrast, who was never considered a good priest by the people, by other priests, or even by himself, finds the courage, despite his many flaws, to exercise his ministry of bringing the Eucharist to the faithful in the face of grave danger and the threat of death.

Another parallel in the novel is the contrast between the whiskey priest and the American outlaw, Calver, the man whom our nameless protagonist visits near the novel's end to hear his confession. Both are wanted men. One is a fugitive from American justice and has fled to Mexico; the other is trying to elude the Mexican authorities, has reluctantly decided to exercise his priestly powers even though it puts him in harm's way. Each man has his moral failings; each man has his own inner demons to deal with. Since the criminal's name, "Calver," so closely resembles the word, "Calvary," the place where Jesus died, one is first led to think that he might represent the good thief, who in Luke's Gospel hangs on cross next to Jesus and repents of his sins (Lk 23:39-43). As it turns out, he resembles more the bad thief, since he is unrepentant and pleads with the priest as he nears death to take his weapons and use them against the police and possible escape. The priest, in turn, shows up drunk and cannot properly administer the sacrament. When seen in this light, the two characters represent an inversion of the event that took place on Calvary.

The fact that the whiskey priest is nameless throughout the novel is yet another parallel that Greene sets up in the novel. By having no name, he has every name. Every priest has sins and weaknesses, some of which may be deeply rooted in his mind and heart and difficult to uproot. In confronting the story of this particular priest, priests reading the novel are brought face-to-face with their own priestly narratives and need to ask themselves what kind of priest they wish to be. Will they dwell on the level of appearances like Padre José and, when difficulties arise, take the path of least resistance, or summon the courage to stand up for the faith in difficult times and face whatever comes? There is a bit of the Padre José and the whiskey priest in every priest and, by way of extension, every believer. Perseverance is a virtue that requires deep soul searching, the kind that delves beneath appearances and struggles to name what one truly believes. For all his human failings, the whiskey priest does what Padre José is either incapable of or unwilling to do. He confronts his dark side and is able to quiet his inner demons and, despite his fears and inadequacies, do what a priest is ordained to do: bring the Body and Blood of Christ to God's people.

The role of the Eucharist in Greene's novels, however, is not limited merely to The Power and the Glory. In *The Heart of the Matter* (1948),[8] for example, he probes the internal world not of a priest, but this time of one of the faithful. Major Henry Scobie, a police officer in a British colony in East Africa, finds himself in an unhappy marriage, has had an affair with another woman, and acting out of pity for both his wife and lover resolves to come up with some sort of a solution. His answer is to commit suicide and making it seem as though he died from natural causes. As the novel unfolds, Scobie is haunted by his fear of death and eternal damnation on account of his affair. Having promised his wife that he would go to Mass with her upon her return from South Africa, he goes to confession but is refused absolution because he is not fully repentant of his affair. Believing he is damned anyway, he receives Holy Communion with his wife at Mass, knowing full well that he is in the state of mortal sin. His plan to kill himself stems from his being caught between two irreconcilable forces in his psyche: his desire to protect his wife and his desire to preserve his relationship with his lover. The Eucharist, in this instance, is an incarnation of the sacred that accuses him of his broken marriage and infidelity. Because neither one can be salvaged, his only solution is to exit the scene. In this instance, the Eucharist functions as a

---

[8] Graham Greene, *The Heart of the Matter* (New York: Viking. Press, 1948).

mirror that forces Scobie to enter into himself and make an honest assessment of his situation. The guilt it imposes on the man leads him to despair and the taking of his life. At the same time, it leaves him with a small glimmer of hope in Fr. Rank, the local priest who refuses him absolution and says he would pray for him, who understands that, in the end, God alone has the authority to judge a person for the life he or she has lived.

One final example of the role the Eucharist plays in Greene's fiction comes in his short story, "The Hint of An Explanation" (1949),[9] which deals with the impact the sacrament has on the inner world of a child. The story begins with two strangers on a long train journey in a compartment that they have all to themselves. As the time passes, they begin talking to one another and discussing a number of topics, finally coming to the topic of God. The narrator of the story is an agnostic, while the other traveler is a Catholic. When the Catholic hears the complaints of the narrator regarding his lack of faith in a God who would allow so much agony in the world, the Catholic responds that we have no answers in this life and have only hints. He then goes on to tell relate one of his early childhood memories about a baker named "Blacker" who was a free thinker with a deep hatred for

---

[9] Graham Greene, "The Hint of Ann Explanation," *Commonweal* (February 11, 1949), https://www.commonwealmagazine.org/hint-explanation.

Catholics and all that they stood for. As the plot unfolds, Blacker, an embodiment of Evil, tries to befriend the young boy by inviting him into his store, letting him play with an electric train set, and telling him that he could have it if he brought him one of the hosts from Sunday Mass. At first, the boy says no, but eventually he succumbs to the allure of play and succeeds in taking the host from his mouth when at Mass and placing it between two small pieces of paper and putting it in his pocket. He then nearly forgets all about it until night fall when he finds the host in his pocket as he undresses for bed and puts it on his nightstand. It is at that point that he realizes that he cannot do what he said he would. The idea of transubstantiation is no longer an abstract theory but is now lodged deep within his psyche. He now realizes that what he had laid beside his bed was "something of infinite value."

When he hears Blacker's whistle outside, he takes the consecrated host lodged between the two small pieces of paper and swallows it, paper and all. When he asks for the host, the boy tells him that he has swallowed it and tells him to go away. Blacker goes away distraught (and weeping), for as the embodiment of Evil, he was probably going to put it under a microscope to assure himself that it was merely a piece of bread, before desecrating it.

As the story ends, the narrator tells the Catholic that he probably owes a lot to Blacker, and the Catholic responds that he does, for he is a happy man. It is at that point that the narrator notices that, when his fellow traveler rises at the end of the journey to take his bag from the rack, his coat collar opens and discloses the collar of a priest. The story demonstrates the powerful sway the Eucharist has on the inner world of children and, in this particular instance, brought happiness and a firm direction to a child's life.

Conclusion

Graham Greene was one of the preeminent English novelists of the twentieth century and his impact on novelists continues to this day. A convert to Catholicism, he used the underlying contours of the faith—the God question, the conflict between good and evil, humanity's sinful condition, redemption through Christ, the mediation of grace through the Church and her sacraments, and more—to create the spiritual and psychological world that the characters of his novels inhabited. This atmosphere penetrates the mindset of his characters and leads them to the decisions they make regarding God, life, others, and ultimately themselves.

Greene's own spiritual journey brought him from being an agnostic to a practicing Catholic to what he would later call a "Catholic agnostic." His attitude toward the Church changed over time and was due, at least in part, to his own struggles with the faith as they applied to his personal life and his exploration of ideas that often led beyond the pale of Catholic orthodoxy. Be that as it may, it is clear that the

Catholic faith influenced him to the point that it had penetrated his own inner world and those of his characters. It would not be far afield to suggest that many of the inner personal struggles of his characters reflect those which he himself experienced and dealt with varying degrees of success and failure. When seen in this light, his fiction is a way he sought to understand and deal with the vying voices in his own inner world.

The Eucharist represents the incursion of the sacred into the outer world Greene's characters inhabit and the inner worlds of their conscious and unconscious minds. For some characters, as in the whiskey priest of *The Power and the Glory*, it is an instrument of healing and self-discovery that calls forth the best in what, by all others counts, would be deemed a failed life, a failed faith, and a failed priesthood. For others, as in Scobie in *The Heart of the Matter*, it has become a dreaded sign of judgment for a life lived out of misplaced pity rather than an authentic search for truth. For the priest in "The Hint of An Explanation," it stands for the childhood discovery of the sacred and the happiness it brings him throughout his adult priestly life. Although these diverse influences stem from Greene's imagination, they also likely point to tensions within his own inner life and his intense (yet precarious) relationship with the Catholic faith. Although the Eucharist stands for the objective presence of the sacred in the world, the characters of "Greeneland" (and perhaps Greene himself) perceive it and react to it differently, depending on where they stand in relation to the faith and the one sacrament that, above all others, represents its source, summit, and very lifeblood.

Reflection Questions

- Have your religious sensibilities changed over time? If so, do the changes in any way resemble those in Greene's life? Why did Greene not like to be called a Catholic novelist? Why did he describe himself later in life as a Catholic agnostic? How is this attitude toward Catholicism reflected in his fiction? Do you sympathize with any of his positions?

- Why does the Eucharist play such a prominent role in many of Greene's novels? Why is he interested in the impact this sacrament has on the inner world of his characters? What positive role does its impact have on them? When negative impact does it have on them. What impact does the Eucharist have on your inner world?

- Greene's spiritual journey led him from being an agnostic to a practicing Catholic and later a hybrid of the two. What has your spiritual journey been like? How would you describe it? What are its main characteristics? Does it in any way resemble that of Greene's? What role does the Eucharist play in it?

Voice Thirteen

Rumer Godden
In this House of Brede

Rumer Godden (1907-98) was born in Sussex, England but spent most of her early life in colonial India in what is now Bangladesh. She and her sisters were sent back to England for their schooling but returned to India at the outbreak of the First World War. Trained as a dancer, she opened a school of dance in Calcutta in 1925 and ran the school for 20 years. She married in 1934, divorced in 1948, remarried in 1949, and had two daughters. She became interested in the Catholic Church in the early 1950s and converted to Catholicism in 1968. The author of some sixty novels, books of poetry, children's books, and non-fictional works, a number of her stories take place in India and many also focus on the lives of women religious. Her most notable works include: *Black Narcissus* (1939) *A Fuge in Time* (1945), *An Episode of Sparrows* (1956), *The Battle of Villa Fiorita* (1963), *In this House of Brede* (1969), and *Five for Sorrow, Ten for Joy* (1979). She was awarded the Whitbread prize for children's literature in 1972 and appointed to the Order of the British Empire in 1994. Her understanding the Eucharist come through most clearly in, *In This House of Brede*, a novel about Benedictine nuns in England in the 1950s and 60s.[1]

Godden's Spiritual Outlook

One of Godden's favorite sayings comes from an old Indian proverb, which she quotes in her autobiography, *A House with Four Rooms* (1989): "Everyone is a house with four rooms, a physical, a mental, and emotional, and a spiritual. Most of us tend to live in one room most of the time but unless we go into every room every day, even if only to keep it aired, we are not a complete person."[2] She led a disciplined life that was dedicated to her writing, working assiduously in both the morning and evening hours, yet also making time for other interests such as opera, dance, Pekinese dogs, and a good whisky. She sought the extraordinary in the midst of the ordinary; holiness, in the woof and warp of everyday life. Reared in the Anglican faith, she had a fascination with India, where she spent much of her childhood and early adult life, especially by the way in which the spiritual world imbued the material, and all of life was counted as sacred.[3]

---

[1] For more on Godden's life and writings, see "Rumer Godden: Literary Trust," https://www.rumergodden.com/biography/ .
[2] Ibid.
[3] Ibid.

A prolific author who wrote in a variety of literary genres, Godden was passionate about her writing and filled her tales with themes related to the search for meaning and the quest of holiness. She always wrote in longhand (and with a fountain pen), likening the author's craft to that of an artist who must dip his brush into the paint to give him time to ponder his next stroke.[4] That nine of her novels were made into films reveals the broad appeal they had on the public and her great success as a literary figure. The wide range of literary genres she employed in her writing manifests her talent as a writer and her willingness to employ various modes of expression in her search for meaning. Her lifelong love of dance represents one way in which she could integrate the physical, mental, emotional, and spiritual in her life; her dedication to her writing, yet another.[5]

As Phyllis Tickle points out in her "Introduction" to the Loyola Classics edition of *In This House of Brede,* Godden studied the world religions and converted to Catholicism in 1968 at the age of sixty, while she was working on Brede.[6] This Benedictine monastery of nuns, she points out, was based on Stanbrook Convent and St. Cecilia's Abbey in Ryde, Isle of Wight. Philippa, the novel's main character, in turn, represents all who search after Christian truth, while the

---

[4] Ibid.

[5] Ibid.

[6] Phyllis Tickle, "Introduction" in *In this House of Brede* by Rumer Godden (Chicago: Loyola Classics, 2005), xi.

monastery itself is a microcosm for the world we inhabit.[7] It is a place where all four rooms of the human person are aired in varying degrees the physical, mental, emotional, and spiritual rooms of their lives. When you read the novel, one other integral dimension (or room) also comes to the fore: the communal. Brede is a religious family, a community of nuns dedicated to God and to one another. Existing as it does at the very heart of the Benedictine way of life, the Mass and the Blessed Sacrament spill over into the rest of the community's life and the lives of its members. Seeing that Gooden converted to Catholicism while she was researching and writing the novel, it is likely that the Eucharist had a similar effect on her own search for holiness.

Godden on the Eucharist

In commenting on her conversion to Catholicism, Godden is known to have said, "I like the way everything is clear and concise. You'll always be forgiven, but you must know the rules."[8] Her fascination with religious life (especially Benedictine monasticism) speaks to this love of clarity and precision. The Rule of St. Benedict cloistered its community members away from the world in order to provide them with a sense of peace, a peace that the world cannot give. That

---

[7] Ibid., ix.
[8] Ibid., xi.

peace was rooted in a well-regulated order of the day organized around the concept of *laus perennis* (continual praise) as manifested in a life dedicated to prayer, spiritual reading, and manual labor. This peace, however, came not without a price: the cost of discipleship involved following in the footsteps of Jesus by taking up one's denying oneself and taking one's cross daily. The opening words of *In This House of Brede* set the tone for all that follows: "The motto was 'Pax,' but the word was set in a circle of thorns. Pax, peace, but what a strange peace, made of unremitting toil and effort, seldom with a seen result; subject to constant interruptions, unexpected demands, short sleep at nights, little comfort, sometimes scant food; beset with disappointment and usually misunderstood; yet peace all the same, undeviating, filled with joy and gratitude and love. 'It is my own peace I give unto you.' Not, notice, the world's peace."[9] Philippa, the novel's main character, leaves the world behind in order to lose herself in the seclusion and anonymity of Benedictine life. The peace she finds there, however, comes about only by placing the will of God and the community before her own. As the novel unfolds, she finds herself only by losing herself in the service of others.

The Eucharist plays a central role within this intentionally organized form of religious life. Although Godden does

---

[9] Rumer Godden, *In This House of Brede* (Chicago: Loyola Classics, 2005), 3.

not betray her craft as a novelist by focusing on the doctrinal dimensions of the faith and although the way she presents the Eucharist in the novel does not necessarily represent her own views (still, she converted to Catholicism while writing the book), she allows the Rule to speak for itself and does her best to depict what life in a Benedictine Abbey would be like in the decades immediately preceding and following the Second Vatican Council (1963-65). The novel is considered one of the best fictional depictions of Benedictine life before the Council and as it tried to adapt to the directives for renewal immediately afterward.

For the nuns of Brede, "the Conventual Mass was the most important act of the day."[10] Although a low Mass was offered at the beginning of each day for those who could not attend because of sickness or essential responsibilities, the Conventual Mass, which was intimately linked to the chanting of the Divine Office, represented the highpoint of their day: "The Office centered round the Mass, giving the day one theme, making of it one continuous prayer. 'Everything we do, outside choir,' said Dame Clare, 'our work, our reading, our private prayer, even our meals in the refectory are simply pauses, meant to prepare ourselves for our real work, the Opus Dei—and that needs discipline.'"[11]

---

[10] Ibid., 105.
[11] Ibid.

Godden also is very good at depicting the human element in the Benedictine way of life. Dame Clare, the assistant novice mistress, points out to her novices that the liturgical year is full of variety for that very reason: "Don't you see, it's like a pageant. Our cardinal has said the liturgy entertains as well as feeds us…Yes, we're not angels but humans… and human nature is made so that it needs variety. The church is like a wise mother and has given us this great cycle of the liturgical year with its different words and colors. You'll see how you will learn to welcome the feast days and the saints days as they come around, each with a different story and, as it were, a different aspect; they grow very dear, though still exacting."[12]

Amidst the business of life at Brede, with all the activities and responsibilities delegated to the various members of the community, they all sensed "the great outlet of the Office and Mass running through the days to bind them to a whole."[13] Indeed, the Blessed Sacrament forms the backdrop against which the drama of Benedictine life unfolds. When Abbess Dame Hester dies soon after Philippa's entrance, the abbey's chaplain comes to administer the last rites: "The abbess had not been able to speak to make her last confession, but Dom Gervase, hastily summoned, had given her absolution; nor could she swallow the holy viaticum, food for the

---

[12] Ibid., 104-5.
[13] Ibid., 493.

unfathomable journey she was to make, nor kiss the crucifix, but the prioress had held it to her lips."[14] When the abbess finally dies, the community mourns her passing for three days which culminate in the celebration of a Solemn Pontifical Requiem Mass.[15] Toward the end of the novel, Dame Emily, who had been the prioress for many years and was now dying of cancer, tells Philippa of her conversion to Catholicism: "When I was eighteen, a high-headed proud young girl…we were on holiday in Folkestone, and on a rainy day when I was bored, having nothing particular to do, I wandered into a church to listen to the music. For me it might have been any church—but it was Catholic. The time was the octave of Corpus Christi, and I heard the priest preach on the Real Presence—"This is my body"— and I thought, If this is true … the rest followed."[16]

The community celebrated *Quarant'Ore*, forty hours of exposition of the Blessed Sacrament on the feast of Corpus Christi and had regular appointed times for solemn exposition.[17] Near the end of the novel, Philippa kneels before the Blessed Sacrament and ponders its deep spiritual significance: "Bowls of flowers surrounded the high altar; the candles made points of flame above them, and, in the center, the disc of the white Host was enthroned in the glittering

---

[14] Ibid., 79.
[15] Ibid., 89.
[16] Ibid., 618.
[17] Ibid., 618-19.

monstrance. Was it fancy because she was so tired, though Philippa, a mere illusion, or was the Host penetrated by a light of its own? A kind of window through which, had she the eyes, she could have looked straight into heaven; but it's only the dying, or the very holy, who have eyes like that, she thought."[18]

One of the central events in the novel concerns the design and installation of a new altar for the main chapel. Ordered by Abbess Hester before her death to be designed and installed by a renowned, internationally famous sculptor, questions arise concerning its exorbitant cost, its appropriateness for a religious community dedicated to poverty, and the way is will influence the celebration of Mass. As it is being constructed, the nuns ponder the possibility of the priest celebrating Mass facing the people, a controversial rubric at the time not permitted before the Second Vatican Council.[19] The nuns' interest in the proceedings of the Council reveals their interest in the world beyond the confines of the monastery walls yet brings to the surface a division within the community between the older sisters who are resistant to change and the younger one who are looking for change simply for the sake of change. Abbess Catherine, who was elected to succeed Abbess Hester tries to steer a middle

---

[18] Ibid., 619.
[19] Ibid., 243.

course between the old and the new.[20] The changing of the altar also reminds us that the holy embraces not only people, but also the very dimensions time and space. The altar, a place where God through human cooperation brings about an actualization of the holy, is both a banquet table and a place of sacrifice. The continuity and close connection between the one and the other reminds the reader that the Church (and Brede itself) has always been in a process of continuity-in-change and change-in-continuity. At the end of the novel, Dame Philippa, the embodiment of the searching pilgrim, embodies this process as she lets go of her dream to live out the rest of her life at Brede and sets out for Japan to plant the seed of Benedictine monasticism on foreign shores.[21]

Some Further Insights

This brief summary of Godden's presentation of the Eucharist in *In this House of Brede* offers an opportunity to delve a bit further into the novel's underlying religious outlook and stance toward the sacrament. What follows are some observations aimed at probing this presentation of the Eucharist in a little more depth.

---

[20] Ibid., 592-604.
[21] Ibid., 635-38.

To begin with, Godden does a superb in highlighting the main characteristics of Benedictine spirituality and the central role played by the Mass and the Opus Dei (the Divine Office). This spirituality sought to sanctify the day through a life of continual prayer dedicated to the chanting of the Divine Office, spiritual reading, and manual labor. All of these activities flowed from and returned to the daily celebration of the Eucharist, the central act of worship of Brede and of all Benedictine monasteries throughout the world. Although the nuns of Brede were divided into choir nuns, whose primary responsibility was the recitation of the hours, claustral nuns, who focused on the manual labor and the physical upkeep of the monastery, and externs, who engaged the community beyond the monastery walls, each sister maintained a certain mixture in varying degrees of all three elements of daily Benedictine life: office, spiritual reading, and manual labor. In the wake of the Second Vatican Council, the distinctions among the sisters themselves would gradually disappear and a categorization that made all members of the community equal members under the abbess or prioress put in place.

Godden also does a very good job of depicting the spiritual battle that goes on within each individual, the battle between God's will and self-will, between humbly obeying the will of one's superiors and one's own individual freedom and autonomy. Dame Agnes describe this battle in her assessment of the novel's protagonist: "Dame Philippa won't have won until she can do what she is asked, what is needed, without a battle."²² As a symbol of the religious seeker, Philippa engages in this battle and goes through a process whereby her will to decide her own destiny diminishes is gently and very gradually replaced by a willingness to serve the needs of the community. There is a clear movement in her life from self-will to conformity to God's will and, one would hope as her journey continues, to an actual uniformity with God's will. Central to this process of conversion is her participation in the life of the community, the most central feature of which is the celebration of Mass and the Divine Office. The Mass, especially, immerses those present in Jesus' selfless, sacrificial death on Calvary, the action par excellence that demonstrated his complete union with the will of his Father.

Brede, we must remember, is a microcosm of the world. It represents the sanctity of time and space and the historical drama of human life that goes within their boundaries. The nuns of the monastery, although bound together by their common search for holiness within the Benedictine tradition, are in various places in their spiritual journey. They have entered the monastery for a number of reasons and have submitted themselves to its strict regimen of life there in order to purify themselves of themselves and allow God's will to reign in their lives. As the novel unfolds, it becomes

---

²² Ibid., 487.

clear that the nuns of Brede have deep spiritual aspirations yet are also very human. The same temptations and earthly attachments found in the world are also present within the monastery walls. While the Eucharist is celebrated on both sides of the monastery walls, it holds a conscious and highly focused place in the life of the community. This intentional Eucharistic dimension sets Brede apart from the rest of the world transforms it into a sign of God building his kingdom in the midst of weak and vulnerable followers.

The peace experienced at Brede is not one free of struggle, pain, and suffering. On the contrary, it is one that comes from embracing the cross of Christ in the particulars of one's life and persevering in following him from day to day, from month to month, and from year to year, until one's earthly sojourn is complete. All of the nuns at Brede are on a journey. This is depicted most eloquently by Godden in the way she juxtaposes the death of Abbess Hester and her passing to new life near the beginning of the novel and Dame Philippa's journey to Japan at the end of the novel.[23] Each is at different stages of her journey. Abbess Hester's is complete, while Dame Philippa is still a wayfaring pilgrim. God has called each of them to leave Brede behind but to take what they have learned from their time there with them. The Eucharist for each of them is *Viaticum*, food for the journey. For Abbess Hester, it will be the last bit of food to touch her lips

---

[23] Ibid., 79, 635-38.

during her earthly pilgrimage. For Dame Philippa, it will continue to be a source of her daily spiritual bread as she faces the challenges ahead. Each has found peace in her earthly passage, a peace the world cannot give.

Finally, the novel takes place during the decades immediately before and after the Second Vatican Council, and many of the tensions experienced in the Church at large are also present within the walls of Brede. The replacing of the old altar with a new, modernized version, one that holds out the possibility of the priest celebrating Mass facing the people, raises questions not only regarding its cost but also the nature of the Liturgy itself. Is the altar a table, and altar? Should the Mass be celebrated in the vernacular or not? If so, how is one to adapt the rhythm and sound of the English language to Latin chant? Should the distinctions between choir nuns and claustral nuns be done away with? To what extent should the Church be open to Christians of other denominations? These questions (and others like them) are of interest to the nuns of Brede, because the way they are answered will affect their lives directly. How the emphasis is laid will say much about how the Mass itself will be celebrated and how the nuns themselves will participate in it. The nuns' interest in the proceedings of the Council reflects their attitude toward change. Some wish to preserve the customs of Brede at all costs; others wish to change with the changing signs of the times. Abbess Catherine, a voice of mediation throughout the novel, seeks a middle ground. As the novel reaches its end, it becomes clear that, Brede has always been in a state of flux (albeit in varying degrees). The Eucharist and the Divine Office themselves have also been subject to change, but their object, purpose, substance, and intent have always remained the same: to give glory and honor to God.

Conclusion

Rumer Godden was one of the most accomplished British authors of the twentieth century. Her sixty books, written in a variety of literary genres and brought into print by more than forty publishing houses, make her one of the most prolific and versatile authors of her day. Her search for meaning and holiness in everyday life, when combined with her fascination with women's religious life and her desire to get in touch with the minutest details of Benedictine monastic life, make her a valuable literary resource for those wishing to trace the religious and spiritual sensitivities of her day.

Although her influence on the Catholic imagination has waned in recent years, her works still maintain their power to immerse her readers in a world dedicated to God and the search for holiness. While researching Benedictine life for *In this House of* Brede (what many consider her masterpiece) she converted to Catholicism in 1968 in the immediate aftermath of the Second Vatican Council, a time when Catholicism itself was undergoing a great changes in its own self-understanding and in the way it related to other Christians, non-Christians, and the outside world in general. Although the vicissitudes of time would impact life at monasteries such as Brede (for better and for worse) in the years to come, the underlying centuries-long tradition of Benedictine spirituality would remain vital as it adapted to the challenges of the day: The strength of a religious tradition consists in its ability to adapt to changing circumstances while at the same time maintaining its own identity.

Faced with the inevitability of change in the midst of life's challenges, one thing remains constant in the monastery of Brede and in the life of the Church at large: the worship rendered to God through the Divine Liturgy. Even if its ritual has changed from the Old Mass to the New, and even if Catholics today have the choice between the Extraordinary Form (what was practiced at Brede) and what is now called the Ordinary Form (the Vatican II Mass), the substance of Liturgy as an immersion into Christ's sacrificial death on Calvary, a foretaste of the heavenly banquet, and a celebration of Christ's presence among his people in the Blessed Sacrament remains constant. In the final analysis, Godden presents the life at Brede as a challenge to all Christians to allow the sacrificial death of Christ to take root in their lives so that they might put off the old self and put on the new, so that Christ might live in them and the peace he offers him by way of the cross might find a place in their hearts.

Reflection Questions

Voice Thirteen: Rumer Godden—*In this House of Brede*

- Do you live in a house with four rooms: the physical, a mental, and emotional, and spiritual? If so, which one do you spend the most time in? Which one do you visit least? Do you try to find each day to move throughout your house? Do you at least try to air them? If not, why not?

- In what sense is the monastery of Brede a microcosm of the world we inhabit? What does it tell us about our world? What does it tell you about your world? With which of the characters do you identify most? Which do you find most off-putting? What role does the Eucharist play in this microcosm?

- What kind of peace does one find in Brede? Is it a peace free of struggle, pain, and suffering? What is the source of this peace? How does one find it? How can it be lost? Have you ever experienced such peace? Would you like to? Can you do so without having to enter a monastery? Do you think of the Eucharist as a sacrament of peace?

Voice Fourteen

Walker Percy
Love in the Ruins

Walker Percy (1916-90), an American philosopher, philologist, and novelist, was born in Birmingham Alabama just before the start of the First World War. His father committed suicide when he was thirteen and his mother died of a suspected suicide some two years later. After their deaths, he and his two younger brothers went to live in Greenville, Mississippi, to live with an older cousin, whom they called "Uncle Will." There, he received a classical Southern upbringing and was exposed to many of the fine literary and cultural tastes prominent in his day. After graduating from high school, he matriculated at the University of North Carolina at Chapel Hill and graduated in 1937 with a major in chemistry. In 1941, he earned an M.D. from Columbia University's College of Physicians and Surgeons in New York, became an intern at Bellevue Hospital in Manhattan, and contracted tuberculosis there while performing an autopsy. Forced to delay his medical career, he spent the next two years in a sanitorium in the Adirondacks of upstate New York. When he was released, he taught pathology for a brief time at Columbia, but had a recurrence of the disease in 1945 and entered another sanitorium in Wallingford,

Connecticut. After he regained his health, he married Mary Townsend in 1946 and both were received into the Catholic Church in 1947. His illness and newfound faith set him on a different career path, since his time in the sanitoriums gave him the opportunity to delve into many of the prominent philosophers and novelists of his time. His decision to turn novelist and essayist was encouraged by his lifelong friend, historian Shelby Foote, with whom he corresponded with for many years right up until his death. His many works include *The Moviegoer* (1961), which won the National Book Award for Fiction in 1962, *The Last Gentleman* (1966), *Love in the Ruins* (1971), *Lancelot* (1977) *The Second Coming* 1980), and *The Thanatos Syndrome* (1987). A collection of his essays appeared in 1975 as *The Message in the Bottle: How Queer Man Is, How Queer Language Is, and What One Has to Do with the Other*. He died of cancer in Covington, Louisiana in 1990 and is buried on the grounds of St. Joseph Benedictine Monastery in St. Benedict, Louisiana.[1]

Percy's Spiritual Outlook

Although he had respect for the social relevance of religion and maintained some nominal ties with his hometown

---

[1] For more on Percy's life, see "A Walker Percy Primer" in *The Walker Percy Project*, https://www.ibiblio.org/wpercy/about-percy/about-percy.html# .

Voice Fourteen: Walker Percy—*Love in the Ruins*

Presbyterian Church, Percy was an agnostic for much of his early life. His spiritual search became much more focused, however, when he was beset with tuberculosis and forced to isolate himself, slow down, undergo treatment, and gradually regain his strength. During his two years recovering from the disease at Trudeau Sanitorium in Saranic Lake in the Adirondack Mountains of upstate New York, he devoted much of his time to reading the works of some of the great philosophers and novelists of his day.

Percy was particularly impressed by the works of Søren Kierkegaard (1813-55), the father of existentialism, whose three modes of existence—the aesthetic, the ethical, and the religious—provided him with an outlook on life that would permeate much of his fiction. The aesthetic man, for Kierkegaard, lives on the surface of life, judges by appearances, and is primarily concerned with satisfying his various needs and pleasures of everyday life. The ethical man, by way of contrast, defines himself according to a strict moral code of conduct. These principles give order to his world and enable him to function in the world and navigate its turbulent waters. When this code is broken or compromised, however, he undergoes a crisis of identity. The religious man, in turn, deals with the ambiguities of life by taking a leap of faith into the absurd. Rather than trying to impose order on the world around him, he simply accepts life as it comes and trusts that, despite the looming darkness, God will not abandon him but bestow peace on him in the midst the surrounding turmoil.[2]

In his novels, Percy offers an interesting mix of characters: some are stuck in a particular mode of existence; others move from one to another, sometimes progressing and at other times regressing; still others are clearly steeped in the religious mode. In developing characters of the latter type, he is careful to avoid having them talk explicitly about the faith, thereby avoiding the blunder of being "edifying."[3] Rather than having them reveal their inwardness by explicitly verbalizing their faith, he has them acting rather humorously in his interactions with others and the world around them. His religious heroes, in other words, are not proselytizing bores, but gleamy-eyed misfits who stick out like a sore thumb by going against the current of world around them.

Percy's conversion to Catholicism in 1947 was the result of a period of deep soul searching brought on by his two bouts with tuberculosis and his search for meaning in life. In reading the works of Thomas Aquinas, he became convinced of the sacramentality of human life and became disenchanted with Kierkegaard's extreme individualism, distaste for reason, and suspicion of science. Although he was still very much indebted to Kierkegaard for giving him a

---

[2] See Linda Whitney Hobson, *Introducing Walker Percy* (Columbia, SC: University of South Carolina Press, 1988), 181-25.

[3] Ibid., 22.

language with which to address some of the most fundamental questions of human existence, he was aware of the limitations of his thought and found in Catholicism a belief system that, at one and the same time, allowed him to reconcile faith and reason, the individual and community, man as object and man as subject, good and evil, and ultimately life and death itself. His thinking on the Eucharist flows from his deep Catholic faith, which he understood was very much discounted by the intellectual elites of his day and under attack in the surrounding culture.[4]

Walker Percy on the Eucharist

Love in the Ruins (1971) is the novel where Percy's views on the Eucharist come to the fore most clearly.[5] In it, Dr. Tom More, the story's protagonist, undergoes a gradual conversion of mind and heart that ultimately leads him to return

---

[4] For the sacramentality of Percy's spiritual outlook, see Rhea Scott Rasnic, "Walker Percy and the Catholic Sacraments," (Ph.D dissertation, Baylor University, 2007), 1-26. For a critique of the centrality of Catholicism in Percy's life and works, see Kieran Quinlan, *Walker Percy: The Last Catholic Novelist* (Baton. Rouge, LA: Louisiana State University, 1996), esp. 195-227.

[5] Walker Percy, *Love in the Ruins: The Adventures of a Bad Catholic at a Time Near the End. Of the World* (New York: Farrar, Straus & Giroux, 1971). For a helpful treatment of the Eucharist in *Love in the Ruins*, see Rasnic, "Walker Percy and the Catholic Sacraments," 82-108.

to the Catholic faith of his childhood and embrace a sacramental understanding of life. The novel's subtitle, "The Adventures of a Bad Catholic at a Time Near the End of the World," indicates the kind of conversion that More would undergo. Unlike his namesake, Sir Thomas More, the sixteenth century lawyer and martyr for the Catholic faith, Dr. More accepts the teachings of the Church but lives a life in direct contradiction to them. An alcoholic and notorious womanizer, he openly admits that in Paradise Estates where he lives he has "stopped eating Christ in Communion, stopped going too mass, and … since fallen into a disorderly life."[6] While he says that "he believes in God and the whole business," he insists that he loves "women best, music and science next, whiskey next, God fourth, and my fellowman hardly at all."[7]

Dr. More believes that science can solve all the world's problems, material as well as spiritual and has invented the Qualitative Quantitative Ontological Lapsometer (QQOL), which he believes can not only diagnose the spiritual ills of modern man, but actually heal them. A brilliant scientist of the first order, he sees himself as a modern-day Messiah, who will cure humanity's wounds by bridging the divide between body and soul that has haunted the human race ever since the Cartesian *Cogito* introduced separation of mind and

---

[6] Percy, *Love in the Ruins*, 6.
[7] Ibid.

body some 300 years ago. Dr. More has fallen victim to what Percy calls "scientism," the mistaken belief common in much of Western culture that is blind to the limitations of science and has a magical (almost religious) faith in its ability to solve all of the world's problems.[8]

The novel takes place "in these dread days of the old violent beloved U.S.A. and of the Christ forgetting Christ-haunted death-dealing Western world."[9] This dystopic setting allows Percy to satirize the philosophy and cultural mindset that have left Western culture in ruins. The solipsism and exaggerated individualism, the subjectivism and relativism regarding truth, the lack of community and the lack of reverence for the common good, have all taken their toll on the heart of modern man. Dr. More's dilemma is that he thinks that science can heal these wounds when, due to his pervasive pride and lack of willingness to confront his own inner demons, he himself is blind to his own spiritual emptiness. The novel is about the gradual shift in his self-understanding that enables him to reject one world view (his belief in scientism) for another (the Catholic faith and its understanding of the sacramentality of life).

If Dr. More is a lapsed Catholic at the beginning of the novel, at its end he has come to fully embrace the Catholic

---

[8] For more on Percy's understanding of the ideology of "scientism," see John F. Desmond, *Walker Percy's Search for Community* (Athens, GA: The University of Georgia Press, 2004), 7.

[9] Percy, *Love in the Ruins*, 3.

faith in both mind and heart. At the outset of the novel, he says he believes in the truths of the Catholic faith but has little remorse for his hedonistic lifestyle and the serious consequences it has for his inner life. By the novel's end, he has come to see that his Lapsometer cannot heal humanity's spiritual wounds and that the remedy for humanity's spiritual ills lies in the Church and the sacraments, especially the Eucharist.

The stark contrast between his life before and after his conversion can best be seen in two scenes from the novel: one before, the other after his conversion. A lapsed Catholic before his conversion, More led a hedonistic lifestyle dedicated to women, music, science, whiskey, and God in that order. One day, when stepping into the Little Napoleon Bar for a drink, he describes his surroundings using religious imagery: "I look at the mirror. Behind the bar towers a mahogany piece, a miniature cathedral, an altarpiece, an intricate business of shelves for bottles, cupboards, stained-glass windows, and a huge mirror whose silvering is blighted with an advancing pox, clusters of vacuoles, expanding naughts."[10] Not long afterwards, he sees his image reflected in the mirror behind the bar: "In the dark mirror there is a dim hollow-eyed Spanish Christ. The pox is spreading on his face. Vacuoles are opening in his chest. It is the new Christ, the spotted Christ, the maculate Christ, the sinful Christ. The old Christ

---

[10] Ibid., 151.

died for our sins and it didn't work, we were not reconciled. The new Christ shall reconcile man with his sins. The new Christ lies drunk in a ditch."[11] Before his conversion More pictures himself as a savior figure. The Lapsometer, he believes, will heal the world's wounds of the world by bridging the dualism of mind and body, what he refers to as the gap between angelism and bestiality. Early on in the novel, he claims: "I can save you America! I know something! I know what's wrong! I hit on something, made a breakthrough, came on a discovery! I can save the terrible God-blessed Americans from themselves! With my invention! Listen to me."[12] Such words indicate that More has moved from being a nominal Christian to a self-proclaimed prophet of scientism. He fails to recognize, however, that he has fallen victim to a messianic complex that rather than healing the mind-body divide actually makes it worse.

More's journey back to the Church and the sacramental life is long and circuitous. Throughout much of the novel, he experiences a tension between cynicism and hope, spiritualism and sensuality, Gnosticism and hedonism, scientism and his heady, abstract, and half-hearted affirmation of the Catholic faith. The death of his daughter, Samantha, the loss of his wife Doris, and his general disgust with his own hedonistic lifestyle (which served in isolating him from God,

---

[11] Ibid., 153.
[12] Ibid., 58.

others, and himself) bring him to a deeper understanding of his faith and helps him to see that it offers a solution to the mind-body dualism that has haunted the Western soul ever since the time of Descartes. For him, the Incarnation with its sacramental outlook on life holds the key to healing the rift in man's soul. Since the Eucharist flows from the mystery of Christ's Incarnation and bridges the gap between mind and body, it initiates a process of healing of More's inner life that eventually brings him to an authentic penitent remorse for his sins. That is not to say that More has resolved all of his problems; he is still very much a work in progress; he still very much wants his Lapsometer to heal the world. But his attitude has changed. He has been humbled. At the end of the novel he goes to confession to Fr. Renaldo Smith, the lackluster priest who heads the local Catholic community:

> "You're sorry for your sins?"
> "Yes. Ashamed rather."
> "That will do. Now say the act of contrition and for your penance I'm going to give you this."
> Through the little window he hands me two articles, an envelope containing ashes and a sackcloth, which is a kind of sleeveless sweater made of black burlap. John XXIV recently revived public penance, a practice of the early Church.
> While he absolves me, I say an act of contrition and pull the sackcloth over my sports coat.

"Go in peace. I'll offer my mass. For you tonight."[13]

More embraces the Catholic faith with renewed vigor and in a very public way: "Father Smith says mass. I eat Christ, drink his blood."[14] He has regained what he had lost. Sinner though he may be, he is reunited with that feeble community of believers who continue to live in faith, hope, and love in the midst of the ruins around them. The novel ends with More barbequing in his sackcloth, downing six drinks of Early Times in six minutes, and taking his wife, Ellen, to bed "for a long winter's nap," where they make love "not under a bush or in a car or on the floor or any such humbug as marked the past peculiar years of Christendom, but at home in bed where all good folk belong."[15]

Some Further Insights

Although much more can be said about Walker's views on the Eucharist, his presentation of Dr. Tom More's conversion represents some of his deepest beliefs and intuitions about the sacrament. The following remarks seek to probe his presentation of Catholicism and the Eucharist in articular in more detail.

---

[13] Ibid., 399.
[14] Ibid., 400.
[15] Ibid., 403.

To begin with, More's development during the course of the novel represents a clear movement from what Kierkegaard would call the "aesthetic man" to the "religious man." This movement entails a fundamental change in attitude in the way the person perceives himself and the world in which he lives. After his conversion, he is no longer the savior, no longer the center of his universe, no longer someone who dreams of winning the Nobel Prize. He still has his scientific interests (the Lapsometer), but they are clearly bowed to a deeper, and much wider, understanding of the meaning of life.

By having More get drunk after his conversion as he is barbecuing while wearing his sackcloth before taking his wife to bed, Walker highlights the sacramentality of life and the reality of God's mediating grace in the midst of human weakness and sinfulness. More's conversion does not necessarily mean an immediate change in his behavior, he escapes the tendency of presenting his hero in an "edifying" manner that would ultimately deflate the message he is trying to convey. Walker's hero deepens his faith, yet remains a sinner, someone in constant need of forgiveness and reconciliation with God, himself, and others.

More's conversion represents a clear movement from scientism to faith. At the end of the novel, what becomes clear is not More's loss of faith in science but his recognition of its limitations. By coming home to his Catholic roots, he is able to see his obsession with diagnosing the world's ills through his Lapsometer in a different light. Rather than being the instrument that would save the world, he sees that as a single diagnostic tool that might further the ultimate healing of the human soul that comes from God alone. More, in other words, sees things in their proper perspective. He is still a sinner (as we all are), but he recognizes his place in God's providential design.

If More is a lapsed Catholic at the beginning of the novel, at its end he anything but edifying. Percy takes care not to portray him in a way that covers over his deep human flaws, which remain after his conversion and will take time to heal and ultimately be transformed. The Church is a community of saints and sinners (mostly sinners), and More clearly numbers himself among the latter. Although his cynicism remains, there is now a light, humorous air about it that enables him (and the reader) to sense the deeper issues at play in life. No human invention can heal humanity of its wounds. More is no longer the self-proclaimed savior of the world but finds love in the ruins of a world that has lost its way and gone sadly awry.

More's return to the faith also means his return to community. The world of Paradise Estates where he lives has lost its center. Its members have all the trappings of prosperity but feel shallow and empty inside. The only ones who have not lost their bearings are the few remaining parishioners of the local Catholic parish led by Fr. Renaldo Smith. They are so few in number that they are hardly even noticed by the larger society. What is more, they are marginalized, even scorned, for holding on to beliefs that the sophisticated citizens of Paradise Estates have long since discarded. More's return to the Church begins a process of healing within his soul. His return to community enables him to find his center and go on with his life with a renewed sense of purpose.

The sacramentality of the Incarnation continues to manifest itself through the Church and her sacraments. The Eucharist, for More, bridges the mind-body divide and enables him to find his center. It accomplishes what his Lapsometer could not: it not only diagnoses but also heals; it connects the material world with the world of spirit; it unites body and soul and does so in a way that transcends science and reveals a world beyond the empirical. More's return to the faith does not deflate his scientific ambitions (he still has hope for his Lapsometer) but gives it new purpose and direction. The inverted values that he lists at the beginning of the novel are now reversed. His discovery of love among the ruins gives him hope for the future of the world and his place in it.

Finally, More finds happiness in the Church and the sacraments, something the decaying world around him so desperately desires. He goes to confession to Fr. Smith, does public penance, and once again is able to eat Jesus and drink his blood. His wife looks on approvingly, but with her Presbyterian mistrust of externals like sackcloth and ashes that Catholics have so often allowed to get in the way of things. At the end of Mass, people confess their sins and pray for the unity of Christians and of the United States. Love, More understands, seeks communion, not isolation. It wishes to bring people together, not separate them according to religion, race, or social status. Despite his faults and failings, at the end of the novel he has come back to his faith, back to his community, and back to himself— as a happy man.

Conclusion

Walker Percy was a devout Catholic whose novels dealt with some of the most basic questions of human existence. His love for science led him to appreciate its limitations, and he was deeply conscious of what it could and could not do. He converted to Catholicism because he found there an approach to human existence that addressed what it means to be fully human, thereby taking into account every aspect of our human makeup. At the same time, he was careful not to fall into the blunder of being "edifying." He would leave that to hagiography, the main purpose of which was to edify. The novel, by way of contrast, was meant to depict reality (and especially human reality) with all its faults and failings, as well as its deepest hopes and aspirations.

Deeply influenced by the thought of existentialist, Søren Kierkegaard, and especially his presentation of the aesthetic, ethical, and religious modes of existence, Walker was put off by the philosopher's suspicion of reason, mistrust of science, and heightened individualism. He borrowed from Kierkegaard what he found to be helpful and integrated it with his Catholic vision of humanity where reason and faith, nature and grace, science and religion, the individual and society complemented one another in a delicate balance that embraced life and death, order and disorder, time and eternity. He had a sacramental view of life that enabled him to embrace the present world and discern in a light and humorous way the divine presence in the midst of life's absurdities.

The character of Dr. Thomas More was not anything like his sixteenth-century namesake, who was beheaded by Henry VIII for his refusal to renounce his Catholic faith. He was much more akin to Percy Walker himself, who came to Catholicism after a struggle with his own human frailty, recognized his own flaws, saw the limitations of science, yet still had a lifelong fascination with the positive role it could play in building up human society. The Eucharist, for More (and for Percy) did for humanity what science could not. It united the material with the spiritual, healed body and soul, brought together the human and the divine—and made humanity whole. It filled the empty void within the human heart with the peace and quiet assurance that it was not alone in the universe and that the looming darkness within the soul and in the world would dissipate and ultimately disappear.

Voice Fourteen: Walker Percy—*Love in the Ruins*

Reflection Questions

- What kind of person do you consider yourself to be? Are you an "aesthetic man?" An "ethical man?" A "religious man?" What kind of person would you like to be? Where are you on that journey? What further steps do you need to take to get there? Have you found any companions on your journey?

- What role does the community of believers play in your life? Do you consider yourself a member of it? Estranged from it? A vital part of it? What lies at the center of this community? What holds it together? What makes it worthwhile continuing to belong to it? Why is it important to celebrate love in the ruins?

- To what extent does the Eucharist hold the community of believers together? How does the sacrament keep the community from falling apart? What does it give the community? How does it sustain it? Do you feel nourished by the sacrament? How does it sustain you? What does it ask of you?

Voice Fifteen

J. F. Powers
Morte D'Urban

James Farl Powers (1917-99), an American novelist and short story writer, was born in Jacksonville, Illinois and studied English and philosophy first at Wright Junior College and later at Northwestern University in Chicago. He was a conscientious objector during World War II and spent thirteen months in jail for his convictions. Powers taught creative writing at several colleges and universities and from 1975-93 was Regents Professor of English and writer-in-residence at St. John's University and the College of St. Benedict in Collegeville, Minnesota. His published works include: *Prince of Darkness* (1947), *Cross Country. St. Paul, Home of the Saints* (1949), *The Presence of Grace* (1956), *Morte D'Urban* (1962), *Lions, Harts, Leaping Does, and Other Stories* (1963), *Look How the Fish Live* (1975), *Wheat that Springeth Green* (1988), *The Old Bird, A Love Story* (1991), *The Stories of J. F. Powers* (1999), the posthumous, *Suitable Accommodations: An Autobiographical Story of Family Life: The Letters of J. F. Powers (1942-1963)*. He was awarded the O. Henry Prize in 1944 for his short story, *Lions, Harts, Leaping Does* and the National Book Award in 1963 for his novel, *Morte D'Urban*. His second novel, *Wheat that Springeth*

Green, was nominated for the National Book Award for fiction in 1988. In 1989, he received an honorary doctorate from St. John's University and the Wethersfield Institute Award for outstanding literary achievement. His humorous, light satirical style focuses on the endearing qualities and foibles of Catholic priests in the period between the end of World War II and the Second Vatican Council. The way he depicts the Eucharist contributes in a particular way to the atmosphere and ambience he seeks to create in this period of post-War American Catholicism.[1]

Powers's Spiritual Outlook

Born into a devout Catholic family, Powers was a regular church goer and practicing Catholic throughout his life. In 1946, he married Betty Wahl and raised with her a family of five children, although he later rather dryly (and quite humorously) ruminated that he and his wife were not really equipped to raise such a large family. A traditional Catholic by his own reckoning, he held to the teachings of the Church yet was deeply dissatisfied with the liturgical changes that entered into the liturgy about by the Second Vatican

---

[1] For more on Powers's life and work, see "J. F. Powers," *Minnesota Historical Society, Minnesota Authors*, https://collections.mnhs.org/mnauthors/10001413 ; John Rosengren, "The Gospel according to J. F. Powers," https://www.johnrosengren.net/powers .

Council. When sometime after the Council someone asked why he sat in the same pew week after week, he quipped that it was the only place in the church where he couldn't hear anything![2]

Powers wrote during what many consider a high point in twentieth-century Catholic literature. His close friend, Jeffrey Meyers says this about him: "In the 1940s, when he [Powers] began to publish, Catholic literature flourished in America. Thomas Merton's mystical *The Seven Storey Mountain* was a bestseller; Jacques Maritain and Etienne Gilson brought out works on Thomist Scholasticism; the poets Allen Tate and Robert Lowell, who expressed his Baroque intensity in *Lord Weary's Castle*, were prominent converts; Flannery O'Connor produced Gothic tales of sin and redemption. Bishop Fulton J. Sheen, a popular promoter of the faith, lectured the nation on television. Powers was not mystical, scholarly, poetical, redemptive, or popular. He lived in Minnesota and Ireland, far from the centers of cultural power, remained aloof from literary politics, and refused to promote himself through readings and interviews."[3] An introvert and recluse who steered clear of the literary limelight

---

[2] See Jon Hassler, "J. F. Powers: R. I. P." *America* (July 17, 1999), https://www.americamagazine.org/issue/100/j-f-powers-rip .

[3] Jeffrey Meyers, "His Bleak Materials: J. F. Powers at One Hundred," *Commonweal* (July 18, 2017), https://www.commonwealmagazine.org/his-bleak-materials .

and was more comfortable living his life on the periphery, Powers unleashed his skill as a novelist and short story writer on a subject that humored him, fascinated him, and at times even troubled him: the Catholic priesthood. No other writer in American literature has captured what it was like to be a Catholic priest in the years after the end of the Second World War and leading up to the Second Vatican Council.

If Bing Crosby depicts the quintessential American Catholic priest at or near the end of World War II in films like *Going My Way* (1944*)* and *The Bells of St. Mary's* (1945), then Father Urban Roche of *Morte D'Urban* represents the same kind of shrewd, committed, charismatic, worldly, and fun-loving priest in the years just prior to the Council. During the twenty-year period of post-war America (1945-65), Catholic priests were helping their flocks find their balance between loyalty to their country and to their Church, to having one foot in the City of God and the other in the City of Man. The election of John F. Kennedy in 1960 as the first Catholic President of the United States pointed to the faithful's coming of age, even while most Catholics knew that many of their fellow countrymen continued to view them with suspicion for the strange kind of hocus-pocus worship they gathered for at each Sunday Mass. Powers lived during this changing period for American Catholicism and had a spiritual outlook that was, at one and the same time, both intensely loyal to the faith yet also willing to engage the wider American public on its own terms.

Powers on the Eucharist

In the prefatory remarks to his novel, *Morte D'Urban*, Powers states, "… all the characters in the book are fictitious, the views expressed by some of them are not necessarily those of the Catholic Church or the author, and any resemblance to actual living persons, living or dead, is coincidental."[4] In this way, he distances both himself and the Catholic Church from the way he presents the faith in the novel. His need for such a disclaimer, however, indicates that some of his characters (and the views they express) likely depict the views and attitudes of real-life individuals and institutions. This holds true for the way he presents the Eucharist in the novel. While it rarely (if ever) takes center stage in the plot's unfolding, it lies in the background and in many ways represents the underlying reason for Father Urban's priestly life and ministry.

Harvey Roche (Father Urban) was born in a heavily Protestant area of Illinois and was very conscious, even as a young boy, that Catholics were looked upon with suspicion by their non-Catholic counterparts. He seemed to understand where they (the Protestants) were coming from and didn't blame them for it: "What troubled them was the hocus-pocus that went on in Catholic churches.… Wasn't it all

---

[4] J. F. Powers, *Morte D'Urban* (New York: New York Review of Books, 1962), viii.

very strange there, in that place, at that time, the fancy vestments, the Latin, the wine? What if Catholics were Protestants, and Protestants were Catholics, and they worshiped in such a manner? What would Catholics think?"[5] Since "hocus-pocus" is a derogatory form of the Latin, *Hoc est corpus meus* ("This is my body"), the young Harvey likely understood that the Protestant suspicion of Catholics had something to do with their understanding of Mass and Holy Communion. This accommodating perspective led Urban to embrace his Catholic identity deeply, yet also instilled in him a desire to be able to reach out to a wider public. He identifies very much with his Catholic priesthood yet does his best to sculpt his remarks to fit his audience, be it Catholic, non-Catholic, or mixed. The same holds true for the way he deals with varying perspectives within his Catholic audiences.

An accomplished public speaker and mission preacher and a member of a dedicated (if undistinguished) religious congregation called the Clementines, Father Urban has spent much of his priestly life on the road, moving from one speaking engagement to the next and raking in huge profits for his order. He views himself as one of the stars of his religious order (a would-be Provincial)—one of their very best. One day, much to his surprise, he finds himself transferred to an obscure, out of the way retreat house (St. Clement's on the Hill) in rural northern Minnesota, where he finds few

---

[5] Ibid., 75.

creaturely comforts and hardly any prospects for doing what he knows best. Out of the limelight, he feels like a fish out of water, while working with the other members this small four-man community to turn what was once a dilapidated poor house into a well-ordered, functioning retreat house. Although he does what is expected of him, he feels out of touch with the two priests and brother stationed with him and maneuvers things in such a way that he is allowed to fill-in for five weeks for the vacationing pastor, Father Phil Smith, of St. Monica's parish in a nearby town where he often helps out on weekends.

At St. Monica's parish, Father Urban energizes the parish, which the pastor had neglected for some time but had recently indicated (possibly under some pressure from the chancery) that he was going to build a new church for the parish. During the pastor's absence, Father Urban begins to turn the parish around. He wins over the housekeeper, Mrs. Burns, by relieving her of her responsibility of answering the phone. He takes the curate, Father Johnny Chumley, under his wing, eases him out of church (and his latent Manicheism), and engages his help in having a parish census, taking an opinion survey of the feasibility of building a new Church, and creating new opportunities for every group in the parish to gather in groups as members of the parish community. In all of this, he is careful not to make participation in these events contingent on their coming back to Mass or an increased participation in the sacramental life of the parish.

Still, the results of his efforts are astounding. Near the end of his time at St. Monica's, he gives a week-long mission which, by all counts, was the most successful one ever held at the parish. As he looks back on his accomplishments in such a short time, he looks back on his record:

- Mrs. Burns, freed from the telephone, given a new lease on life.
- Johnny Chumley rehabilitated.
- People polled on a new church—and pollinated.
- Parish life now a reality.
- Attendance at daily mass up 150 percent (eight-ten people now make it).
- Mission—most successful in history of parish.
- All-around good work for the Order.
- Mrs. Thwaites.[6]

Mrs. Thwaites, a wealthy shut-in to whom he brought daily Communion, seems to take him into her confidence and is a possible donor for his order. As the plot unfolds, he soon discovers that this was not to be the case.

In all of this, the Eucharist is what distinguishes the Catholic community from the larger society and ties them together. As he is about to leave the parish, Father Urban looks back with gratitude at his time at St. Monica's: "…he

---

[6] Ibid., 176-77.

was going to miss the deep satisfaction there was in doing the work of a parish priest—his daily Mass meant even more to him at St. Monica's. He had done well there in the last five weeks. Could he have done better? He did not think so. His record would speak for itself."[7] At his sermon during his closing mission, he has this to say to the parishioners in attendance: "Plant your gardens and orchards with the good seed and the green saplings of pious works, attendance at Holy Mass, regular confession, frequent reception of the Sacrament of Sacraments! Do these things, and leave the rest to God! Do these things, and the warm sun of God's merciful love will shine upon you and yours! Do these things, and the gentle rain of God's mercy will fall upon you and yours! Now and for all time! *Now! Forever! If!*"[8]

Father Urban does not hold a limited view of the priesthood that confined itself to the Church and the sacraments. Rather, he believes that a priest should engage his parishioners and the larger society in which they find themselves. He believes a priest could be both a "priest-priest" and a "priest promoter," someone who is faithful to the Church's sacramental ministry yet also enters the lives of the people he serves.[9] A good pastor, he believes, is able strike a fine balance between active lay participation and strong priestly

---

[7] Ibid., 176.
[8] Ibid., 171.
[9] Ibid., 154-55.

leadership: "The most successful parishes," according to Father Urban," "were those where more was going on that met the eye, where, behind the scenes, a gifted pastor or assistant pulled the strings. God, it seemed, ran those parishes, which was as it should be."[10] Although his main work as a priest has been that of a parish mission preacher, Father Urban's time at St. Monica's deepens his respect for the life of the parish priest, who lives behind the scenes (like the Blessed Sacrament itself) and feeds his flock daily with the Sacrament of Sacraments.

Some Further Insights

Although the above brief summary of Powers's presentation of the Eucharist in *Morte D'Urban* is by no means exhaustive, it offers an opportunity to delve a bit further into the novel's underlying religious outlook and stance toward the sacrament. What follows are some observations aimed at probing this presentation of the Eucharist in a little more depth.

To begin with, although Powers makes it clear that the views expressed by some of the characters in the novel are not necessarily those of the Catholic Church or even his own, he has a keen awareness of what American Catholic culture was like in the interim period between the end of the Second World

---

[10] Ibid., 165.

War and the opening of the Second Vatican Council. During this time, the Church was in its ascendancy but still looked upon with suspicion by the wider society. For this reason, it maintained, at one and the same time, a desire to set itself apart from yet also to be accepted by American culture as a whole. In *Morte D'Urban*, Powers embodies in himself that unique blend of the parochial and patriotic that characterized American Catholicism of the period. It is clear throughout the novel that, while the Eucharist is rarely mentioned, it forms the backdrop against which Catholic life unfolds and, as the Sacrament of Sacraments (as Father Urban aptly calls it) is the glue that holds the community together.

Powers's knowledge of Catholic culture extends to the relationship between the diocesan and religious priesthood. A member of the Clementines, a religious order dedicated to mission preaching, retreat work, and education, Father Urban has for most of his priesthood been involved in what the Church typically refers to as the *extraordinary care* of the faithful, as opposed to the *ordinary care* provided by the diocesan priesthood on a daily basis in the parishes. His time at St. Monica's parish, however, gives him a hefty taste of what ordinary parish life is like—and he thoroughly enjoys it! He realizes that specialized ministries can cause a priest to fall out of touch with what the priesthood is all about. He tells the story "about the old Clementine priest, too long a seminary professor, who had witnessed a street accident and cried out, "For God's sake—call a priest!"¹¹ Urban takes very well to the ordinary care of souls which focuses on entering people's lives, meeting them where they are, engaging them on their own ground and, of course, celebrating the sacraments.

For all the activities he organizes for the parishioners of St. Monica's— card parties for the seniors, square dancing for the young married, to rock-and-roll dances for the teens, sports films for the Men's Club, theater parties for the children (to name but a few) —Father Urban is careful not to use these activities as bait to lure his parishioners to the communion rail. He is dead set against the practice of Frs. Cox and Box at the cathedral parish, who were known to insert short films of a religious nature between at the all-cartoon parties they hosted for children at the local theater. In Urban's mind, "…it wouldn't be fair to the kids or to the exhibitor, a Jew, who was already taking a loss on the deal."¹² The Eucharist, for Urban, stands on its own and has no need of perks or incentives to establish its importance or support its legitimacy. There is no need to lure parishioners with a carrot on a stick in order to get them to confess their sins and receive Holy Communion. Simply entering into people's lives and living in communion with them will, in time, bring them

---

[11] Ibid., 158.
[12] Ibid., 166.

around and help them to understand precisely what it means to receive Holy Communion.

Powers has an uncanny ability of portraying in a light, humorous and even satirical way the many facets of what it meant to be a Catholic priest in the 50s and early 60s. Unlike his friend, Msgr. Renton, the pastor of the cathedral parish, who considers anything done outside administering the sacraments a waste of a priest's time, Urban has a hand in everything that goes on in his religious community, the parish he helps out at, and the larger community. He even "rehabilitates" Father Johnny Chumley, the young curate at St. Monica's who was spending nearly all of his time in church and gets him to take a more active role in reaching out to the parishioners of St. Monica's by working on the parish census and working with the young people of the parish. A priest's work, for Urban, includes not only the celebration of the sacraments (as important as that is), but also reaching out to the people and sharing in their lives. He is also very conscious of the politics that goes on behind the scenes on the parish, diocesan, and even within his own religious order. Rather than shying away from such entanglements, Urban tries to steer them to his own benefit and to the benefit of the Clementines.

Finally, if Powers uses Catholicism and the priesthood as the narrative backdrop against which the plot and character development of his novels and short stories unfold, then the Eucharist can be thought as the backdrop against the backdrop. Although the sacrament rarely takes center stage in any of the scenes of his stories, it is always there in the background in both thought and action. Celebrating Mass is what Catholic priests do. Going to Sunday (and sometimes even daily) Mass is what Catholics do, at least those who are practicing their faith. It is what sets them apart, what gives them their identity as Catholics. The sacrament even lurks in the back of the minds of those who have stopped practicing the faith (and even those who have rejected it) as a symbol of that they have left behind and have forever forsaken. The Eucharist lies at the heart of American Catholic culture and identity. Powers has no need to focus on it or emphasize its importance. In post-World War II Catholic America, it was simply taken for granted.

Conclusion

One of the preeminent American authors of the twentieth century, J. F. Powers did not seek the limelight, nor did he promote himself and his work as was typical of most other novelists of his day. Although the focus of his fiction, the Catholic priesthood, did not naturally draw the attention of the wider reading public, he was awarded national honors for his clarity of style, subtle humor, character development, and satirical wit. A lifelong Catholic, he gave his readers an insider's view of 1950s and early 1960s Catholicism, the period between the end of the Second World War and the start of the Second Vatican Council.

In his novel, *Morte D'Urban*, Powers describes an insular American Catholic culture that seeks acceptance of the wider American society and, as a result, finds itself in danger of losing its religious bearings. Father Urban Roche, the novel's main character, is eloquent, suave, calculating, personable, self-promoting, political, and staunchly Catholic individual—and a real operator! He considers himself a star of his religious order, the Clementines, and actively pursues its (and his own) well-being—or at least what he thinks it should be. Although Powers distances himself from the views of his characters, his knowledge of American Catholic culture in his day enables him to touch upon a number relevant themes of universal significance.

As the novel unfolds, Urban undergoes a deep spiritual struggle between the life he has chosen and the possibilities of what might have been. He recognizes that his way of life has left him with many acquaintances but no true friends. His relationships are mostly transactional and generally fall apart. When he offends his benefactors or refuses to buy into their warped sense of values, they leave him high and dry, and he has nowhere to turn but to God, his undistinguished religious family, the Clementines. In subtle reference to baptism and his vocation to the priesthood and religious life, he twice finds himself wading into a lake and swimming away from power, possessions and pleasure to the safety of his religious community. In a subtle reference to Christ's crowing with thorns, he twice finds himself crowned on the head: once with a golf ball driven by the local bishop and once by the high heel spike of a shoe thrown at him by Sally Hopwood, a woman who failed to seduce him. At one point, he even loses his shoes (while swimming too safety), a subtle reference to Jesus' exhortation to his disciples to take off their shoes and shake the dust of their feet before those who do not welcome them.

Knocked off his high horse and deeply humbled, Urban is a changed man. Although the members of his Province elect him as their Provincial (a kind of coronation, since it was what he had aspired to for most of his religious life), he proves largely ineffective at the helm and winds up leading sheepishly from behind rather than boldly from the front. He now feels much more at home at St. Clement's Hill in rural north Minnesota (an assignment on the periphery of the Province that he dreaded when he first received it), than at the Provincial headquarters in Chicago. He now sees that he has been living a lie and that he must now face the truth about himself. As the novel's title suggests, Father Urban Roche does indeed die, but it is the false, sophisticated, overly confident and self-absorbed Urban who passes away. The mask he wore, the false "persona" through which he lived most of his life as a priest and religious, has fractured, split apart, fragmented, and simply faded away. Like the bread that is broken and shared at Eucharist, Urban himself has become a broken yet much humbler, more authentic, and blessed human being. Being hit on the head (not once but twice!) has finally knocked some sense into him.

Reflection Questions

- Why does Powers call his novel, *Morte D'Urban*? What kind of death does Urban experience? How would you describe it? A conversion? A type of baptism? What changes occur in his life? What caused these changes? Have you ever experienced something similar?

- How would you describe Urban's understanding of the priesthood? Does it change in any way during the course of the novel? If so, what caused his change in outlook? Is Urban happy with this change in himself? To what extent has he become a humbler, more modest priest?

- How would you describe the role the Eucharist plays in American Catholic culture? Is it negligible? On the periphery? In its very heart and center? A quiet backdrop? What role does the Eucharist play in your own life? How would you describe it? Where should it be? Where would you like it to be?

Voice Sixteen

Flannery O'Connor
A Temple of the Holy Ghost

Flannery O'Connor (1925-1964), one of the prominent American fiction writers of the twentieth century, was born in Savannah, Georgia to devout Catholic parents. In 1938, her family moved to Milledgeville in central Georgia. She attended Georgia State College for Women, where she majored in social science and was the editor of and contributing author to the *Corinthian*, the college's literary magazine. In 1945, she received a scholarship to study journalism at the State University of Iowa and, after a semester in that discipline, decided to switch to creative writing under Paul Engle, head of the Iowa Writers' Workshop. She completed her M.F.A degree in 1947, won the Rinehart-Iowa Fiction Award and for spent several months at Yaddo, an artists' retreat in Saratoga Springs, New York, and some time in Manhattan and Milledgeville. In 1949, she moved to Ridgefield, Connecticut and lived nearly two years in the garage apartment of her good friends Sally and Robert Fitzgerald. In 1950, she came down with lupus, a deadly disease that eventually took her life. This diagnosis prompted a move in 1951 back to the family farm, Andalusia, just outside Milledgeville, where she would spend the rest of her life writing fiction, answering letters, raising peacocks, and practicing her Catholic faith. She published her first novel, *Wise Blood*, in 1952 and won a number of literary awards for her fiction in her remaining years. She succumbed to the disease on August 3, 1964. In 1972, her posthumous collection, *The Complete Stories*, received the National Book Award. In 1979, *The Habit of Being: Letters of Flannery O'Connor*, edited by her longtime friend, Sally Fitzgerald, hit the literary world and received excellent reviews.[1]

O'Connor's Spiritual Outlook

O'Connor's spiritual outlook stems from her devout Catholic upbringing. Her parents came from two of Georgia's oldest Catholic families and taught her to practice the faith and to love it, despite the flaws exhibited by many of its members. During her early childhood in Savannah, she was educated by nuns in the local parochial school. When she moved to Milledgeville at the age of thirteen, she attended the local public high school, for lack of a Catholic alternative. Because the atmosphere in the Deep South at the time was prone to bigotry and hostile to the Catholic minority, she learned the necessity of delving beneath the externals of her

---

[1] All biographical references in this section and the following one come from "Flannery O'Connor (1925-1964)" in *New Georgia Encyclopedia*, https://www.georgiaencyclopedia.org/ articles/arts-culture/flannery-oconnor-1925-1964.

faith, identifying its essentials, and embracing it with both mind and heart.

O'Connor's father died of lupus when she was just fifteen, the same disease that would eventually take her own life. This tragic loss at such an early age made a deep impression on her and caused her to probe the meaning of life, appreciate its preciousness, and mourn its eventual demise. Beneath the appearances of things, she could sense the ongoing struggle between life and death, and looked to Christ and his Church for the remedy. She was saddened by and impatient with those self-righteous Catholics who practiced a shallow, surface version of their faith and who criticized the Church because of the flaws of its members without taking into account the internal movement of the Spirit. She took Jesus' words in Luke's gospel to heart, "I have come to call not the righteous but sinners to repentance" (Lk 5:32).

O'Connor believed that the Church, with all its flaws and imperfections, was the body of Christ and that Christ loved it as he loved his own self. Whether good or bad, those who accepted the Church's teachings were members of Christ's body and had recourse to the sacraments in their struggle to break evil's hold on them and walk the way of holiness. Rather than judging others, the Catholic faithful should put aside any tendencies they might have toward self-righteousness and become more conscious of their own sinful tendencies. In the words of Christ, "You hypocrite, first take the log out of your own eye, and then you will see clearly to take the speck out of your neighbor's eye" (Mt 7:5). Rather than being smug and self-satisfied, she believed all Catholics should come out of their stupor of complacency and strive to lead holy lives and walk the way of virtue.

Much of O'Connor's fiction has to do with those who give lip service to faith, but do not believe it deep down inside. The character of Mrs. May in the short story, *Greenleaf*, fits this description: "She was a good Christian woman with a large respect for religion," O'Connor writes, "though she did not, of course, believe any of it was true."[2] Such people attach themselves to the externals of the faith, but have failed to penetrate its deep inner meaning. Much of her fiction also focuses on those who have turned the practice of religion to an empty, yet lucrative, cultural artifact. The character of Hoover Shoats, who in her novel, *Wise Blood*, changes his name to Onnie Jay Holy and grows rich in his ministry at the "Holy Church of Christ Without Christ," is one such example.[3] These are just two examples in O'Connor's fiction of how she presents Christianity as having been compromised by the secular outlook of the modern world.

The spiritual poverty of the characters in O'Connor's fiction is a symptom of a world that has abandoned Christ and,

---

[2] Flannery O'Connor, "Greenleaf," in *Flannery O'Connor: The Complete Stories* (New York: Farrar, Straus and Giroux, 1979), 316.

[3] Flannery O'Connor, *Wise Blood* in *3 by Flannery O'Connor* (New York: Signet, 1962), 82-89.

as a result, become ugly, even grotesque. Writing in her southern gothic style, O'Connor depicts a world that has rejected the redemption offered it by Christ. In her writing, she seeks to heighten the reader's sensitivity to the need for redemption. Evil flourishes in a world without Christ. Catholicism, she believed, was the only remedy to the world's descent into evil. The Eucharist, for her, was central to the world's redemption.[4]

O'Connor's Teaching on the Eucharist

O'Connor's deep love for the Eucharist comes through in her fiction and especially in her letters. In one letter, she recounts an incident at a party hosted by the novelist Mary McCarthy, an ex-Catholic and now a nonbeliever, who said that she said that she had once thought of the Eucharist as the Holy Ghost, but now thinks of it as merely a very good symbol. To which O'Connor replied: "'Well, if it's a symbol, to hell with it.' That was all the defense I was capable of but I realize now that this is all I will ever be able to say about it, outside of a story, except that it is the center of existence for

---

[4] For more on O'Connor's spiritual outlook, see George N. Niederauer, "Flannery O'Connor's Religious Vision," *America* (December 24, 2007), https://www.americamagazine.org/issue/639/article/flannery-oconnors-religious-vision.

me; all the rest of life is expendable."⁵

For O'Connor, the Eucharist was more than a mere symbol. She was a sacramental realist, who believed that the sacrifice of the Mass made the bloody event of Calvary present in an unbloody way, that the consecrated bread and wine contained the Real Presence of Jesus' resurrected body and blood, and that the entire celebration was a foretaste of the heavenly banquet. The Eucharist was the center of existence, because it brought the sacrificial offering and love Jesus, the Redeemer, into our midst. All else was insignificant and paled in comparison. If it was only a symbol, then it had no meaning for her. She was wary of those who sought to rationalize this great mystery of the Catholic faith by reducing it to facile ideas and neat human concepts. Her heart would resonate with the Second Vatican Councils depiction of the Eucharist as "the source and summit o the Christian life."⁶

Of all her short stories, O'Connor's "A Temple of the Holy of the Holy Ghost" contains the most clearly evident Catholic themes and has much to say about the Eucharist. Told through the eyes of a twelve year old girl from a devout Catholic family, the story relates the child's time with two

---

⁵ Sally Fitzgerald, ed., *The Habit of Being: Letters of Flannery O'Connor* (New York: Vintage Books, 1979), 124-25.

⁶ Second Vatican Council, *Lumen gentian* ("The Dogmatic Constitution on the Church"), no. 11 in Austin Flannery, gen. ed *Vatican Council II: The Conciliar and Post Conciliar Documents* (Northport, NY: Costello, 1981), 362.

fourteen year old cousins, Susan and Joanne, who ridicule the advice given them by a nun at their convent school, Mount St. Scholastica, that the best way to handle boys who wish to have their way with them is simply to shout out, "Stop sir! I am a temple of the Holy Ghost!"[7]

During their visit, it is arranged that Wendell and Cory Wilkens, two sixteen-year-old farm boys from the Church of God, will take the two girls to the local fair. When they first meet, the boys and girls look each other over from a distance and start singing of religious songs back and forth. The boys, who according to the twelve year old, "were both going to be Church of God preachers because you don't have to know nothing to be one," start out with "I've Found a Friend in Jesus" and then "The Old Rugged Cross." The girls giggle and respond by singing the Latin "Tantum Ergo."[8] Not understanding what the girls were singing, Wendell responds, "That must be Jew singing."[9] The girls giggle at him, but twelve year old, who was eavesdropping, standing on a barrel hidden in some bushes on the side of the house, stamps her foot on the barrel and says, "You big dumb ox! . . . You big dumb Church of God ox!"[10] The scene depicts the prejudices on both sides of the religious Catholic/Protestant divide. The

---

[7] Flannery O'Connor, "A Temple of the Holy Ghost," in *Flannery O'Connor: The Complete Stories*, 238.

[8] Ibid., 240-41.

[9] Ibid., 241

[10] Ibid.

"Tantum Ego," written by Thomas Aquinas who in his youth was sometimes likened to a dumb ox, is one of the hymns used during Benediction and Exposition of the Blessed Sacrament and underscores the Catholic belief in the Real Presence, one of the main differences between Protestant and Catholic teaching. The scene also depicts how some believers possess a very shallow understanding of the faith, while others a much more profound, childlike trust in God. The words of Jesus come to mind, "Amen, I say to you, whoever does not accept the kingdom of God like a child will not enter it" (Mk 10:15).

The older girls return at about a quarter to twelve. Their giggling wakes the twelve year old, who gets them to tell her about the hermaphrodite freak they had encountered at the fair that night and how this half man/half woman and kept telling the audience, "This is the way He wanted me to be and I ain't disputing His way," and later, "I am a temple of the Holy Ghost."[11] As it turns out, the police at the instigation of some local Protestant preachers shut down the fair. That night, while lying in bed, the child thanks God that she does not belong a church of the self-righteous, but of sinners. She knows she is a sinner, a freak, and that she will never be a saint (although maybe a martyr if they killed her quickly).[12]

The next day, the girls are brought back to Mount Saint

---

[11] Ibid., 245-46.
[12] Ibid., 243.

Scholastica in their brown uniforms. The child and her mother come with them and are asked to stay for Benediction by one of the nuns. The child was not happy about this at first but realizing that she is in the presence of God, she begins prays: "Hep me not to be so mean, she began mechanically Hep me not to give her so much sass. Hep me not to talk like I do. Her mind began to get quiet and then empty but when the priest raised the monstrance with the Host shining ivory-colored in the center of it, she was thinking of the tent at the fair that had the freak in it. The freak was saying, "I don't dispute hit. This is the way He wanted me to be."[13] The story ends with some beautiful Eucharistic imagery: "Her mother let the conversation drop and the child's round face was lost in thought. She turned it toward the window and looked out over a stretch of pastureland that rose and fell with a gathering greenness until it touched the dark woods. The sun was a huge red ball like an elevated Host drenched in blood and when it sank out of sight, it left a line in the sky like a red clay road hanging over the trees."[14]

Some Further Insights

---

[13] Ibid., 248.

[14] Ibid. For more on O'Connor's understanding of the Eucharist, see Stephen Sparrow, "This is My Body: The Mystery of the Incarnate God in Flannery O'Connor's Short Story 'A Temple of The Holy Ghost,'"(February, 2006), http://www.flanneryoconnor.org/ssmybody.html.

Although the above summary of O'Connor's views on the Eucharist does not do justice to the richness of her appreciation of the sacrament, it provides a solid backdrop against which the following observations come to light.

To begin with, O'Connor was keenly aware that the Catholic faith in the Real Presence could be compromised by worldly attitudes influencing the Catholic faithful. The ridicule that Susan and Joanne have for the nun's advice to ward off the sexual advances of men by saying that they are temples of the Holy Spirit represents an adolescent scorn for the faith that could easily overflow into other areas. At the same time, she was also conscious of the impact devotional Catholic practices such as Benediction could have on young children. One wonders if the twelve year old will eventually become like Susan and Joanne, or if Susan and Joanne will eventually come to a deeper understanding of their faith.

For O'Connor, the Catholic Church was meant to be a home for sinners who looked to its sacraments as a source of healing. It was a home for the child and her mother, the nuns at Mount Saint Scholastica, and even students like Susan and Joanne. At the end of the story, the Eucharistic imagery present in the setting sun as it dips below the horizon brings a more universal dimension to the sacrament. The Eucharist can be viewed as the sacrament of the new creation. It is home not to the self-righteous, but to the broken people of the world, to the Freak in the circus tent and to the freak who lurks deep down inside each of us. One wonders if O'Connor viewed herself in this way with regard to her lupus: "This is the way He wanted me to be and I ain't disputing His way."[15]

O'Connor would be very much at home with Pope Francis's description of the Church as a field hospital.[16] It is a very big tent with all kinds of people in it, each of whom has sores to be cleansed and wounds in need of healing. The Eucharist, for her, is the center of existence and is the source of the Church's healing, transforming power. It is, we might say, the "medicine of immortality."[17] These words of Ignatius of Antioch would resonate deep within her soul. The Blessed Sacrament, she understands, is more than a mere symbol, since it brings the believer into the presence of God himself. By partaking of the Eucharist, the believers receive the Body and Blood of Jesus Christ, who suffered and died for the sins of humanity and who rose again on the third day. As a result, each person becomes a temple of the Holy Spirit. The ridicule of Susan and Joanne does not displace the affirmation of the Freak. By virtue of our sinfulness, we are all freaks in

---

[15] Ibid., 245.

[16] Antonio Spadaro, "A Big Heart Open to God: An Interview with Pope Francis, *America* (September 30, 2013), https://www.americamagazine.org/faith/2013/09/30/big-heart-open-god-interview-pope-francis.

[17] Ignatius of Antioch, "Letter to the Ephesians," 20.2 in *Early Christian Fathers*, Cyril C. Richardson, ed. (New York: Macmillan, 1970), 93.

the eyes of God in need of healing. God alone can heal us. In the Eucharist, he meets us where we are and slowly draws us to himself.

O'Connor understood the need for Catholics to push back against the world's secularizing tendencies and its negative impact on the Catholic faithful. Her terse response to Mary McCarthy ("Well, if it's a symbol, to hell with it.") demonstrates her willingness to voice her objections to the rationalizing tendencies that the modern world. Raised in an environment that was hostile to Catholicism, she recognized the importance of probing one's faith more deeply and defending it when it came under attack, was ridiculed, or simply discounted. She wanted to preserve the mystery of the faith and preserve it from those eternal, reductive, and rationalizing tendencies that have attacked it for centuries and continued to do so in her day. She knew that the meaning of the Church and its greatest treasure, the Eucharist, lies beyond the powers of human comprehension and could never be fully explained. The Eucharist, like the Church, is the body of Christ and will always remain a mystery.

Like the child in "A Temple of the Holy Ghost," O'Connor knew that belief in the Eucharist must be simple, devout, and childlike. It asks us to put aside all ridicule and skepticism and to rid ourselves of our tendencies toward self-righteousness that trap us in ourselves and prevent us from growing in our spiritual lives. As Catholics, we must recognize that the Eucharist, not the fallen and wounded self, lies at the center of the moral universe. The sacrament bids us to come out of themselves and place Christ at the center of our lives. To be a temple of the Holy Ghost means that a person is a child of God, someone who calls God, "*Abba*, Father!" (Rom 8:15), who accepts the mystery Eucharist with childlike faith, and who, despite ones flaws and weaknesses, understands that, in the end, faith, hope, and love are the only things of enduring value and that all else is secondary.

The Eucharist, for O'Connor, is also a sacrament of hope. In "A Temple of the Holy Ghost," the child prays from her heart, asking God to help her become a better person. She knows she is not a saint, turns to God for assistance, yet also recognizes that God loves her just as she is. The words of the Freak resonate inside her: "I don't dispute it. This is the way He wanted me to be."[18] The desire to be a better person, to become holy, is a mainstay of Catholic spirituality. This aspect of faith, however, does not discount the truth that God loves us just as we are. We seek to become holy, not because God will love us more, but because we wish to become more and more like him. This element of hope comes through in the story's ending with the sun, "a huge red ball like an elevated Host drenched in blood" sinks over the gathering greenness and the dark woods, leaving a red line in the sky hovering over the trees.[19] The Eucharist puts us in touch with

---

[18] Flannery O'Connor, "A Temple of the Holy Ghost," 248.
[19] Ibid.

the passion and death of Christ. The sun sinks over the western sky only to rise the next day to help us begin life anew.

Finally, much of O'Connor's fiction depicts a grotesque world that has rejected God's love and wallows in the aftermath of the evil that has been unleashed from the human heart. This unredeemed world, dark and dreary as it is, forces us to delve beneath the surface of life and to focus on things that really matter. In doing so, we become aware of our own hardness of heart and seek a remedy for the pain and suffering in which we are immersed. O'Connor's fiction shakes us to the core and prepares our hearts to hear the Gospel message as if for the first time. By immersing us in the world of the unredeemed, it kindles in us a hope for a better world, the one originally envisioned by Christ, not the one that has been distorted so often by his would-be followers. When seen in this light, the Eucharist is a concrete sign that God has not abandoned this world. Much more than a symbol, it is the center of existence and promises to transform even the grotesque world of O'Connor's fiction in God's own good time.

Conclusion

Flannery O'Connor was an eccentric woman from the Deep South and with an even deeper Southern drawl. She had a natural talent for the craft of writing and in her short life developed that talent into making her one of the most prominent literary American voices of her day. Among Catholics, she is revered as a standard bearer for the quality and depth that Catholic authors should aspire to. Her fiction and correspondence show her to be a woman of deep faith who firmly believed that what appeared to be irredeemable was not outside the reach of the purview of God's plan of redemption.

O'Connor's fiction is in the style of Southern gothic. She paints an irrational world peopled with grotesque characters, who act on impulse and are alienated from themselves, others, and the light of divine grace. In the midst of this darkness, there is little hope for those who hold merely to the external trappings of the Christian faith. In the face of such darkness, the evil forces that have been unleashed in the world by the unruly passions of the human heart easily swallow up such people. The dark humor of it all is that such people often come to their senses when it is too late, when the unfolding tragedy has already taken its toll.

O'Connor's writing bids her readers to delve beneath their half-hearted convictions and go to the heart of things, to the quiet beneath the chaos, to the gentle being beneath the growing turmoil. Her spiritual outlook was shaped by her devout Catholic upbringing and the awareness of the need to push back against the moral bankruptcy of her day and the secularizing tendencies of the modern word. She had little time for the subtle (and not so subtle) sarcasm that nonbelievers hurled against her faith and even less time for those self-righteous who judged others while being unaware of their vapid moral smugness. She believed that the Catholic Church was the body of Christ made up of a wide assortment of personalities, all of whom were spiritual pilgrims journeying through a fallen world with the Eucharist for their food and sustenance.

Reflection Questions

- Much of O'Connor's fiction depicts a grotesque world that has rejected God's love and wallows in the aftermath of the evil that has been unleashed from the human heart. Do you agree with her that Catholicism is the only remedy to the world's descent into evil and that the Eucharist is central to the world's redemption? Why is the Eucharist a sacrament of hope?

- Why did O'Connor choose to write so much about those who gave lip service to faith, but do not believe it deep down inside? Do you think the majority of believers fall under this category? Do you know anyone like this? Do find in any of this a reflection of your own self? How does grace get through to such people? How does grace get through to you? What role does the Eucharist play in all of this?

- O'Connor was a sacramental realist. For her the Eucharist was more than just a symbol, since it immersed us in Christ's paschal mystery. How do you view the Eucharist? Are you a sacramental realist? Do you believe the Eucharist is more than a mere symbol. Do you believe it manifests the Real Presence of Christ? Do you believe that the Mass immerses us in Christ's passion, death, and resurrection?

Voice Seventeen

Basil Pennington
Wine of Faith, Bread of Life

Dom M. Basil Pennington, O.C.S.O. (1931-2005) was a Trappist monk and one of the founders of the Centering Prayer Movement.[1] He entered St. Joseph's Abbey in Spencer Massachusetts in 1951, made his first profession in 1953, and was ordained a priest in 1957. In 1959, he received a licentiate degree in theology from The Pontifical University of St. Thomas (Angelicum) and in 1963 another in canon law from the Pontifical Gregorian University. In the late 1960s, he was instrumental in the establishment of Cistercian Publications and was one of the organizers of the First International Cistercian Studies Symposium. In the 1970s his interest in Eastern Orthodoxy led to an extended stay at Mount Athos in Greece. After holding various positions in formation at St. Joseph's Abbey, he was made superior of Assumption Abbey in Ava, Missouri in 2000 and later that same year was elected Abbot of the Monastery of the Holy Spirit in Conyers, Georgia. He retired to St. Joseph's Abbey in 2002 and remained there until his death in 2005. The author of more than sixty books, he was an internationally

---

[1] For more on the Centering Prayer Movement, see http://www.contemplativeoutreach.org.

known author, lecturer, retreat master, and spiritual director. His teaching on the Eucharist reflects his vast knowledge of the spiritual life and the life of contemplation.[2]

Pennington's Spiritual Outlook

As a Trappist monk, Pennington was shaped by the spirituality of St. Benedict of Nursia (c. 480-547), the founder of the Benedictine tradition and the father of Western monasticism. The *Rule of Benedict* moderated the rigorous asceticism of the desert fathers of the East and shifted the focus of monasticism from a solitary pursuit of God in the style of hermits and anchorites to the pursuit of holiness through a life in community dedicated to prayer, spiritual reading, and manual labor.[3] The goal of Benedictine monasticism was to sanctify the day through continual prayer (*laus perennis*). Chanting the Psalter, spiritual reading (*lectio divina*), and manual labor were viewed a way of sanctifying the day and giving and praise to God. The Eucharistic liturgy was an essential feature of Benedictine life.[4] The Trappists were a

---

[2] For more on Pennington's life, see https://www.findagrave.com/cgi-bin/fg.cgi?page=gr&GRid=27717764.

[3] See *The Rule of Benedict*, trans. Anthony C. Meisel and M. L. del Mastro (Garden City, NY: Image Books, 1975).

[4] Karl Bihlmeyer and Hermann Tüchle, *Church History*, trans. Victor E. Mills and Francis J. Muller, vols. 1-3 (Westminster: Newman Press, 1966-68), 1:367-71.

reform of the Cistercians, themselves a reform of Benedictine monasticism. They were, we might say, a reform of a reform. Officially known as Cistercians of the Strict Observance, they dedicated themselves to following the Rule to the letter.[5]

Pennington's spiritual outlook was also shaped by his studies at two of the great Pontifical universities in Rome, the Angelicum and Gregorian universities. At the former, the Dominicans gave him a foundation in the thought of Thomas Aquinas and scholastic theology: dogmatic, moral, ascetical, and mystical. At the latter, where he studied canon law, the Jesuits taught him to appreciate the role of law in the organization and life of the Church. This background served him well when he returned to St. Joseph's Abbey and took on various roles in the theological and spiritual formation of the younger monks. As a professor of both canon law and spirituality, he shaped the spiritual outlook of many young Trappists during the years of the Second Vatican Council and beyond.

Pennington's approach to the mysteries of the faith was blended. Catholic spirituality can be either kataphatic or apophatic: it can emphasize the capacity of language to convey positive truths about the mystery of God (the kataphatic); or it can see that language ultimately falls short of saying anything meaningful about the infinite and employ

---

[5] Ibid., 3:226.

instead the way of negation (the apophatic). If Pennington's spiritual outlook was shaped by the largely kataphatic tendencies of Benedictine monasticism, scholastic theology, and canon law, it was also greatly influenced by his involvement in the largely apophatic tendencies of the Centering Prayer Movement. As with fellow Trappists Thomas Keating and William Meninger, he authored a series of books in the 1970s and 80s that focused on casting out of one's mind all thoughts and images in order to rest in the gentle but all so elusive presence of God. This apophatic approach to prayer has its roots in the thought of an early sixth-century Syrian monk called the Pseudo-Dionysius, whose treatise, *Mystical Theology*, emphasized the approach to God by way of negation rather than affirmation.[6] Centuries later, the "way of negation" was promoted in the West by the anonymous author of the late-fourteenth-century Middle English treatise, *The Cloud of Unknowing*.[7] The Centering Prayer Movement presents the underlying themes of this treatise in a way that can be easily understood and practiced by today's spiritual seekers. The way to God, it states, lies not through the mind, but through the heart. One must throw into the "cloud of forgetting" all thoughts, ideas, and concepts, and, instead, knock on the "cloud of unknowing" with a fervent heart repeating

---

[6] See *Pseudo-Dionysius: The Complete Works*, trans. Colm Luibheid (New York/Mahwah, NJ: Paulist Press, 1987), 133-41.

[7] See Dennis J. Billy, *The Cloud of Unknowing: Spiritual Commentary* (Liguori, MO: Liguori Publications, 2014).

again and again a single word to channel one's deep fervor and desire to God.

Pennington's teaching on the Eucharist has aspects of both the kataphatic and apophatic approaches to God. The juxtaposition of the "way of affirmation" and the "way of negation" reveal a presence that goes beyond mere affirmation and mere negation to reveal the living God of Abraham, Isaac, and Jacob. In the Eucharist, God reveals his unconditional love for us and we, in turn, are overwhelmed and rendered speechless by the sheer gratuity of Christ's sacrificial presence and presence in our midst.

Pennington Teaching on the Eucharist

Pennington's book, *The Eucharist: Wine of Faith, Bread of Life* provides a vivid picture of his views toward the sacrament of the Last Supper.[8] He says in his Introduction that he wrote the book out of a need to do so some good motivational reading on the Mass and, not being able to find any that helped, decided to write one himself. By motivational reading he means a book that generally encourages us "to live according to the fullness of the reality of our Christed person."[9] More particularly, it can mean "responding to a

---

[8] M. Basil Pennington, *The Eucharist: Wine of Faith, Bread of Life* (Liguori, MO: Liguori Publications, 2000).
[9] Ibid., xiii.

need of the moment such as, for example, a struggle with prayer, a need for forgiveness, or the problem of the Mass losing its meaning."[10] By responding to his own personal need to probe the mystery of the Eucharist more deeply, he provides his readers with an invaluable tool for understanding the central it plays role in their own lives.

In the book, Pennington goes through the various parts of the Mass and discusses them in the light of the Church's rich liturgical tradition, relevant stories, and his own personal experience. When treating the Introductory Rites, he reminds us that the Eucharist is a time for coming together and normally begins with the ringing of a bell to summon those who can gather around the altar physically and invite those who cannot to send their hearts.[11] He also points out that the earliest Eucharistic celebrations took place in homes and that the Church should be looked upon as the place where a family gathers: "Here is where we come together to share our common story. Here is where we recall our common covenant. Here is where we drink and eat together. Here is where we come together as a family—the family of God—gathered in our family home in joy."[12] He writes of our need to humble and purify ourselves when we gather to celebrate the sacrament and says that the penitential rite

---

[10] Ibid., xiii.
[11] Ibid., 4.
[12] Ibid., 14.

should not be prayed in a perfunctory manner, but in a way that callus us to *metanoia* or a radical change of heart.[13] Only then can we give praise and glory to God, when we sing or recite the Gloria, and collect ourselves properly at the opening prayer.[14]

When treating the Liturgy of the Word, Pennington reminds us that "the liturgy is a school: it effectively teaches us and leads us into reality if we are attentive to what is happening, what is being said."[15] The readings, he maintains, involve both proclamation and response. The Bread of God's Word must be broken and shared, by means of bold proclamation, attentive listening, and solid reflection. The homilist plays an important role in translating the Gospel narrative: "We want to hear his lived experience of the story. We want to hear how he is experiencing the story lived out in us, all of us together in the community of the Christ-living-today. He helps us get in touch with the story as it is unfolding in our lives. He wipes some of the film from our eyes of faith so that we see something more of the enthralling wonder of salvation history coming to its consummation in us. The homilist is not exegeting a text, he is sharing an event in which we are all participating."[16]

---

[13] Ibid., 19-20.
[14] Ibid., 21-24.
[15] Ibid., 25.
[16] Ibid., 41.

Pennington spends most of the book on the Liturgy of the Eucharist. He says it is unfortunate that the Offertory Rite "can be a hurried thing, done with little time for reflection and virtually no community participation."[17] He refers to the Preface as that part of the Eucharistic Prayer that "invites us to transcend our particular gathering, or rather, bring our gathering into the great communion of all worshipers of all times, of all saints and angels."[18] The words of Institution, he says, make Christ's sacrificial death "ever present in God's eternal NOW, coming to be present in our historical now."[19] He then goes through each of the four Eucharistic Prayers and shows how the first preserves "a very stable tradition" of the Roman Canon,[20] the second recalls the Canon of Saint Hippolytus and emphasizes the role of Jesus as our mediator,[21] the third is a new prayer that brings to the fore "the role of the Holy Spirit, through creation and salvation history, in the gathering of a godly people *from east to west*,"[22] and the fourth is based on "the *Anaphora* attributed to St. Basil the Great."[23] He also spends considerable time

---

[17] Ibid., 51.
[18] Ibid., 57.
[19] Ibid., 62.
[20] Ibid., 71.
[21] Ibid., 77.
[22] Ibid., 89.
[23] Ibid., 100.

discussing the three Eucharistic Prayers for Children[24] and the two Eucharistic Prayers for Masses of Reconciliation,[25] reminding us that the Church provides us with many choices to adapt the Eucharist to a variety of circumstances. To the presiders at Eucharist, he emphasizes one very important point: "Our priesthood is a ministerial priesthood because it ministers to the priesthood of all the faithful."[26] What is more, he points out the importance of being centered as one presides over the Eucharist: "There is then a real interconnection between the time the priest spends in his room or in the cell of his heart in centering or contemplative prayer and his presiding successfully at the liturgical assembly."[27]

When treating the Communion Rite, Pennington sees the priest's role as mediator changing when he leads the congregation in the Lord's Prayer: "He had been with Christ, all to the Father. Now he turns to the other party of the mediation, to us, and invites us to give voice ourselves to this prayer to the Father, for we have truly been reconciled and made most dear children in Christ."[28] Although the reception of Holy Communion preserves two traditions—reception in the hand and reception on the tongue—,[29] he points

---

[24] Ibid., 107-23.
[25] Ibid., 124-38.
[26] Ibid., 139.
[27] Ibid., 148.
[28] Ibid., 152.
[29] Ibid., 162.

out that the recipient participates more actively when receiving it by hand and can thus become more deeply aware of his or her sharing in the priesthood of Christ.[30] The Concluding Rites, he says, remind us that we are called to carry the effects of the Eucharist into life: "We are sent, it is a mission, to make the passion of Christ healingly present in our world today."[31] The very name, "Mass," he says, comes from the final words of the Roman rite: "*Ite, missa est*" (Literally, "Go, it [the assembly] is dismissed.") and emphasizes one crucial point: "This moment of dismissal gave its name to the whole because of its prime importance. It does sum up the whole and charges each one to take it—the whole infinitely empowering experience of Calvary and Communion—out into the world."[32]

Some Further Insights

Many other things can be said of Pennington's approach to the Eucharist. The above description, while not comprehensive, underscores the central role it played in his life and points out some of the ways in which it influenced his thought. The follow remarks seek to probe a little more

---

[30] Ibid., 163.
[31] Ibid., 170.
[32] Ibid.

deeply into his understanding of this great sacrament and how it shaped his approach to life in general.

To begin with, Pennington was very much aware that the Church's sacramental system was an expression of the kataphatic (positive) approach to the mystery of the divine. He believed that God was capable of revealing himself to humanity and actually did so though the person of Jesus Christ. As the soteriological principle of St. Athanasius of Alexandria (c. 296-373) —"God became human so that humanity might become divine"—suggests, God's has the ability to enter the world he created in order to redeem and ultimately divinize it. For Pennington, God reveals himself through words of Scripture, through the person and flesh of Jesus Christ, and through the sacraments of the Church. The Eucharist, for him, was a continuation of the divinizing process begun in the mystery of the Incarnation and now extended to humanity and ultimately the whole of creation.

Pennington was also aware, however, that the Eucharist does not exhaust the mystery of Christ and that, we must ultimately put aside all attempts to explain it and simply rest in silence before it, allowing ourselves to be absorbed in the mysterious silence of God. Pennington's emphasis on the role played by silence in the Liturgy brings to the surface the apophatic (negative) dimension of the Eucharist. The God who reveals also conceals. The Eucharist is, at one and the same time, the visible presence of God in our midst and an invisible absence veiled beneath the appearances of bread and wine. This already-but-not-yet combination of presence and absence highlights the eschatological dimension of the Eucharist. As our food for the journey, it points to both the hear-and-now and to world beyond. It reminds us that Jesus him accompanies us on our journey into Eternity and that he reveals and conceals himself along the way to help us grown in faith and love for him.

For Pennington, therefore, the Eucharist expresses both the kataphatic (positive) and apophatic (negative) approaches to the mystery of the divine. This approach, in effect, juxtaposes the revelatory dimension of God with his elusive tendency to conceal and creates a healthy tension in Catholic theology and sacramental practice. It allows God to reveal himself in time and space, while at the same time veiling himself in mystery. It prevents us, on the one hand, from ever making an idol of him from the material world and, on the other hand, from making him distant and unapproachable because of his transcendent nature. If the mystery of the Trinity itself asserts that God is transcendent, incarnate, and immanent, and if the mystery of the Incarnation asserts that the Word of God has become human and walked this earth in the person of Jesus Christ, then the mystery of the Eucharist asserts that the bread and wine that has been changed into the Body and Blood of Christ and has become the primary means by which we ourselves can share in his life and mission.

In his exposition of the various parts of the Mass, Pennington is very conscious that God loves variety and that the Church images this love in its sacramental system. He likens the Church to a good Jewish Mother who piles so much food on her guest's plate that he or she has to pick and choose what to eat.[33] Sunday liturgies, for example, have three readings and contain so much spiritual nourishment for us to digest that we must stop for a moment when they are finished so that we can focus on what has touched us personally to help us grow. What is more, the Liturgy provides us with many choices regarding the singing, penitential rite, the profession of faith, the Eucharistic prayers, and the Memorial Acclamation. Such choice reflects both our freedom as the sons and daughters of God, and the need to adapt the Eucharist celebration to the circumstances of daily life. The various rites with the Church, moreover, reflect God's love for the differences among people and remind us that communion does not mean uniformity, but a union of hearts with the mystery of the Triune God.

Finally, Pennington displays a profound understanding of the divine simplicity that permeates the celebration of the Eucharist. He recognizes that the Eucharist has its roots in a simple meal and that Our Lord chose to use the common food of bread and wine to transform into his body and blood. His emphasis on the simplicity of the Liturgy stems, in part,

---

[33] Ibid., 32.

from his Trappist formation, which steered away from the liturgical trappings that had accumulated in the Benedictine tradition and focused instead on austere surroundings and simple chant tones in its liturgical celebrations. It also comes from his experience of centering prayer and the awareness that we can say more by saying less and that silence itself puts us in touch with the silence of God himself, who speaks to our hearts and puts us in touch with the divine simplicity. The Eucharist, he believes, gives us the chance to stand before the God who loves and cares for us as he loves and cares for his own Son. It reminds us that we are God's children and that he touches the depths of our being, lays bare our souls, and dwells there us mysteriously in his divine simplicity.

Conclusion

M. Basil Pennington was an influential spiritual writer, retreat director, and spiritual guide in the last decades of the twentieth century and early years of the new millennium. He possessed a firm grounding in both the kataphatic and apophatic traditions of Christianity and used that knowledge to probe more deeply the mysteries of the Christian faith. As one of the founders of the Centering Prayer Movement, he did much to translate the contemplative dimension of the Christian mystical tradition to the spiritual mindset and cultural sensitivities of his contemporaries.

In his teaching on the Eucharist, Pennington shows how the liturgical reforms of the Second Vatican Council spring from the tradition, yet speak to the concerns of modern man. In keeping with his scholastic and canonical training, he proceeds in a very orderly fashion, going through the various parts of the Mass and explaining them in a way that is concise, accurate, and easy to understand. He writes as one who has not only celebrated the Eucharist, but also as one who has lived it. His insights into the Mass convey a sense of wisdom and sound practical knowledge that only comes from a longstanding loving relationship with the sacrament could instill. The Eucharist, for Pennington, "is a reality that pervades our lives and our world."[34]

Pennington's teaching on the Eucharist reminds us of the depth of the Catholic teaching on the Eucharist and our need to ponder its mysteries from a variety of vantage points. His use of the kataphatic and apophatic traditions to interpret these mysteries reminds us that the Eucharist can be understood, but never fully grasped. By juxtaposing them, he reveals a tension within the Godhead that is resolved only by the divine simplicity. His appreciation of silence as an appropriate backdrop against which the celebration of the Eucharist unfolds reminds us we are all called to enter into that silence, rest in it, and share in the inner, mystical life of God himself.

---

[34] Ibid., 171

Reflection Questions

- To what extent does the Eucharist represent a kataphatic approach to the faith? To what extent does it espouse an apophatic approach? How do these two approaches of positive and negative theology relate to one another? Which of the two is dominant in the theology of the sacrament? Which do you prefer?

- What does Pennington mean by "the reality of our Christed person?" To what extent is this already a realty? To what extent is it a hope? To what extent does it involve a journey, one that normally lasts a lifetime? What role does the Eucharist play in our becoming more and more conformed to Christ? What role does it play in your life?

- What does Pennington mean by the "divine simplicity?" How does Christ embody this simplicity? How is it embodied in the Eucharist? To what extent is the purpose of the Eucharist to reveal this simplicity to others? To what extent is this simplicity present in your own life? How do you deal with the lack of such simplicity in your life?

Voice Eighteen

Henri Nouwen
With Burning Hearts

Henri J. M. Nouwen (1932-1996), a Dutch priest, psychologist, pastoral theologian, and spiritual writer, was one of the most widely read Catholic authors of his day. The oldest of four children, he did his priestly training at the major seminary in Rijsenburg, was ordained a priest for the archdiocese of Utrecht in 1957, and studied clinical psychology at the Catholic University at the University of Nijmegen from 1957-64. The author of some 39 books and numerous academic and popular articles, he taught at Notre Dame, the Catholic Theological University of Utrecht, Yale Divinity School, and Harvard Divinity School. He also had extended stays at St. John's University in Collegeville, Minnesota, the Pontifical North American College in Rome, the Trappist Monastery of the Genesee in New York, and theological centers in Bolivia and Peru, and the L'Arche Community in France. In 1986, he joined the L'Arche Daybreak Community in Richmond Hill, Ontario and remained associated with it for the rest of his life. His teaching on the Eucharist reflects his deep concern for the healing of the physical, psychological, spiritual, and social wounds of God's people.[1]

Nouwen's Spiritual Outlook

Throughout his life, Nouwen was interested in drawing connections between the Christian faith and daily life. He was not afraid to write about his personal struggles with loneliness, his need for intimacy, his sexual identity, and his own struggle with depression. These deeply personal issues struck a chord in his readers and attracted followers from many other religious traditions, both within the Catholic Church and outside of it. His willingness to share such private concerns with his readers gave a ring of authenticity to his writings that lent credence to the saying, "The most personal is the most universal." His need to connect with others carried over to his literary works. Because of this, he was able to touch his readers' hearts and convey to them a sense that they were his fellow companions on life's journey. His choice of the personal diary as a way of conveying his insights into the spiritual life made him, in many respects, an "open book" that others could read and find traces of their own stories and personal struggles.

---

[1] For more on Nouwen's life, see *Henri Nouwen Society*, http://henrinouwen.org/about-henri/his-life/.

Voice Eighteen: Henri Nouwen—*With Burning Hearts*

In one of his early works, *The Wounded Healer*,[2] Nouwen presents a theme reflected throughout his writings: "In our woundedness, we can become a source of life for others." This sentiment reflects the words of the Apostle Paul:

> But we have this treasure in clay jars, so that it may be made clear that this extraordinary power belongs to God and does not come from us. We are afflicted in every way, but not crushed; perplexed, but not driven to despair; persecuted, but not forsaken; struck down, but not destroyed; always carrying in the body the death of Jesus, so that the life of Jesus may also be made visible in our bodies. For while we live, we are always being given up to death for Jesus' sake, so that the life of Jesus may be made visible in our mortal flesh. So death is at work in us, but life in you. (2Cor 4:7-12)

Nouwen's spiritual outlook was thoroughly Christ-centered. Like Paul, he looked to the sufferings of Christ to find meaning in his own daily struggles and found healing in the wounds of the Risen Lord. If Jesus was the Wounded Healer par excellence, then Nouwen saw himself as one of Jesus' weak, vulnerable disciples, who ministered to others from

---

[2] Henri J. M. Nouwen, *The Wounded Healer: Ministry in Contemporary Society* (New York: Image Books, 1972).

his own woundedness and, in doing so, became for them a source of life and hope.

Nouwen's relationship to Jesus was central to his life and carried over to his relationship with others which, at times, became strained and the cause of much pain. Through Jesus, he saw the need to forgive those who had hurt him and from whom he had become estranged. In his book, *The Return of the Prodigal Son*,[3] he interpreted Rembrandt's painting of the famous parable in Luke 15:11-32 to bring home to his readers that we are all beloved by God and that, if we receive the Father's forgiveness, we must also be willing to extend it to others. Doing so was no easy feat, but he maintained that all things were possible with Jesus' help. In his mind, we are all returning prodigals in need of the Father's unconditional love and mercy. Jesus, the Wounded Healer, heals our wounds and enables us to be a healing balm for others. He invites us to share in the drama of his redemptive suffering and be nourished by the sacramental fellowship of his body and blood.

Nouwen and the Eucharist

The Eucharist was central to Nouwen's faith, priesthood, and ministry. He saw it as a way of reaching out to people

---

[3] Henri J. M. Nouwen, *The Return of the Prodigal Son: A Story of Homecoming* (New York: Image Books, 1992).

and inviting them to share in the fellowship of Jesus. Ever since he was a child, he had a profound sense of Jesus' presence in the sacramental mystery of the breaking bread and passing the cup. For him, the Eucharist was an action of Christ given to his followers not only as a way of remembering him, but also as a way of having his living presence ripple through the corridors of time and space. He once wrote: "The Eucharist is the most ordinary and the most divine gesture imaginable. That is the truth of Jesus. So human, yet so divine; so familiar, yet so mysterious; close, yet so revealing!"[4] For him, this simple ritual revealed the mysterious nature of God's love for humanity: "It is the story of God who wants to come close to us, so close that we can see him with our own eyes, touch him with our own hands; so close that there is nothing between us and him, nothing that separates, nothing that divides, nothing that creates distance."[5] The Eucharist, in his mind, was an unconditional action of hospitality that forged unity among those participating despite their differing beliefs and practices. It was the sacrament of table fellowship that celebrated life and bridged the gap separating those who gathered for it. In this sense, it was for him a sacrament of unity.

---

[4] Henri J. M. Nouwen, *With Burning Hearts: A Meditation on the Eucharistic Life* (Maryknoll, NY: Orbis Books, 1994), 67.
[5] Ibid.

As a Catholic, Nouwen believed in Jesus' real presence in the consecrated bread and wine. He wanted that presence to be a unifying and transforming force in the daily lives of those he served. For this reason, he sometimes departed from normal Catholic sacramental practice by inviting everyone present to partake of the sacrament, regardless of their religious tradition or denominational background.[6] This departure stemmed from his firm belief that Jesus entered our world to bring people together and to heal their wounds. The Eucharist, in his mind, brought Jesus, the Wounded Healer, into our midst and allowed him to touch us and make us whole. To put it simply: Jesus ate with sinners and tax collectors during his earthly life; he continues to do so today in his post-resurrectional existence through the Eucharist. What is more, Nouwen believed that Jesus' presence in the Eucharist had a unifying and transforming effect not only on humanity, but on the whole of creation. The transformation of bread and wine into the body and blood of Christ were but the first signs of the world's divinizing *theosis*. The Eucharist, for him, was the sacrament of the new creation.

This sacrament came not without great cost. Nouwen was very much aware that the Eucharist was the sacrament of the suffering Christ and that it was instituted the night

---

[6] See Michael O'Laughlin, *God's Beloved: A Spiritual Biography of Henri Nouwen* (Maryknoll, NY: Orbis Books, 2004), 116-23.

before his horrific death. He understood that the transformation of the humanity and, indeed, of the whole world came at a great price and that Jesus' suffering and death on the cross was the means chosen by God to achieve it. The Eucharist, for him, was a time for us to unite our sufferings with those of Christ. He understood that celebrating Eucharist required a willingness to drink of the cup from which Jesus drank. In his respect, the Eucharist was, at one and the same time, a cup of sorrow, a cup of joy, and a cup of blessings.[7] It was a celebration of life and death, a gesture that put us in touch with matters of ultimate concern and helped us to understand them. He knew that life was defined, at least in part, by the reality of death—and vice versa. For him, to celebrate Eucharist was to celebrate life and death by looking beyond them and drinking in joys and heartaches of the present moment. The sacrament was a way of finding the eternal in the present moment. It gave flavor to life and enabled us to savor its subtle tastes.

Some Further Insights

While this brief description of Nouwen's approach to the Eucharist does not exhaust his views on the sacrament, it does give us with a sense of his general concerns and helps

---

[7] Henri J. M. Nouwen, *Can You Drink This Cup?* (Notre Dame, IN: Ave Maria Press, 1996), 31, 41, 63.

us to understand his use of it in ministry. The following remarks expand on this description with the hope of providing deeper insights into the place of the Eucharist in his life and thought.

To begin with, it is important to point out that Nouwen's understanding of the Eucharist evolved over time and reflected the times and circumstances in which he lived. Raised in a devout Catholic family in the 1930s and 40s, he entered the seminary at an early age and was shaped by the theology and spirituality of the pre-Vatican II Church. His view toward the Eucharist changed with the teachings of the Council, which sought to make the Liturgy more accessible by introducing the vernacular, having the priest face the congregation, and including more lay involvement. These changes in practice brought on a period of experimentation in the Liturgy that Nouwen was familiar with as a young priest and participated in throughout his priestly ministry.

What is more, his being a professor in ecumenical and interreligious environments such as the divinity schools at Harvard and Yale likely contributed to his going beyond normal Catholic practice to a wider interpretation of Eucharistic participation. We can also imagine that his visit to South America, his stay with the Trappists at Genesee, and his life at the L'Arche Daybreak community (to mention but a few of the many places he visited) also contributed to approach to the sacrament. Nouwen was a widely traveled teacher and lecturer. He incorporated his experiences on the road into his

Voice Eighteen: Henri Nouwen—*With Burning Hearts*

growing understanding of Jesus and the Christ event. These experiences gave him a deep appreciation of our common humanity and the way the Eucharist could help us celebrate it.

Nouwen's training as a clinical psychologist also impacted his approach to the Eucharist. Aware of the frailty and poverty of the human condition, he is more concerned with the direct impact the Eucharist had on people's lives than with the fine points of theology. He used psychology as a tool in pastoral theology and saw the Eucharist as a way of bringing Jesus into people's in a very real and palpable way. That is not to say that he was not concerned with sound theology, but only that his priorities regarding the Eucharist were more focused on the bonds of fellowship it created and the healing it mediated in the midst of our wounds and common brokenness.

The Eucharist, for Nouwen, also had important anthropological implications, not the least of which was a deeper understanding of our bodies as an integral dimension of our human makeup. His own words speak for themselves: "The greatest mystery of the Christian faith is that God came to us in a body, suffered with us in a body, rose in the body, and gave us his body as good. No religion takes the body as seriously as the Christian religion. The body is not seen as the enemy or as a prison of the Spirit, but celebrated as the Spirit's temple. Through Jesus' birth, life, death, and resurrection, the human body has become part of the life of God.

By eating the body of Christ, our own fragile bodies are becoming intimately connected with the risen Christ and thus prepared to be lifted up with him into the divine life."[8]

Nouwen's approach to the Eucharist was thoroughly Christocentric. For him, the sacramental Christ was continuous with the Jesus who walked this earth, was crucified, and conquered death. For him, the Jesus of history and the Christ of faith were one and the same person. The Eucharist, in other words, made the Risen Lord palpably present in our lives: "It is the presence of Jesus coming among us, real and concrete that gives us hope. It is eating and drinking here that creates the desire for the heavenly banquet, it is finding a home now that makes us long for the father's house with its many dwelling places."[9] The Eucharist provided people with an opportunity to encounter the same Risen Lord whom the two disciples had encountered on the road to Emmaus.

The Eucharist, for Nouwen, was the sacrament of God's unconditional love for humanity manifested in the symbolism of a meal and characterized most strikingly in the hospitality of those gathered around the table of the Lord. Through it, God extended his unconditional love to us by virtue of our common humanity and invited us to share in his divine life

---

[8] Ibid., 118.

[9] Henri J. M. Nouwen, *Lifesigns: Intimacy, Fecundity, and Ecstasy in Christian Perspective* (New York: Doubleday, 1989), 122.

by partaking of his body and blood. Doing so enables us to celebrate life and to mourn its passing. The sacrament, for him, was a visible sign of the kingdom that was, at one and the same time, but in our midst and still to come.

For Nouwen, the Eucharist brought Jesus, the Wounded Healer, into our midst as food and drink. Partaking in the Eucharist meant opening our own wounds, presenting them to Jesus, and allowing him to touch us with his healing presence and unite them with his own. In his resurrected state, the wounds of his passion and death have become a soothing and healing balm. They exist there in a transformed state that he promises to share with us and make our own. Whenever we eat the body and drink the blood of Jesus the power of that transformation comes to us. Our wounds are opened, cleansed, cared for, healed, and ultimately divinized. What is more, as members of his body, our lives are now mysteriously tied up with the life of the Risen Lord.

The Eucharist also put Nouwen in touch with the deep hunger that touches all human lives. He relates one such experience when he distributed Holy Communion at a Good Friday service at the L'Arche Community in France: "I took the chalice and started to move among those whom I had seen coming to the cross, looked at their hungry eyes, and said, 'The body of Christ ... the body of Christ ... the body of Christ' countless times. The small community became all of humanity, and I knew that all I needed to say my whole life long was 'Take and eat. This is the body of Christ.'"[10] This small community was, for him, a microcosm of the whole human family. The Eucharist was the food that eased its pain and satisfied it deep spiritual hungers.

The Eucharist, for Nouwen, also makes us more sensitive to the whole of nature. It delves beneath appearances and helps us ponder the meaning of much deeper realities. His words again speak or themselves: "We will never fully understand the meaning of the sacramental signs of bread and wine when they do not make us realize that the whole of nature is a sacrament pointing to a reality beyond itself. The presence of Christ in the Eucharist becomes a 'special problem' only when we have lost our sense of his presence in all that is, grows, lies, and dies. What happens during a Sunday celebration can only be a real celebration when it reminds us in the fullest sense of what continually happens every day in the world which surrounds us. Bread is more than bread, wine is more than wine: it is God with us—not as an isolated event once a week but as the concentration of a mystery about which all of nature speaks day and night."[11]

Finally, it bears noting that, despite his departure from normal Catholic practice (at least with regard to reception of Holy Communion), Nouwen embraced the three major

---

[10] Ibid., 121.

[11] Henri J. M. Nouwen, *Seeds of Hope: A Henri Nouwen Reader*, ed. Robert Durback (New York: Bantam Books, 1989), 100.

elements of Catholic Eucharistic teaching of banquet, presence, and sacrifice. The Eucharist, he believed, was a sacred meal and a foreshadowing of a heavenly banquet. It brought real presence of Jesus into our midst in the form of bread and wine. It healed the wounds of the world by putting us in contact with Jesus' sacrificial suffering and death. Nouwen presented these themes in a way that met people where they were, addressed their needs, and took their own suffering and personal sensitivities into account. In this respect he was an interpreter of the Catholic tradition for the people of his day, someone very much in touch with his own wounds and personal frailties, who shared them with others, and encouraged them to do the same.

Conclusion

Henri J. M. Nouwen was one of the most influential spiritual authors of his day. His writings touched on a wide range of issues and were flavored by his own struggles and experiences. He was a restless man always traveling, moving from place to place, searching for that ever-elusive peace of mind and heart. Throughout his wanderings, the Eucharist gave him glimpses of that peace, nourished his hope of one day finding it in all its fullness, and gave him the courage to face the fragmented and broken world to which he belonged.

The Eucharist was one of the mainstays of Nouwen's spiritual journey. It was always there for him, always an important part of his life. It nourished him from his early childhood and accompanied him throughout his priestly training, scholarly activity, and pastoral ministry. It put him in touch with Jesus, the Wounded Healer, and gave him a sense of the type of person God was calling him to become. It represented God's unconditional love for humanity and was a celebration of life and death. It put him in it in touch with the drama hidden beneath the appearances of things. It encouraged him to take deep, hearty draughts of life. It invited him to share in the divine hospitality and encouraged him to go and do likewise.

Nouwen was both a free spirit and a conflicted soul. He suffered greatly from his own personal insecurities, but he was also given the grace to face them squarely and to share his struggles with others. He tried not to put on any masks when he wrote for he knew that, in the end, the truth would be revealed. He believed in the power of the language to cut through worldly pretensions and touch the heart. He believed even more in the power of God to break through the boundaries of time and space and be with his people. The Eucharist, for him, was precisely that: "God with us," here and now. It was God *being* with us, *living* with us, *suffering* with us, *dying* with us, and, ultimately, *rising* with us. It was a seed of hope pointing to something both still to come and already present beneath the appearances of bread and wine. It was a celebration of life and a joyous expectation of the fullness of life yet to come.

Voice Eighteen: Henri Nouwen—*With Burning Hearts*

Reflection Questions

- Do you agree with Nouwen that in our woundedness we become a source of healing for others? Have you ever experienced such healing? Has your woundedness ever been a source of healing for others? How deeply are you in touch with your wounds? How are they related to the wounds of Jesus? To what extend have his wounds been a source of healing for you?

- Do you agree with Nouwen that Jesus' presence in the Eucharist has a unifying and transforming effect not only on humanity, but on the whole of creation? If so, can you point to concrete examples around you where this is so? To what extent has the Eucharist had a unifying and transforming effect on your own life?

- Nouwen believed the Eucharist brought Jesus, the Wounded Healer, into our midst as food and drink. What does it mean to consume Jesus, the Wounded Healer? In doing so, do his wounds become our wounds? Do our wounds become his? Do we ourselves take on the role of wounded healers for those around us? To what extend is the Eucharist itself a sacrament of healing?

Voice Nineteen

Jon Hassler
North of Hope

Jon Hassler (1933-2008), an American novelist and short story writer, was Regents Professor Emeritus and Writer-in-Residence at St. John's University in Collegeville, Minnesota. He was born in Minneapolis, studied English at St. John's, and eventually earned an M. A. in English from the University of North Dakota. After teaching English at a number of Minneapolis high schools, he taught at Bemidji State University and Brainerd Community College, before going to St. John's as Writer-in-Residence in 1980. The author of twelve novels and two short story collections, he wrote about small-town life in northern Minnesota and the people who lived in them. Although known as a regional writer, the characters he creates and the stories that unfold around them touch upon themes with universal significance. His works include: *Staggerford* (1977), *Simon's Night* (1979), *The Love Hunter* (1981), *A Green Journey* (1985), *Grand Opening* (1987), *North of Hope* (1990), *Dear James* (1993), *Rookery Blues* (1995), *The Dean's List* (1998), *Keepsakes and Other Stories* (2000), *Rufus at the Door and Other* Stories (2000), *The Staggerford Flood* (2002), *The Staggerford Murders* (2004), and *The New Woman* (20005). Catholicism often provides a narrative backdrop for his characters as they struggle with their past, question the choices they have made, try to deal with the loneliness in which they find themselves, and struggle to come to terms with the meaning of their lives and, indeed, with life itself. The Eucharist is present in his stories, but usually on the periphery and, like the Real Presence itself, difficult to see, except through the eyes of faith.[1]

Hassler's Spiritual Outlook

Hassler has been called the last "Catholic novelist," not in the sense that he presents orthodox Catholic doctrine in a way that edifies his readers, but because Catholicism offers the existential backdrop against which he develops his characters and hatches his plots. A master storyteller, he uses Catholicism to convey his thoughts about the human situation in all its bright, dark, and shadowy dimensions. Although he did not live an exemplary life (he was twice divorced and remarried a third time), Catholicism always lingers in the background of his novels and short stories. While small-town Minnesota provides the setting for his stories, he uses it to explore many of the most universal questions of human existence: the meaning of life, the struggle between good and

---

[1] For more on Jon Hassler's biography, see "Jon Hassler: The Official Website," http://www.jonhassler.net. See also, "Jon Hassler/ Biographical Information," http://www.ar.cc.mn.us/stankey/Literat/Hassler/Hassler1.htm .

evil, the power of choice in the face of trying circumstances. He also uses humor as a way of deflecting and coping with the emptiness and loneliness in life that can at times seem overwhelming.[2]

Some say that Hassler does for the post-Vatican II Church what J. F. Powers did for the pre-Vatican II Church. That is to say that he captures a particular mindset that embodies a particular era in the life of the Church. Hassler himself notes that the priests in Powers's *Morte d'Urban* (1962) and *Wheat That Springeth Green* (1988) differ greatly from Fr. Frank Healy in *North of Hope*: "Where they seem to be more urbane and they're older and more cynical, Frank isn't so cynical. Frank is a better priest, I think, than those guys."[3] Hassler describes a world in which the people who inhabit it (including its priests) struggle with their own human frailties and seek to come to terms with their need for love and their tendency to fill it with false hopes and wrongful imaginings. It is a world in which choice matters and where grace, while not always accepted, is never far away. If "grace perfects

---

[2] See Andrew Greeley, "The Last Catholic Novelist: The grace-filled fiction of Jon Hassler," *America* (Novermber 3, 2008), https://www.americamagazine.org/issue/674/ bookings/last-catholic-novelist.

[3] See Joseph Plut, "Conversation with Jon Hassler: North of Hope," *Renascence* 55/2(Winter, 2003): 145-162, 175, https://search.proquest.com/docview/194939040?pq-origsite=gscholar&fromopenview=true.

nature," as Aquinas would have it, it is fair to say that Hassler presents us with a world where human beings, embattled as they are by life's petty betrayals and inner wounds, are embraced by the transforming power of love and its perennial capacity to endure.

Although Hassler steeps his readers in the atmosphere of small-town Minnesota, he captures the drama of human existence in a way that transcends time and place. Many of his characters reflect persons he has met in his own life, while the places he describes can be seen in the very places where he himself has lived and worked. He admits, for example, that the character of Fr. Frank Healy in *North of Hope* is based thirty-seven percent on his own life, while Aquinas Academy is partially based on St. John's University in Collegeville, Minnesota, where he taught and was for many years writer-in-residence. The Catholic imagination looms so large in Hassler's stories and shapes the way in which his characters become themselves and his plots unfold. For this reason, it should not be surprising that the Eucharist, being a major fixture in the Catholic worldview, would hold a prominent (if not always visible) place in his writing.[4]

---

[4] Ibid.

Hassler on the Eucharist

One of the best places to view Hassler's presentation of the Eucharist comes in what many consider his masterpiece, *North of Hope*.[5] This novel traces the story of Frank Healy, a young boy whose mother dies at the age of eleven and whose father retreats into himself after her death. With his home life in disarray, Frank gravitates towards Fr. Adrian Lawrence, his saintly pastor, and the motherly (and often intrusive) care of Eunice Pfeiffer, the rectory housekeeper, both of whom influence him during his adolescence and beyond.

As the plot unfolds, Frank develops a friendship with a new girl in town, Libby Girard, whose beauty captures his attention from the first moment he lays his eyes on her and which continues throughout their time together in high school and, in many ways, throughout his whole life. Though friends with Frank, Libby takes a downward turn, as she gets pregnant by another boy she is dating, leaves high school to get married, lives on a farm, leaves her husband some three years later, and eventually moves back to Minneapolis with her mother and daughter. Frank, in turn, decides to enter Aquinas Seminary, a secluded, all-male campus with strict rules and limited access to the outside world. He does so through the influence of Fr. Adrian, whom he considers a saint, and inspired by the many heroic stories he had heard

---

[5] Jon Hassler, *North of Hope* (Chicago: Loyola Classics, 1990).

about Fr. Zell, one of the early missionary priests to the region, who collapsed and froze to death on Christmas day in 1893 while crossing a large ice-covered lake while on his way to celebrate Mass on the opposite shore. Also influencing his decision was learning from Eunice Pfeiffer that before her death his mother had told her that she wanted him to be a priest.

After his seminary studies and priestly ordination, Fr. Frank spends most of his priestly life as a teacher and baseball coach at Aquinas Academy, the high school seminary on the grounds for young men considering the priesthood. When the Academy closes some twenty-five years later, he undergoes a vocational crisis that eventually opens up a big leak in soul and sends him first to the cathedral and later as an assistant to Fr. Adrian Lawrence (aka "Loving Kindness") to his home parish of St. Ann's in Linden Falls, Minnesota and Our Lady's mission on the nearby Basswood Indian Reservation.

At various times in the novel, Frank senses this leak that has opened up in his soul, even while he celebrates Mass and experiences a number of homiletic blackouts from the pulpit. His vocational search is complicated by the reappearance of Libby Girard on the Basswood Reservation as a nurse in the local clinic with her third husband, Dr. Tom Pearson. Libby is very unhappy and seems like a lost soul. She has been married three times and her daughter, Verna, sexually abused by Libby's second and third husbands, has suffered breakdowns and has been hospitalized numerous times. Libby looks to Frank as a source of comfort and possible long-time friendship, perhaps even marriage. Frank, in response is forced to encounter his own intentions and motivations for becoming a priest. Much of it involves his mother's dying wish that he become a priest. With the closing of the seminary which he knew was coming for many years, he goes into an emotional tailspin and depression. In reflecting back on his life, he states, "In all this time, I haven't once felt that I've moved anyone's soul closer to God, my own included."[6] In looking back, he sees himself "bringing up the end of a long line of distinguished teacher-priests and discovered that he had scarcely been a priest at all."[7] He asks his bishop to be stationed in his home parish of St. Ann's as the assistant to Fr. Lawrence with the hope regaining his equilibrium and rekindling some of his lost priestly zeal. By returning home, he hopes to go back to the origins of his priestly vocation get a fresh start.

One example of how the Eucharist plays a role in Frank's embrace of his priesthood comes in a passage where he celebrates Mass for the Second Sunday of Advent in the Our Lady's Church on the Basswood Reservation for a congregation of about 50 Ojibway Indians (about twenty percent of the Catholics living on the reservation). Wearing purple

---

[6] Ibid., 224.
[7] Ibid., 225.

vestments, he recited the opening prayers at the altar and looking out on the congregation, saw written on their sad, wrinkled faces the whole history of the suffering and injustices done to the Ojibway nation down through the years. At the Gospel, "everyone, even the children, stood at stiff attention and appeared to concentrate on every phrase as though the Word of God were grim and sobering news."[8] During his homily, "the entire congregation, making slits of their eyes, might have been peering into a snow squall."[9] In his homily, "he spoke of the healing power of the sacraments and as he concluded with the story of Father Zell dying on Sovereign Lake in the service of his savior, he felt once again the same old priestly zeal that had carried him through the seminary to ordination. It warmed him. It actually made him tingle. He hadn't felt this sure of himself for a long time. For a few moments thereafter, crossing from the pulpit to the altar and there reciting the offertory prayers, he felt that Our Lady's Church in Basswood, dusty and cold and half-empty, was exactly where he belonged at this time in his life. He felt that by allying himself with this small band of Indians in this tiny clearing in the woods, he might somehow come to understand his destiny. Here something would happen, he didn't know what, to justify his life as a priest."[10] This small ray of

---

[8] Ibid., 183.
[9] Ibid.
[10] Ibid., 185.

light, however, would not last even through the duration of the Mass. Soon after the consecration, he felt his optimism slipping away and by the Our Father he was having a hard time keeping his spirits up and felt that the air had gone out of him, like a punctured football. By communion time, he found himself asking cynical questions about his desire to imitate Father Zell: "Was it truly a longing to be of service to God and humankind? Couldn't it just as likely be a death wish?"[11] At the end of the novel, when he discovers years later that his mother really said, "I hope Frank will want to be a priest" and not "I want Frank to be a priest,"[12] he realizes that he has passed his vocational crisis and no longer questions his priestly identity: "It was clear that his mother had allowed him more volition than Eunice, but really, would it have made a difference? Would he have taken his life in a different direction? If so, it was much too late to imagine what that other direction might have been. We are what we are, he told himself. For better or worse—I am a priest."[13]

Frank comes to terms with his relationship with Libby and reaffirms his commitment to the priesthood. His ministry at St. Ann's in Linden Falls and to the Ojibway Indians at the Basswood Church of Our Lady plays no small part in this discernment. Hassler describes it thus: "He [Frank] sus-

---

[11] Ibid.
[12] Ibid, 661.
[13] Ibid.

pected that he was actually doing some of his parishioners some good. Both at St. Ann's and at Our Lady's, he could sense a vague kind of spiritual unity taking shape around him. More and more people were coming to him and opening up to their souls and either asking for advice or—more often—asking for confirmation of the advice they'd been giving themselves. More and more of his people were receiving the sacraments; he sensed a heightened regard for the Eucharist, and he might be the only priest in the diocese—indeed, in America—to report an upswing in the number of confessions. He was becoming increasingly aware of himself as surrounded by two small communities of faith, one Indian, on white, and being nourished by them as he strove to nourish them. They did not follow him as much as cluster around him. He was not so much their leader as their center. They were not his followers; they were his family."[14] Conscious of the limits of what he is now able to give her, Frank now knows that he cannot love Libby as a wife or a lover, but only as a sister. He has found his true home. The people in these two small rural communities, believers and unbelievers alike, have plugged the running leak in his soul, given him a sense of belonging, and enabled him to rediscover his priestly calling—and for that, he is ever so grateful.

---

[14] Ibid., 569-70.

Some Further Insights

Although the above brief summary of Hassler's spiritual outlook and view toward the Eucharist is by no means exhaustive, it offers an opportunity to delve a bit further into his underlying religious outlook and the challenge it presents today's world. What follows are some observations aimed at probing his understanding of the Eucharist in a little more depth.

To begin with, it bears noting that the main characters in the novel —Frank and Libby—come from dysfunctional families, whose influence informs the decisions they make in life. When his mother dies when he is eleven and his father becomes something of a recluse, Frank finds solace in his local parish. The pastor, Fr. Lawrence, he believes, is a saint, while the rectory's housekeeper, Eunice Pfeiffer, tries (unsuccessfully) to take the place of his mother. Libby, in turn, has a father who is frequently drunk, abuses his wife, and eventually abandons the family altogether. These similar yet different family backgrounds lead them to make very different life choices. Libby marries at a young age, has a child (who is sexually abused and mentally unstable as a result) and reappears on the scene when Frank is already ordained a priest some twenty-five years and is currently undergoing a vocational crisis. Frank, in turn, enters the seminary fed with dreams of heroic self-sacrifice for the good of humanity (as embodied by Father Zell and the early missionaries to the rural northern areas of Minnesota) and the understanding that his mother wanted him to become a priest. The Eucharist, in Frank's mind, in intimately related to the priesthood. A priest celebrates Mass. He preaches and consecrates the bread and wine, transforming it into Jesus' body and blood. His vocational crisis ultimately comes down to a choice between Libby and the Eucharist, between his childhood friend with whom he was (and still is) deeply in love or service to the people of God, which in this case are the people of St. Ann's parish and the Ojibway Nation in Our Lady's Church on the Basswood Reservation.

Hassler uses the Eucharist as a way of highlighting Frank's vocational crisis. The leak in his heart, the drain on his priestly zeal caused by the closing of Aquinas Academy, the homiletic blackouts, the depression and lack of focus, the drinking, the confusion he experiences as a result of his friendship with and attraction to Libby, all seem to converge when he celebrates Mass as the leak in heart turns into a gaping hole. Even if he is able to recapture momentarily the apostolic zeal that motivated his hero, Father Zell, the mood soon dissipates and gives way to an existential struggle over the authenticity his priestly calling. Even though he was a great teacher and baseball coach in the minor seminary, he wonders if, in all his priestly life, he had ever helped someone draw closer to God. He wonders if he has made the right decision so many years ago when he entered the seminary immediately after high school. He goes to his home parish and to Father Adrian Lawrence, his childhood pastor, in one last attempt to salvage his vocation. There, he hopes to be immersed in the ordinary duties of priestly life, the most important of which is the daily celebration of Mass for the parishioners of St. Ann's in Linden and Our Lady's chapel on the Basswood Reservation. Although Hassler weaves the sacrament in quiet, unobtrusive ways into his novel, there is little or no doubt that it is intimately tied to the priestly vocation. Celebrating Mass for God's people is what a priest does. Frank's decision at the end of the novel to embrace his priesthood is an embrace of the Eucharist.

Another way Hassler presents the Eucharist by looking at the priests in the novel who have influenced Frank in either positive or negative ways. Three in particular stand out. First, there is Father Zell, the frontier priest of northern Minnesota who covered vast tracts of land (often by foot) in the early twentieth century to bring the Gospel to the Indians of the region. Frank had heard stories about him as a boy and was fascinated by the determination and zeal of this early priestly pioneer, who froze to death from exhaustion while walking across the icy surface of Sovereign Lake in the dead of winter while traveling from one shore to the other to celebrate Mass for his faithful flock. He even defends Zell against those who said the priest had been imprudent (even reckless) by trying to keep the Eucharistic fast even though he knew he had a long, arduous journey by foot ahead of him. Zell, in Frank's mind, kept the fast out of his love for the Eucharist and his belief that God would protect him while carrying out his priestly endeavors. Another priestly influence in Frank's life is Father Adrian Lawrence, his saintly childhood pastor, who is a father figure for him after the death of his mother at an early age and his real father turns inward on himself, becoming a distant and brooding distant recluse. Father Adrian, whose nickname among the priests of the diocese is "Loving Kindness," is a gentle, saintly figure who loves the priesthood and the people of the parish he serves. In Frank's mind, he may not be as brave and heroic as Father Zell, but he is a stable fixture at St. Ann's parish, is loved by the people, affirms them, and gives them a sense of comfort and belonging. Frank turns to him during his vocational crisis and hopes to recover his priestly identity through him. On the negative side, there is Father De Smet, the young associate whose place he takes at St. Ann's and who now serves as an associate at the wealthy Cathedral parish in Barrington. Father De Smet dresses well, likes his liquor, is a social climber, and has only a superficial sense of the Gospel's relevance for the lives of the people he serves. De Smet is an example of the kind of cleric Frank does not want to become. If he cannot be like Father Zell, he'll take "Loving Kindness" over De Smet any day. The way each of these priests celebrates Mass, moreover, is quite different: Father Zell gives his life to bring the Eucharist to his people; his entire life is a sermon. Father Adrian sees the sacrament as the center of parish life; he loves to preach about the importance of being kind to one another (hence his sobriquet, "Loving Kindness"). For Father De Smet, celebrating Mass is something he simply does pro forma; his sermons have little (if anything) to do with the Gospel.

Franks deals with his vocational crisis against the backdrop of the rural northern Minnesota landscape, in particular the town of Linden Falls and the Basswood Indian reservation. Hassler points out that the linden and basswood trees are the same and bring a sense of unity what seems like two very different cultures—one white; the other, Indian—that coexist in such close proximity to one another.[15] Having lost his mother at such a young age, it is interesting that the churches in these towns are names after venerable motherly figures in the Christian tradition: St. Ann, the patroness of the church in Linden Falls, is the mother of the Blessed Mother; and Our Lady's chapel in Basswood, is named after Mary, the mother of Jesus. Mothers bring a sense of warmth and belonging to family life, and these churches do something similar for Frank in that they fill a void in his life that his mother left behind (he barely remembers her) and that the intrusive (and often nagging) Eunice Pfeiffer cannot fill. He finds a special sense of belonging at Our Lady's chapel in Basswood, where at one point he makes says this prayer:

---

[15] Plut, "Conversation with Jon Hassler: North of Hope," 145-162, 175, https://search.proquest.com/docview/194939040?pq-origsite=gscholar&fromopenview=true.

"Dear God, if it's numbers you're after, we might as well board this place up, but, please, let's carry on here for a while longer. I don't understand why—maybe it's because I'm such an outsider everywhere else—but I feel more at home in this clapboard church in this desolate outpost of humanity than in any place I've been since the academy shut down."[16] It's almost as if St. Ann's in Linden Falls and Our Lady's chapel on the Basswood Reservation are actual characters in the novel. They are a significant part of the spiritual landscape that leads Frank into the seminary, priestly ordination, and eventually a mid-life vocational crisis. They provide for him the soothing, motherly presence that he has been looking for much of his life. Since the primary purpose of these churches is to offer a sacred space where the priest can celebrate Mass with the people, it follows that this comforting motherly influence would also have an effect on Frank's understanding of his priestly ministry.

Finally, throughout the novel Frank searches for a sense of communion with himself, others, God, and the world around him. He thought he had found it at Aquinas Academy during his time there as a teacher, baseball coach, and later as headmaster. When it closes due lack of vocations, however, his world collapses in on itself and he begins to question his own priestly identity. His crisis heightens with the appearance of Libby, a childhood friend, whom he loved dearly at the time

---

[16] Hassler, *North of Hope*, 432.

and, in many respects, still does. As the novel unfolds, Frank experiences the leak in his soul that is slowly draining him of his love for the priesthood. His struggle extends through most of the novel and is resolved when he comes to the realization that God has called him to establish bonds with his people, especially those in difficulty: Libby and her daughter, Verna, Fr. Adrian and the shut-ins of St. Ann's parish, the parishioners at Our Lady's chapel on the Basswood Reservation, and (perhaps most off all) himself. This sense of communion brings him peace and begins to repair the leak within his soul. He comes to see that most people have leaks in their souls and that part of his priestly vocation is not to plug the leak but to share it with others so that they will share theirs with him and together let God fill their inner emptiness with a sense of his ever-elusive presence. Hope yearns for fulfillment and can be found even in the most desolate of places, even in the rural, small town wintry northern regions of Minnesota. The priesthood, Frank learns, is all about building communion, that is to say, breaking open the bread of our lives and sharing it with one another.

Conclusion

In his novels, Hassler liked to use small-town settings to touch upon many of the universal themes of human existence: loneliness, depression, the meaning of life, relationships—to name but a few. He chose the rural setting of northern Minnesota, because it was the culture and geographical landscape with which he was most familiar. Although he wrote from his actual experience of the northern mid-West, he was more than a regional writer. His skills in descriptive writing and character development enabled him to transcend the local color and treat themes that, in one way or another, affect every human heart. This ability to capture the universal in the particular, the extraordinary in the ordinary, sets him apart from the writers of his day and numbers him among the great American novelists of his generation.

Catholicism, for Hassler, provides the underlying spiritual atmosphere within which his novels would unfold. In *North of Hope*, what many consider his masterpiece, the Eucharist offers a quiet backdrop against which the plot develops and the characters, especially Frank and Libby, come to an understanding of their place in the world. The Catholic faith, we might say, offers the spiritual context within which Hassler treats universal themes of interest to every human heart, even those that seem estranged from traditional Catholic practice and belief. When seen in this light, *North of Hope* brings to the fore the importance of deciding for oneself the direction one wishes to take in life.

In the final analysis, Catholicism provides a narrative backdrop for Hassler's characters as they struggle with their past, question the choices they have made, and try to deal with the loneliness in which they find themselves. His characters struggle to come to terms with the meaning of their lives and with Life itself. The Eucharist is present in nearly all of Hassler's stories, but usually on the periphery and, like the Real Presence itself, difficult to see, except through the eyes of faith. It is almost always associated with the person of the priest: Father Zell in past generations, Father Adrian Lawrence in more recent times, and Father Frank Healy in the present. The latter's decision to remain faithful to his vocation and embrace his priesthood and humble (yet so important) duties within the Church, indicates that, in the end, the Eucharist is all about the Body of Christ and its quiet, mysterious, and often hidden presence in the believing (and even unbelieving) community of wounded humanity.

Reflection Questions

- Frank experiences a leak in his heart that drains his priestly zeal and makes him wonder if he made the right vocational decision. Have you ever experience a leak in your heart that made you question the direction your life has taken? If so how, did you deal with it? How did Frank deal with it?

- How would you describe the difference between Fr. Zell, Fr Adrian Lawrence, and Fr. De Smet? Which one inspires Frank? Which one helps him the most? Which one gives him only negative example? How would you characterize Fr. Frank? What priests in your life have inspire or helped you? Which ones have been a negative influence on you?

- Frank searches for a sense of communion with himself, others, God, and the world around him. What is the relationship between Eucharist and community? To what extent is the sacrament the center around which the St. Ann's in Linden Falls and Our Lady's chapel on the Basswood Reservation are built? Does the same hold true for your own faith community?

Voice Twenty

Ron Hansen
Mariette in Ecstasy

Ron Hansen (1947-), an American novelist, essayist, and university professor, was born in Omaha, Nebraska, earned a B.A. in English at Creighton University (1970), an M.F.A. from the Iowa Writer's Workshop (1974), and an M.A. in Spirituality from Santa Clara University (1995), where he presently teaches fiction and screenwriting as the Gerard Manly Hopkins, S.J. Professor of the Arts and Humanities. Early in his career he also held a Wallace Stegner Creative Writing Fellowship at Stanford University. The recipient of numerous awards and fellowships, his works include *Desperadoes: A Novel* (1979), *The Assassination of Jesse James by the Coward Robert Ford: A Novel* (1983), *The Shadowmaker*, children's book (1987), *Nebraska: Stories* (1989), *Mariette in Ecstasy: A Novel* (1991), *Atticus: A Novel*, a finalist for the National Book Award (1996), *Hitler's Niece: A Novel* (1999), *A Stay Against Confusion: Essays on Faith and Fiction* (2001), *Isn't It Romantic?: An Entertainment* (2003), and *Exiles* (2008). Several of these works have been adapted for movies and theater. A devout Catholic, he was ordained to the permanent diaconate in 2007 and continues to write on a wide variety of secular and religious themes.[1]

Hansen's Spiritual Outlook

Hansen has written extensively on the impact his Catholic faith had on his vocation as a writer. In his Preface to *A Stay Against Confusion*, he observes: "Looking back on my childhood now, I find that church-going and religion were in good part the origin of my vocation as a writer, for along with Catholicism's feast for the senses, its ethical concerns, its insistence on seeing God in all things, and the high status it gave to scripture, drama, and art, there was a connotation in Catholicism's liturgies that storytelling mattered."[2] "Each Mass," he continues, "was a narrative steeped in meaning and metaphor, helping the faithful to not only remember the past but to make it present here and now, and to bind ourselves into a sharing group that, ideally, we could continue the public ministry of Jesus in the world."[3] It should be of no surprise to us that his love of the Mass would eventually lead him to become a permanent deacon in the Church with the

---

[1] See *Santa Clara University, Department of English,* "Ron Hansen," https://www.scu.edu/english/faculty-staff/ron-hansen/ .

[2] Ron. Hansen, *A Stay Against Confusion: Essays on Faith and Fiction* (New York: HarperCollins, 2001), xii.

[3] Ibid.

liturgical responsibilities and those pertaining to service in the community.

Hansen states that another important influence in his vocation as a writer was his desire to live out in his imagination "other lives and possibilities."[4] Using a broad description from *The Oxford Companion to the Bible* of sacraments as "occasions of encounter between God and the believer, where the reality of God's gracious actions needs to be accepted,"[5] he speaks of the sacramental nature of writing insofar that it "provides occasions of encounter between humanity and God."[6] Writing, for him, is a way the author can mediate for his or her readers an encounter with the divine. The imagination is an important vehicle that brings this about, since it encourages both author and reader to look for the extraordinary in the midst of the ordinary. In doing so, it immerses them in a world that leads them to the threshold of the sacred, where humanity brushes shoulders with the divine, and where the divine reveals itself in the most unexpected of places.

Hansen agrees with G. K. Chesterton that "[a] small artist is content with art; a great artist is content with nothing except everything."[7] Everything, for him, is "the mystery of

---

[4] Ibid., xiii.
[5] Ibid., 3.
[6] Ibid.
[7] Ibid., 6.

the Holy Being as it was, and is, incarnated in human life."[8] In trying to capture the presence of the divine in human affairs, he tries to avoid the smug moralizing and rigid ethical conformity that characterized so many Catholic authors of the forties and fifties.[9] Following the example of Jesus, whose allusive parables pushed the boundaries of the commonly held perceptions of his hearers, he seeks in his writing to convey an experience of the human that invites an even deeper experience of the sacred. He embraces Nathan Mitchell's idea that "[s]ymbols are places to live, breathing spaces that help us discover what possibilities life offers."[10] "The job of fiction writers," Hansen maintains, "is to fashion those symbols and give their readers the feeling that life has great significance, that something is going on here that matters."[11] When seen in this light, the sacramental nature of writing shines through most clearly when it plumbs the depths of Pierre Teilhard de Chardin's formula for happiness: to be, to love, and to worship.[12] As one can well imagine, to speak of worship, from a Catholic writer's perspective, must in some way point to Eucharist.

---

[8] Ibid.
[9] Ibid., 10.
[10] Ibid., 13.
[11] Ibid.
[12] Ibid.

Hansen on the Eucharist

Hansen ends, *A Stay Against Confusion*, with a chapter entitled, "Eucharist." In this chapter, he reflects back on his childhood experience of receiving his First Holy Communion in 1955 at Immaculate Conception Church in Omaha, Nebraska. He contrasts what that experience was like in his childhood with the sixties and seventies when society itself was in a rebellious mode and when he himself was going through a time of insubordination, would miss Mass on occasion, and eventually came to a stark realization: "I discovered that when I did not go to Mass I missed it. I felt serenity there, even joy, it seemed to make things good and right; and as my attendance at Mass increased in frequency, my sense of rhythm, history, and logic of the liturgy also grew. Weather, busyness, and the doldrums could still hold me at bay but for the most part I was hooked. A daily."[13] At the end of the chapter, he reflects on his experience of being a eucharistic minister: "It is a gift to me, that giving: it's the glorious feeling I have when I am writing as well as I can, when I feel I am, in ways I have no control of, an instrument of the Holy Being; for I have just an inkling of what Jesus felt when he looked on his friends in mercy and aching love, and I have a

---

[13] Ibid., 258.

sense of why, just before he died, he established this gracious sacrament of himself."[14]

The sacraments mediate the divine to the human, and the Eucharist, being the "sacrament of sacraments," does this in a special way, since it brings the sacrifice and nourishing presence of Christ himself into our very midst. Since Hansen views writing itself from a sacramental standpoint, it should not be surprising that his attitudes toward the Eucharist would eventually make their way into his writing. Such is the case in his novel, *Mariette in Ecstasy*, which he describes as "a parable of a young woman's quest for God."[15] Mariette, a seventeen-year old postulant at Our Lady of Sorrows, the Church and Priory of the Sisters of the Crucifixion, has received the stigmata and has been the cause of rancor and division in the community. Some sisters think she is putting on a show; others, that she is mentally deranged, while still others believe she is a saint. At one point, Mother Saint-Raphael has this to say to the nuns of the priory: "Wondrous things do happen here, but they take place amidst great tranquility. We shall make it our duty to preserve that. We shall try to find a natural explanation of these phenomena if we can, and we shall deny they are holy gifts to Mariette until there is no other alternative. We know there are miracles in the Gospels, but we show them disrespect if we dispose

---

[14] Ibid., 261.
[15] Ibid., 12.

ourselves to believe in the simply fabulous. And we must keep in mind that there are a good many more pages in holy scripture that show how little pleasure God takes in astounding us with His power."[16]

In a chapter of *A Stay Against Confusion* entitled, "Stigmata," Hansen says that Mother Saint-Raphael is speaking for himself: "Wondrous things do happen in life, but generally in the ordinary ways of faith and healing and love. Then there are phenomena like the stigmata for which there is no natural explanation, and which seem so grossly old-fashioned, as misplaced in our modern times as witchcraft and sorcery. Mariette Baptiste was, for me, the real thing, a stigmatic; but I inserted an element of questionableness because in my research that seemed standard even in those instances in which the anomalies seemed authentic and all medical science could do was scratch its head in puzzlement."[17]

A close reading of the novel shows that the liturgy is an important backdrop against which the Mariette's drama unfolds. Each of its three major parts is subdivided according the various feast days of Our Lord, Our Blessed Mother, and the saints, whom the sisters of the monastery celebrate in according with the liturgical calendar of the Church. Many of the scenes, moreover, have the sisters sharing their meals in common and are reminiscent of the many meals that the

---

[16] Ibid., 177.
[17] Ibid., 177-78.

Lord himself shared with his disciples. What is more, the Blessed Sacrament reserved in the tabernacle of the priory church provides a quiet still point around which all of the sisters, regardless of their attitude toward Mariette (and, indeed, Mariette herself) display deep love, reverence, and respect. Hansen's descriptions of the rhythm of work the sisters do throughout the day displays the sense of peace and tranquility one would expect to find at a monastery dedicated their Lord and Savior. Different as they are from one another, the sisters of Our Lady of Sorrows priory seek to live a strictly regimented religious life meant to unite them with the suffering and death of their Lord. Although Mariette bears in her body the visible signs of Jesus' passion, her stigmata upsets that rhythm. Since there is reasonable doubt concerning the validity of her wounds (her own father tells the sisters they are being duped), she is sent home so that the tranquility of the community can be restored. One gets the sense in reading the closing pages of the novel, however, that once outside the convent Mariette's suffering has moved from the merely physical to the spiritual. Although, as the years pass, the signs of the stigmata are long past, the reader get a sense that Mariette has lived with a deep sadness over what might have been. Still, her relationship with the Lord is as strong as ever. The closing words of the novel emphasize the freedom he bestows upon those he seek him: "And Christ still sends me roses. We try to be formed and held and kept by him, but instead he offers us freedom. And now when I try to know his will, his kindness floods me, his great love overwhelms me, and I hear him whisper, Surprise me."[18]

Some Further Insights

Although these examples of Hansen's views on the Eucharist do not exhaust his understanding of the sacrament or its impact on his vocation as a writer, they provide the general contours within which a fuller presentation can unfold. The remarks that follow seek to delve a bit more deeply into his attitude toward the Eucharist.

To begin with, Catholic rites and liturgical calendar are deeply embedded in the very structure of the novel, giving us a sense that its characters are immersed in a rhythm of the sacred. That rhythm is upset by Mariette's stigmata and the ecstatic experiences that accompany it. The purpose of the strict daily *horarium* followed by the nuns is to sanctify the day (indeed, time itself) by taking time out at various points of the day to render glory and praise to God. The Mass is the highlight of the day, when Jesus's sacrifice on the cross enters the world of the convent in a very real and mysterious way and blesses the community with his glorified presence in the consecrated elements. Mariette participates in the worship of the community and encounters the mystery of Jesus' passion

---

[18] Ron Hansen, *Mariette in Ecstasy: A Novel* (new York: Harper Perennial, 1991), 179.

and death very deeply and personally. The marks on her hands, feet, and side show that Jesus' passion has touched her in a real and palpable way and given her a sense of peace and joy that sets her apart from the other members of the community. The different (and very human) reactions to her stigmata on the part of various members of the community say as much about them as they do about her, perhaps more. Although the Eucharist is a remedy for the humanity's weak and sinful tendencies, the healing process usually takes place during the course of a lifetime, and even beyond. Mariette's intense experiences upset the community's daily routine an divides it by drawing attention more to Mariette than to Christ.

Although the novel deeply embeds the Catholic rites and liturgical calendar into its very structure, its style at times appears to be very stunted and disjointed. Hansen uses this style to give us fleeting glimpses into the life of community which spans the gamut of human emotion from jealously and pride, to loyalty and love, to accusation, gossip, and pity. The juxtaposition of this truncated and disjointed style over the deeply embedded liturgical calendar that gives the novel its underlying narrative structure creates a tension between sacred time (*Kairos*) and chronological time (*Chronos*) that is sustained throughout the novel. Although the purpose of life at the Church and Priory of the Sisters of the Crucifixion is to sanctify life by turning *Chronos* into *Kairos*, there is a clear tension in the life of the community that Mariette's stigmata highlights all the more. Mariette, it appears, has been so taken up into sacred time that her presence in the community makes many of the sisters feel uncomfortable, as if they were inferior religious unable to sustain the rigors of the vowed life and community living. Mariette is variously perceived as a saint, who challenges the community to higher things, a deranged and mentally-ill postulant with visions of grandeur unfit for humble convent life, or someone possessed by a demon playing a sophisticated trick on the community at its own expense. The fact that Mariette is able to maintain her sense of peace and joy in the Lord as a member of the laity for years after her expulsion from the convent says something about the authenticity of her experience and her ability to live within the tension between *Kairos* and *Chronos*.

Mariette comes to a unique insight at the novel's end in a letter she addresses to Mother Philomène: "And Christ still sends me roses. We try to be formed and held by him, but instead he offers us freedom. And now when I try to know his will, his kindness floods me, his great love overwhelms me, and I hear him whisper, Surprise me."[19] The Christian life is all about uniting one's will with God's. Such is the nature of holiness, the quest to receive God's will as one's own. Scriptural precedents abound. Mary, the mother of Jesus responds to the Angel Gabriel, "Here I am, the servant of the

---

[19] Ibid.

Lord; let it be with me according to your word" (Lk 1:38). Jesus himself prays in the garden of Gethsemane, "…not my will but yours be done" (Lk 22:42). In the Lord's Prayer, he also teaches his disciples to say, "Your kingdom come. Your will be done, on earth as it is in heaven" (Mt 6:10). By the end of the novel, Mariette's relationship with Christ has moved from the physical manifestation of the stigmata to the deep inner wisdom of knowing that, when one truly loves God, one's will is completely united with his. His will becomes one's own—and vice versa. Mariette's words are reminiscent of St. Augustine when he says, "Love God and do as you will." Such is the freedom of the sons and daughters of God. The freedom of which Mariette speaks is the freedom to do the good. If one truly loves God, one's will is completely one with his, so much so that one would always act in a kind and loving manner. When such a person seeks God's will, God responds by saying, "Surprise me. Let your will be done."

The order of the day listed at the beginning of the novel indicates that the life of the Sisters of the Crucifixion revolves around Mass and the recitation of the Divine Office. The close link between the Eucharist and the identity of the community is highlighted by the fact that both are linked with Jesus' sacrifice on Calvary: the former immerses the believing community into Jesus' sacrificial offering on the cross in an unbloody manner, while the latter has taken "The Crucifixion" for its very name, that brutal form of punishment chosen by the Romans to intimidate the nations they conquered. What seems to be lacking in much of the novel is any emphasis on Christ's resurrection. In some ways, this emphasis on Christ's passion represents the typical spirituality of early twentieth-century Catholicism, the time period during which the novel unfolds. The spirituality of that time emphasized Christ's passion and death as the key moment when Jesus redeemed the world. Such an emphasis, however, is only part of the picture, since the cross leads to the empty tomb and the proclamation that Christ has risen. When seen in this light, Mariette is the only character in the novel who embodies both. She is a Christ figure (and an enigmatic one, at that), someone who bears the marks of the crucifixion in her body, but who also bears in her soul the peace and joy of the Holy Spirit, one of the main fruits of the Christ's resurrection. It is interesting to note that, as the novel unfolds, her stigmata disappears entirely and that she is at peace with all that has happened, an indication that she has passed through her time for suffering and relishes in the knowledge "that he loves me more, now that I am despised, than when I was so richly admired in the past."[20] Her thirty years outside of convent life has been a blessing to her, something she never would have imagined when she was asked to leave.

Finally, the novel describes a very specific model of religious life, one that might be described in H. Richard Niebhur's

---

[20] Hansen, *Mariette in Ecstasy*, 179.

terms as being "Christ against the World."[21] The Sisters of the Crucifixion live largely apart from the world and are worried that, because of Mariette's notoriety, worldly attitudes and values will infiltrate its cloister boundaries and cause it to compromise its high ideals. This attitude toward religious life was very common for the monastic setting of early twentieth-century religious life, and Hansen does an excellent job of capturing the spiritual (and also very human) dynamics involved in such a religious mindset. Because of her stigmata, Mariette becomes something of a celebrity in her small, isolated town in upstate New York. People flock to the Sunday Mass at the convent with the hope of seeing the person whom they revere as a saint. The fear within the convent is that the eyes of the faithful are being drawn to someone other than Christ. As Hansen himself suggests, also at work in the novel is the general suspicion many have of anyone who is the recipient of extraordinary graces such as the stigmata.[22] This is why Mariette has become a source of division within the community. Although some consider her a saint, others think she is deranged and still others believe she is possessed by the Evil One. Mariette's expulsion from the community and her capacity to maintain her peaceful, spiritual demeanor, despite the fact that she was now looked

---

[21] H. Richard Niebuhr, *Christ and Culture* (New York: Harper Torchbooks, 1951), 45-82.

[22] Hansen, *A Stay Against Confusion*, 177-78, 190.

upon with suspicion and ridicule by the townspeople, says something about the authenticity of her spiritual journey. Expelled from the convent, she lives in obscurity for the rest of her life among the very people who were once so fascinated by her and who now treat her with quiet disdain. In the past (and sometimes even today) a stigma was often attached to those who entered religious life and then left it. Mariette, a victim of these same worldly attitudes, is able to bring the suffering, crucified, yet risen Christ into the world of Arcadia, New York, a town named after an ancient Greek city, whose mythological king who taught his subjects, among other things, the art of baking bread. Like Christ, at the novel's end Mariette can be seen as a leaven given to the world as an instrument of its quiet, gentle (and very hidden) transformation.

Conclusion

An accomplished American novelist and devout Roman Catholic, Ron Hansen has explored the relationship between the role of faith in his work in a number of essays written over the years and collected in a single volume entitled, *A Stay Against Confusion.* The title comes from a line in the Preface to Robert Frost's *Collected Poems,* where the poet says poetry brings clarity to life and gives us "a momentary stay against confusion."²³ A professor of fiction and. screenwriting at Santa Clara University, he has written several novels, a number of which take up themes specifically relate to the deep spiritual themes of sin, faith, and redemption. In his novel, *Mariette in Ecstasy,* he explores such themes in a very open and explicit manner.

Hansen's Catholic upbringing has played a large role in his writer's vocation, because it reinforces the idea that storytelling matters in life and that writing itself can be seen as having a sacramental purpose in helping people find the extraordinary in the midst of the ordinary circumstances of daily life. Writing, for him, is a way in which an author mediates an experience of the holy to his or her reading audience. Through a focused use of the imagination as a primary vehicle for facilitating this divine-human encounter, the author delves beneath appearances, by an array of images and symbols to explore the depths of human experience and to uncover hitherto unseen purpose and significance in life.

Hansen writes of the serenity and joy he experienced when attending Mass and of his sense of being an instrument of Holy Being when serving as a Eucharistic minister. One would imagine that, as a permanent deacon, this sense of service (*diakonia*) and his appreciation of Jesus' institution of the sacrament would be highlighted all the more. In *Mariette in Ecstasy*, the Mass, Tabernacle, and Catholic liturgical

---

²³ Ibid., xvii.

calendar provide the backdrop against which the drama within the Church and Priory of The Sisters of the Crucifixion unfolds. The community's order of the day, which revolves around the Mass and the recitation of the Divine Office, is meant to provide a spiritual rhythm that sanctifies the day and brings a sense of peace and tranquility to the lives of the sisters. Although Mariette's stigmata upsets that peace and is one of the reasons for her being expelled from the community, she remains faithful to her love for Christ for the rest of her life as a Catholic laywoman and demonstrates that, despite the stigma (and disgrace) associated with one who has left the convent, peace and holiness are still possible outside of the bounds of cloister life. To the reader, Mariette is a Christ figure, someone who, as the novel unfolds, has taught members of the faithful on both sides of the priory walls the spiritual art of baking bread.

Reflection Questions

- What role do extraordinary phenomena like the stigmata play in the life of faith? Why are they given? What purpose do they serve in the life of a community? Do you agree with Hansen that "[w]ondrous things do happen in life, but generally in the ordinary ways of faith and healing and love?" What experiences of faith, healing, and love have you had?

- Why is Mariette a source of division in her community? Why do some sisters think she is a saint, while others believe she is mentally ill or possibly even possessed? What judgments did you make about her during the course of the novel? What was your assessment of her at the novel's end?

- To what extent is Mariette a Christ figure? To what extent do her wounds go beyond the physical but embrace the psychological as well as the spiritual? Have you ever been rejected by a group you longed to belong to? Have you ever been rejected or looked down upon by the people in your town or even your own family? What evidence of holiness does Mariette display throughout the novel?

Conclusion

"God became human so that humanity might become divine." These words of an ancient Church father remind us that God entered our world so that we might enter his. The Eucharist is the way God choose to bring about this reality. In giving us his body and blood to eat and drink, Jesus allows us to share in his glorified, resurrected existence and enter into the presence of the Father. Through this sacrament, he makes our narrative his, and his narrative our own.

The authors presented in this volume weave the Eucharist into their creative writing in any number of ways. Some make it stand out as the centerpiece of their narratives. Others use it as a stable backdrop against which their narratives unfold. Still others use it as a symbol of a deeper reality that lies beneath the surface of life. In some ways, the role the Eucharist plays in their narratives reflects the place it holds in their own lives. In other ways, it is a commentary on how the sacrament is viewed by the believing community and possibly even the wider culture. Like Jesus' presence in the tabernacle, the role the sacrament plays in their writing often lies hidden in the background. Although at times barely detectable, it is always a stable (yet, ever elusive) presence.

The Eucharist is a sacrament of beauty, mystery, meaning, wonder—and so very much more! Its beauty both attracts and transforms. It leads us into the mystery of God, the Church, and our very selves. It reveals to us the meaning of who we are and the world in which we find ourselves. It fills us with wonder at the depth of God's love for us. It sends us forth with renewed hope to proclaim this reality to others. The voices presented in this volume affirm that the Eucharist is the visible, palpable sign and reality of God's continual and ongoing presence with his people. They remind us that, in the end, God asks of us nothing more than to let go of ourselves and allow him to enter the warp and woof of our daily lives. To do so would be to set out on an adventure that no one would dare imagine.

www.ingramcontent.com/pod-product-compliance
Lightning Source LLC
Chambersburg PA
CBHW051108230426
43667CB00014B/2494